# COLLECTING ART

*Masterpieces, Markets and Money*

# COLLECTING ART

*Masterpieces, Markets and Money*

Eileen Chanin

CRAFTSMAN HOUSE

COLLECTING ART: *Masterpieces, Markets and Money*

First published 1990 by Craftsman House,
Upper Level, 108 Pacific Highway, Roseville, NSW 2069, Australia

ISBN 976 8097 00 0

*Typesetting, Layout and Design*   Netan Pty Limited, Sydney
*Printer*   Globe Press, Melbourne

*~ For Adrian and Roland ~*

# CONTENTS

Acknowledgements   ix
Introduction   xi

**1 Collecting**   **1**
Why Collect At All?
Judging Value: Price and Quality
Buying and Selling: Many Markets
Money and Taste, Specialisation and Connoisseurship

**2 The Art Market: Auctions**   **21**
A Dollar and a Dream
Perils of Auctions
How Do You Know When a Price Is Right?
Hype
Auctions vs Dealers
How to Buy and How to Sell at Auction
Mega-Star Business

**3 The Art Market: Dealers**   **45**
Dealing with Dealers
Buying and Selling with Dealers
The Business of Art
Consultants
Art Fairs

**4 The Contemporary Market**   **59**
The Unique Contemporary Market
Selecting Talent on the Cutting Edge of Contemporary Art
Commercial Galleries
Artists-Gallery Relationships
Artists' Rights

**5 Art as Investment**   **71**
High Art and Big Money
The Success of Art as Investment
Art Funds: Depreciation, Gifts, Bequests and Tax Deductions

**6 Protecting Your Treasures**   **89**
Display and Storage,
   Framing and Looking After Paper
Conservation and Restoration
Art Loans
Cataloguing and Record-Keeping
Security
Insurance
Valuations

**7 Fakes, Forgeries, Fraud, Replicas**   **115**
Provenance and Attributions
Limited Editions
Export Controls

Footnotes   129
Appendix: Collectors Marketplace Directory   145
Bibliography   153
Index   157

# ACKNOWLEDGEMENTS

There are many to whom I owe thanks for their thoughts and assistance. I'd particularly like to thank Nevill Drury who commissioned and published this book. Without Jackie De Diana's patient typing of the manuscript this never would have reached him. To Andrew Durham at the Australian National Gallery, my thanks for his thoughts on conservation. Allan Byrne of the National Centre for Cultural Heritage Science Studies, the University of Canberra, most generously gave me the benefit of his conservation experience, for which I am grateful. David Broit, Indemnity Corporation, gave me valuable advice on insurance. From Christie's, Sue Hewitt's opinions on auctions were much appreciated. Christie's in particular were of great help with my enquiries about sales and my requests for illustrations; as were Leonard Joel, Rushtons, and Sotheby's.

# INTRODUCTION

This is a book dedicated to the spirit and traditions of collecting art. It offers up-to-date practical advice on questions most frequently asked about collecting art, including a review of recent trade and collecting in international and Australian markets. It looks at developing an eye and expertise, identifies some hazards which buyers and sellers should beware of, explains buying and selling, looks at money and art, and advises on looking after a collection.

It is a book for collectors who are art-lovers, rather than art-speculators (who principally acquire works of art with little interest in art per se beyond the profit art may nett them). The collector acquires works of art for the pleasure they give. At the very least, collectors enjoy living with art and show as much of their collection as they can where they live or work. Real collectors are art *aficionados* who read about art, visit museums, may even be a museum trustee or volunteer, and may often number artists among their friends. Though it considers art and money, this book is not about the art of making money from art. This book is for art-lovers who prefer to exercise their personal preferences when collecting and who, in the course of buying and living with work they like, may set fashions and perhaps then may also reap considerable financial benefit, in addition to the many other pleasures art collecting offers.

This is a book to accompany looking at and enjoying art. It focuses on collecting the more traditional fine art objects, namely paintings, sculpture and graphics. However, the principles for collecting fine art discussed here apply to collecting other 'rare collectibles' like rare musical instruments, jewellery, or antiques.

Collecting in all its many forms has always involved gathering numbers of chosen desired objects, collected often at a cost in money or time. Collectors enjoy collecting. Collecting not only transmutes all sorts of objects from things of use into ends in themselves, but as an activity collecting is an end in itself. What mainly delights collectors is gaining possession of and enjoying their prizes. This book is for them.

> *... to collect nothing at all is to descend below*
> *the level of magpies and marmots.*

Gerard Reitlinger
*The Economics of Taste, the Rise and Fall of Picture Prices: 1760–1960, Vol 1*

> *The masterpiece should appear as the flower to the painter —*
> *perfect in its bud as in its bloom —*
> *with no reason to explain its presence —*
> *no mission to fulfil.*

James McNeill Whistler
*The Gentle Art of Making Enemies, 1890*

> *To collect is to gather objects belonging to a particular category the*
> *collector happens to fancy; and art collecting is a form of collecting*
> *in which the category is, broadly speaking, works of art.*

Joseph Alsop
*The Rare Art Tradition*

# 1

# COLLECTING

*'A painting has no more spiritual message or meaning than an exquisite fragment of Venetian glass or a blue tile from the wall of Damascus: it is a beautifully coloured surface, nothing more.'*

Oscar Wilde, *The English Renaissance in Art*, 1882

*'Remember that the most beautiful things in the world are the most useless; peacocks and lilies for instance.'*

John Ruskin *The Stones of Venice*, 1851–3

## Why Collect At All?

Reasons for collecting vary. They range from pleasure to greed. Fuelled by the desire to have and to keep, people buy art for all kinds of reasons, whether these range from simple aesthetic attraction, or from extra aesthetic considerations such as those of fashion, as a way of self-expression, from curiosity and open experiment, for investment, from covetousness, or the desire to gain prestige through display of wealth or embellishment of private life.

Certainly collecting art has distinguished wealth and power from the Roman Emperors, the Doges, the military dictators of the 19th and 20th centuries, the American 'robber barons' to today's collecting moguls. Throughout history, art has always followed empire. However, the instinct to collect and hoard also exists among animals and children. Collecting is not for millionaires only, and true collecting is more than satisfying the urge to accumulate.

Many forms of human collecting can be detected in so many different societies over so enormously long a span of time. In remains from the Stone Age, fairly soon after the emergence of *Homo sapiens*, archeologists have found more than one indisputable collection. The earliest was found at the so-called Cave of the Hyena in France, excavated by Andre Leroi-Gourhan, which contained a small but obviously man-made assemblage of *objets trouvés*, such as a fossil skull and an oddly shaped lump of iron pyrites. Art collecting in the Western world began with the Greeks and spread to Rome, where Roman collecting resembled modern millionaire collecting. The world's earliest fairly solidly documented art collector was King Attalus I of Pergamum, who began to reign in 241 B.C. During the Middle Ages art objects like precious Eastern silks and Byzantine silverware were sought as luxuries. Antique ornaments set with jewels and reliquaries were sought as talismans, symbols of power, and sacred furnishings as accessories for buildings and tombs. The desire for elegant interior decoration was the motivation behind much collecting and even explains the nature of what was collected, particularly sculpture. Cosimo De Medici (*Pater Patriae*) was the first magnate-collector of classical art on a really large scale from Italian history. One of the most remarkable collections was that assembled by England's Charles I, from around 1616 to 1640. After he was beheaded in 1648 the Commonwealth sold off his collection, the most remarkable sale of works of art then seen. Works from his incomparable collection are now the pride of just about every art museum in the Western world and superb memorials to Charles' discrimination and love of art.

In the more recent museum age, collecting has made great works of art into major ends in themselves, museums serving as they once did for princely powers, but now for public states, as 'ornaments' and proof of the grandeur of significant states and cultures. Museums acquire to fill gaps and broaden their specialised collections.[1] They buy in relation to the strengths and weaknesses of their collections, usually acknowledging that concentrated collections are better than historical surveys. Universities buy art for study purposes or for the enlightenment of their academic and student communities. Corporations look to the humanising role of art, which they use to embellish the working environment. Most privileged is the private collector who buys only for himself or herself and whose only restrictions may be funds, space, taste and knowledge.

Art collecting can be a dangerous affair. Those who begin possessing often become possessed. True collecting — as distinct from decorating, status seeking or investing — can be a madness. Collecting art with its strong spiritual and aesthetic power as an end-in-itself is probably the most passionate manifestation of the collecting mania.

Covetousness can become a neurosis such as in the case of a gluttony for ownership and need for possession, or a compulsive tendency to classify and regularise objects. Heredity may be part of a collector's psychology, for whom objects are stamped with family prestige and history. Another incentive to collecting exists where objects are regarded as symbols of status and money to affirm dynastic prestige and offer posterity.[2] Examples are bequests like those from Joseph Mellon, Samuel Kress and Joseph E. Widener to the National Gallery in Washington; and Samuel Courtauld whose pioneering support of modern art in Britain resulted in the Courtauld Institute.[3] For these collectors, wanting to keep together after they were dead what they had gathered in life, their enjoyment of collecting was made additionally keen by the satisfaction that their bequests ensured their posterity. Many public collections have developed from such private 'larval' museums of private ownership like the Wallace Collection in London, the Musée Guimet and

Cognac-Jay Museum in Paris, the Barnes Collection and the Morgan and Huntington libraries in the United States, and the Hinton collection at Armidale in Australia.

Collecting is a personal affair and true collections reflect the collector's own personal judgment. True collecting demonstrates individuality, when a collector's judgments affirm his or her individualism from general opinion and prevailing taste. True collectors are beings of developed perception and intuition. They enjoy the veneration of art and sure connoisseurship. They don't consider the practical possibilities of objects. They are spurred by a love of beauty, as subjective as this may be. They regard objects as a departure point to continual, fresh, intellectual pursuit. Through objects they uncover and rediscover the past. By their preservation of objects, collectors make the history of civilisations and cultures available to future generations. Through them the values and standards of any age are submitted to future alterations in perspective, because ways of seeing change with the passage of time.

Collecting, art history and the art market are closely linked. No market exists without collectors. Collectors determine what becomes desirable and, in their competition for objects, a market operates accordingly. Competition among collectors creates rarities. As objects considered ultra-desirable for which collectors compete become scarcer or unobtainable, so competition among collectors for these 'collectibles' intensifies. A specialised market to supply the demand results. As soon as enough collectors compete for the same works of art, they create a market which dealers come to supply. Collectors also require their prizes to belong to categories identified and endorsed by history. History clarifies the importance of objects and provides authentication. The shared bloodstream of ideas and critical viewpoints of art history and art collecting determine ways of seeing and in turn ways of collecting. They certainly increase opportunities for enjoyment. Prices on the market are also affected by the interaction between art collecting and art history. Super prices are paid for any ultra-desired work of quality that can be art historically labelled. Faking begins wherever there is a brisk market. Revision also occurs when collectors who find themselves unable to pay super prices look at other areas from which they may collect. They revalue history and objects to subsequently affect prices as the 'new' collectibles in turn become more desirable, therefore less obtainable, and more expensive.

One of the interesting undercurrents of the history of 20th century art and the art market is the way in which modern movements in art have influenced the demand for works of other kinds. The 'rediscovery' of El Greco, for example, before World War I, was related to the development of the new Expressionist school in Germany and Austria. Early German Expressionists in Dresden and the Fauves in Paris, through their contact with African and Oceanian art, incorporated into their work some of the vigour and freshness of these cultures. Although the artefacts of Africa, the South Pacific, and similar areas had until then been regarded primarily as curios, they began to achieve a new status, becoming objects of interest to the art market within a relatively short time. The Blaue Reiter movement, which began in 1911, presented in its famous Almanac, a wide variety of primitive forms as sources from which modern art could derive stimulation. These included not only those of the art of Africa and of the Pacific but also those of pre-Columbian periods, of folk art, and indeed, of every kind of expression that is considered 'unsophisticated'. The interest artists expressed in pre-Columbian art was, in subsequent decades, taken up by collectors. Export restrictions imposed by the countries of origin tended to augment scarcity and further raise prices of pre-Columbian work. Before World War II, works by the German Expressionists could not be sold extensively. However, alongside an increasing shortage of works by favoured French Moderns, and especially following the impressive 1957 exhibition at New York's Museum of Modern Art, German Expressionist works have enjoyed growing vogue and related prices.

With the number of first-rank works available for purchase constantly decreasing, the prices of these are being driven up, leading to a trend to 'rediscover' secondary artists in order to fill the ensuing gap. This produces a kind of stock market of taste, on which works of art of all sorts go up and down in estimation all over the world. Although some neglected artists have thus been rescued from undeserved obscurity, the market's search for more material has also led to capricious selling of works ranging from minor sketches to studio sweepings, and works by 'also-ran' artists, often touted as masterpieces ready to be snatched up at bargain rates and 'guaranteed' to increase enormously in value. All of which demonstrates the necessity for exercising cool judgment and connoisseurship in the art market.

*‘Nowadays people know the price of everything
and the value of nothing.’*

Oscar Wilde's definition of a cynic

## Judging Value: Price and Quality

What intrinsic value does a work of art have? A work of art is a commodity for which a market is created and maintained by financially interested parties who are no different than the operators of any other legal sort of market. The market value of the art object is derived from its exchange value — that is, the price a buyer is prepared to pay for the object. This has nothing to do with the sum values of the object's properties, like the cost of materials and labour required in the making of the object. Marcel Duchamp (1887–1968) aimed to demonstrate this with his 'Readymade' *Urinal* of 1917. He assumed his urinal would not be contradicted as a commodity because the readymade object had no value in terms of labour and material costs. Ironically, his 'readymade' became the art object he intended it could never be. It has become the best example of the fetishised art object. One of the eight white porcelain urinals based on Duchamp's 1917 'readymade' and issued in 1964 by the Galleria Schwarz in Milan was bought on 29 April 1989 for US$68,750 at Sotheby's, New York against an estimate of $2,000–2,500. It was one of the high points of the Andy Warhol sale. The buyer's *need* for the object and exchange of this sum for it determined the *value* of that need and the value of the urinal, the art object. The ultimate value in the market then is the value of the need any single person has for an object. Price is dictated by supply and demand.

When Japanese paper maker Daishowa's Chairman Ryoei Saito was revealed in May 1990 as the mystery bidder at New York auctions in which he spent US$160.6 million on two late 19th century European paintings, paying US$82.5 million for Van Gogh's sombre portrait of Dr Gachet and US$78.1 million for Renoir's scintillating *Au Moulin de la Galette*, of 1876, the highest prices ever paid for works of art — he commented he did not think the prices expensive. Of the Van Gogh he said, 'It cost 5 billion yen more than I expected, but that's nothing. Next I want the Renoir' and his acquisitions cost him US$82,401 per square inch of canvas.

The art market makes valuations in a less theoretical manner than does art criticism. The value placed on works of art by the art market will differ from, and can have little relation if any to, the critical value placed on the same work. Other elements seemingly unrelated to the work can affect value. Additional elements can affect the need any single person has for an object and so can influence that object's value. These elements can include the artistic merit of the work: is it a 'museum picture' or a 'private collector's picture'? That is, is it important and most representative, or decorative and attractive? The art historical importance of a piece can affect value: did the work have an influence or has it been influenced? Documentation and provenance qualifies the work's pedigree and influences value. Value can be affected by the nature of attribution the work has: a scholar's opinion, and which scholar; and a contemporary attribution. Individual works of art are traded at individual prices established by the individual place of each work of art in the prevailing art collectors' opinion. Art history has the essential role of supplying attribution, establishing opinion and authenticating what is offered on the market. Besides the state of the object's condition, the title and subject of the work can influence value. Paintings of cemeteries and of portraits are more difficult to place. Style and fashionability, which is receptivity to a style, decides whether the work is scarce or otherwise. Value is created by other elements such as the reputation of the seller, determined competition between two bidders, or local chauvinism for an object of native value. Price can be affected if the object completes a collector's series which the collector must then have. Even photographic reproductions affect values. Charles Blackman's portrait of a child, well-known through colour reproduction in

Alan McCulloch's *Encyclopedia of Australian Art,* raised interest when offered at Rushton's sale of 6 July 1987 to fetch a then record A$32,000.[4]

Value in contemporary art is less often equated with the 'fictional factors' affecting values of non-contemporary work. With contemporary art, value is often equated with the sense of personal discovery of an artist and the artist's work, and the pleasure this gives the connoisseur or collector. Additional value to the contemporary art collector is the satisfaction — some would call it inverted snobbery — that comes with collecting the difficult or non-fashionable artist, whose work is often bought ahead of the market and so for modest prices. The contemporary field offers the greatest selection of high-quality work by little-known artists who may be on the ascendant or rising stars. The adventurous collector of contemporary art with sharp eyes and strong legs earns price advantages, as does any collector who anticipates rather than follows fashion.

Obviously, different buyers buy different work of different values for different reasons — whether speculative, faddish, for decorative reasons, or from considerable commitment. Like being well-dressed, the value of art has little to do with monetary value. The best work is not necessarily the most expensive. A Van Gogh drawing of top quality is unlikely to go cheaply but a marvellous contemporary drawing may. A less fashionable piece may not lend itself so well to advertising and may not be so prominently publicised because it has to be described and explained instead of being easily labelled with a fashionable name that clicks. Such a less fashionable piece may be an excellent buy. It is always best to buy when focus shifts away from periods or styles. There are many instances in the history of collecting of courageous individuals who swam against the tide to collect what was disregarded at the time to enjoy the obvious benefits. What is neglected in the art market is as revealing as what is pursued, and what is underappreciated is often undervalued.

Buying drawings — which are often overlooked — demonstrates the rewards to be gained from individual patient connoisseurship. Drawings are unique statements offering clues to an artist's working process. Being unique works, drawings are free from the worry which arises in the field of prints — of restrikes, or reproductions sold as originals, or falsely numbered editions. Generally intimate, often small, drawings are introspective, tentative and best when frankly personal. Drawings free artists from the restrictions paintings pose through their material scale and persuasive sense of finish. Drawings allow artists to rapidly notate and visualise many ideas. Drawings offer artists a hands-on connection with their expression which becomes an integral part of the viewer's experience. The immediacy of drawings gets you closer to an artist faster than paintings do. You feel you are sharing the moment when they were done. With paper, artists can work in a quicker, more spontaneous way and drawings show the anatomy of an artist's thinking more clearly — the bare bones of their work. They provide a diary to the artist's development, and give the most unusual insight into the artist. As Degas defined it: 'Drawing is not what you see but what you must make others see.'[5] Drawings, demand to be tracked down. Give them time and they reward.

Collectors looking for works that are cheaper or easier to come by than the great collectors' prizes, look elsewhere and their comparisons lead to important revaluations, which in turn develop further markets. American landscapists of the 19th century like Cole, Inness, Moran, Church and Bierstadt could be bought cheaply and easily in the early 1970s. Their prices escalated as collectors turned to buy their work, on finding prices for French Impressionist paintings which they would have preferred to buy were rising to levels then considered astronomical and certainly beyond their reach. Their collecting of American 19th century 'Luminists', as they came to be labelled, developed the market and values paid for this work. Lesser works of art are automatically promoted as soon as works by the great masters become unobtainable. The major art collectors' prizes have been the works of long-recognised old masters, or works of lesser artists promoted to 'old master' standing by the rarity of higher prizes, or works by artists believed likely to be the 'old masters of the future', as the notable Philadelphian collector Dr Albert C. Barnes called them. Notoriously difficult and parsimonious, Barnes bought works nobody else seemed to want, making his most rewarding purchases during the Depression of the 1930s, when masterpieces by Matisse and Cézanne among others went begging.

Where power declines, money grows short or order dissolves into disorder, there are always opportunities for collectors. Many collecting opportunities have arisen from the misfortunes of others. Andrew W. Mellon bought many of the pictures for his National Gallery from The Hermitage, sold by order of Josef Stalin badly needing foreign exchange. It is thought collecting in Rome began following Rome's sacking of Corinth in 146 B.C., the spoils from which flooded into Rome. While Europe's monarchs were shocked by Charles I's public beheading at Whitehall, they were successful bidders at the sale of the King's collection, and included Philip IV of Spain, Cardinal Mazarin, and the Hapsburg Archduke Leopold Wilhelm. More recently collectors of Khmer art have bought sculpture from Angkor Wat and other Khmer monuments from refugees and starving Cambodians. A clear-headed collector can turn a recession to his advantage, since it can often provide him with his best opportunities of buying well, and he can use a boom to weed out and trade up.

By all means shop around. Compare prices, which you will see can fluctuate widely and vary from object to object because condition and quality alter price by a significant factor. However, remember that too great a preoccupation with price can be counter-productive. A weakness for buying bargains can be one of the worst faults that can afflict a new collector. Bargain hunting clouds judgment and leaves the new collector prey to unscrupulous offers of works available at bargain prices because they are not genuine. If the piece is good and rare, someone else will step in and buy it while you cogitate. If you like a thing, and it suits you, and you can afford it, buy.

## Buying and Selling: Many Markets

The art market is many markets. To speak of the 'art market' is to refer to the very many markets of special interest like contemporary and oriental art which often bear little relation to each other and are only tenuously linked by the fact that objects within each field of interest, being fine art objects, are commonly considered collectibles. Markets are where these collectibles are traded. Just as objects themselves differ, so where, when, and how objects are traded vary.

Art, like other commodities, can be sold in a variety of ways. Trading occurs at auction, in galleries, through private dealers, at art fairs, and direct sales made between a vendor with a work to sell and a buyer wanting it. Each situation offers buyer and seller different opportunities. Though few lists exist telling you where to go to best buy or sell work, there are ways to identify the various markets and their levels.

Basically the market is two-tiered, with many sectors. The art market is comprised of a symbiotic relationship between the secondary market of the auction saleroom where works are resold and prices are determined in a kind of public free-for-all, and the private market, where prices are discretionary and carefully negotiated. Within these two tiers many sectors exist.

Special interests qualify markets which are further distinguished by period or medium. For example, the international print markets range from Old Master European prints, the Moderns (principally of either French, German or British schools), and contemporary prints (principally dominated by American Masters like Jasper Johns and Frank Stella).[6] Within Australian Painting different markets exist for work from the Colonial and Impressionist schools, the Moderns, and contemporary painting. National chauvinism and local history aids the Australian market. Colonial and Impressionist paintings are acclaimed and esteemed as part of Australia's historical and cultural heritage. Buyers look for Australian points of reference. European works never fare as well. Consequently there is a great deal of costly nostalgia and provincial flotsam within the Australian market with often an absence in Australian sales of paintings to set the market on fire. Stock turns over, but good money is paid for fresh, visually strong and appealing pictures. Another market altogether is that for Aboriginal painting.

The much publicised and glamourised international market sees the trading of works by artists and schools of work for which there is international demand, usually of Masters ranging from Antiquities, Old Master Paintings, the Impressionists and Moderns, and Masters of French Art Deco like Louis Majorelle, the undisputed Master cabinet maker of the 1900 era. The international market favours leading exponents from major schools or periods of world history.

Markets can be geographical and regional. National markets exist of work by artists generally not known beyond their country of origin or practice, as is principally the case with Australian painting. This is not to say collectors internationally do not buy Australian Art, as demonstrated by the healthy results Sotheby's netted from their sale devoted only to Australian Impressionists held in London in late 1988; and the high prices paid in Sotheby's London sale in May 1989 of topographical pictures by Australian artists, where, for example, a large unframed oil depicting a steam launch on a river in Victoria painted in 1891 by James Alfred Turner (1860–1910) and estimated to sell between A$13,000 to A$25,000, was bought for A$79,200 by an Australian dealer. Generally, though, works by Australian artists sold in London are bought by Australians. Australian artists enjoy healthy support for their work within a national Australian market and are little known internationally.

Because most trade of Australian art outside Australia occurs in Britain it is worth looking at the market for Australian art in the United Kingdom and how that market has developed. Despite a long history of Australian artists working in England, few are represented in British museum collections. The Tate's collection of modern Australian art consists of seven Frances Hodgkins and five Roy de Maistres, both whom were accepted as part of the British art scene, rather than as Australians. Russell Drysdale, Ian Fairweather and Godfrey Miller are represented by one painting each; Brett Whiteley by two works; Arthur Boyd and Lawrence Daws by several prints. Arthur Boyd and Sidney Nolan can be regarded as much British as they are Australian artists. They both live in England. Generally, when accepted, Australian art is considered in Britain to be part of the British scene.

Australian art is principally sold in England at auction through Topographical sales (which combine modern and colonial pictures from Africa, the East, Australasia and the Americas), and Modern British sales, which include artists (like Frances Hodgkins, Roy de Maistre, Boyd and Nolan) who are integral to, or associated with, British art history. Australian artists never appear in the internationally based Impressionist, Modern or Contemporary art sales in London or New York, because their market is still considered to be highly localised. In December 1988 Christie's, South Kensington (CSK) held the first-ever sale devoted to Australian Impressionist and Modern Art. This makes CSK the major (or only) venue for such sales in Europe. This is one of a series of commercial promotions by London's auction houses of 'neglected' regional schools, as was done with the Dutch some twenty years ago, the Italians with their academic painters, the American Primitives and Landscapes of the Far West, and 19th century Scandinavian pictures in more recent times. As has generally been the pattern with sales in England of Australian art, most work seems to return to Australia. Exceptions are the early modern artists whose work is indistinguishable in style or subject matter from mainstream European modes, such as Derwent Lees (1885–1931) who often resembles Augustus John, and Charles Conder (1868–1909) who is sought after (though the best prices for Conder, who was only in Australia for six years, are raised by Australian demand). In most cases prices in the saleroom are stimulated from Australia. Christie's sale offered works of variable quality, the duller of which failed to sell. They did not reach prices near those paid in Australia for similar work by similar artists. Take, for example, a recent Clifton Pugh, which though it doubled its estimate at £3,300 came nowhere near the A$40–50,000 range paid in Australia for Pugh's work. Works sold in London are mostly bought by Australian buyers, to be returned to Australia where higher prices may be received.

Things are a little different in London's primary market where there is more likelihood of a market developing for Australian art. At least this market is now being developed by several British dealers. Whether triggered by the Bicentennial or not, the last two years have seen many exhibitions of work by Australian artists at London's commercial galleries: Ray Crooke at Agnews, Graham Fransella at Rebecca Hossack, Tim Storrier at Fischer, Jeffrey Makin at Bernard Jacobson, Peter Booth at Albemarle Gallery, and Rodick Carmichael at the Scottish Gallery, to name a few. And these were selling to British and American clients, not only to Australians. This is important because only if this happens will the market for Australian art develop beyond a presently localised home-based market to one with more international dimensions.

Another example of a market which principally draws national interest is that for American Indian Art which is most strongly supported within the United States, especially in the South-West. Americana and Australiana, despite their respective charm, remain localised markets.

An interesting twist to internationalising domestic markets is the recent entry of Soviet art into the art mainstream. Largely unknown until *glasnost*, Soviet art is now hot — considered as one of the last virgin markets in the art world. Since the Reagan-Gorbachev summit brought news of *glasnost*, a passion for 'made in the USSR' has been growing, much like there was a passion for Chinese civilisation in the early 1970s. Soviet culture, for so many years closed to the West and now opening up with high political blessing, is proving irresistibly attractive as demand grows worldwide for Russian art of the unofficial avant-garde. On 7 July, 1988 Sotheby's organised the first international art auction of Soviet art in Moscow. The pre-auction estimate of US$1 million for 119 mostly contemporary paintings proved to be modest. The sale totalled a remarkable US$3.4 million, more than tripling the auction house's best expectations. Among living Soviet artists whose work was for sale, chief interest centred on forty-three year old Muscovite, Grisha Bruskin. One of his six works sold fetched US$407,166, way above an estimate of US$24,000 to US$30,000. This was the highest sum ever paid for the work of a living Soviet artist. In vogue, Russian art was catapulted from a very local situation into the mainstream of collecting and collectors. Price levels, however, have yet to be clearly pegged by mainstream market activities beyond the exhilarating prices hyped by a special sale. A second public sale of Soviet art demonstrated the volatility of the new market. In October 1988 in New York, Guernsey's (a smaller auctioneer that specialises mostly in collectibles) offered nearly 900 Russian works ranging from early 20th century avant-garde and vintage propaganda posters to work from the Socialist Realist School and living artists largely unknown in the West. This first auction of Soviet art outside the Soviet Union was a disaster, with the majority of works failing to sell well.

**'*Taste is the legitimate offspring of nature, educated by propriety; fashion is the bastard of vanity, classed by art.*'**

Henry Fuseli, *Aphorisms On Art*, 1789

## Money and Taste, Specialisation and Connoisseurship

Art and money have always gone hand-in-hand. Art has always been regarded as the luxury of the privileged and the moneyed, glorifying power — whether of the Crown, the State, or the Church. Art now carries the additional weight of the value of expression. It is art's expression of human spirit that gives art the spiritual force it holds. It is coy to bemoan the present very public alliance between art and money. The present age of art-money or moneyed-art is not new. Speculation has always been associated with art, as have taste and fashion.

Money may usually be necessary in order to follow fashion, which is not necessarily taste. To exercise taste it is not necessary to follow fashion nor to have money. Money is not essential for taste, particularly when buying against fashion. All that is then required is certainty of judgment, supported by specialisation, from connoisseurship. This is knowing the subject. This is evaluating the object: is it really what it is represented to be? Where did it come from? What kind of condition is it in? Is it a good buy?

The connoisseur today is an art collector on a budget. Passionate and persevering art lovers manage to find affordable works by choosing appropriate fields and then buying at the right place and the right time. For this you must be a judge of both art and character. Beware a bargain which is really a swindle. Smart shoppers need to know where to buy and when to buy. When a particular field is in vogue, prices may be inflated. Fashion equals high prices. However, vendors are not eager to sell when prices are deflated in a down market. A booming market tends to lure out more choice and desirable offerings.

Buying is not for millionaires only. Many of the dullest collections have been built with a limitless cheque book. Many exciting collections have been built on a modest income. Somehow you do not associate Turner with the turmoil of limited domestic space or Gainsborough with the garage. Yet an English schoolteacher, Stowers Johnson, lives in an ordinary house that is crammed floor to ceiling with an outstanding collection of paintings: Italian, Spanish, Flemish, Primitive, Mannerist, 19th century, Baroque, and 20th century. Twenty years ago, when the collection was smaller, it was exhibited in London and caused a stir. Paul Getty congratulated Stowers Johnson on his collection. It was put together without money. It was built up by commonsense: he bought an unattributed portrait of Samuel Johnson by Joshua Reynolds because he recognised the subject's face. His joy of discovery outweighed any consideration of value.

The story of Australian steelworker Bob Sredersas is another good illustration of how to buy well and enjoyably without a fortune. Before his death in 1982, Crimean-born Bob Sredersas presented almost one hundred works of paintings, antique china and Pacific artefacts to the city of Wollongong. Sredersas was one of thousands of European displaced persons who migrated to Australia in 1950. Known to auctioneers as 'Mr Bob' from Wollongong, as appears on the invoices of all his purchases, he built a collection combining intuition with basic research, limited to and buying only what was appearing in Sydney's auction rooms from 1956 on. He bought his first purchase, Sydney Long's *Herring Fleet at Sea* for one guinea. With his collection acting as a catalyst for the establishment of the Wollongong City Gallery, in which a gallery has been named in his honour, Sredersas could feel satisfied. 'When I came to Wollongong there were many factories, building and bridges. People before me had built them. But I too can do something for future generations. You must not forget that we are only temporarily in this world but the human race will stay. Something must be done for future generations, future citizens.'[7]

There are many examples throughout history of collections assembled on shoestrings and enterprise. A great collection was assembled in 18th century Venice by Fra Carlo Lodoli. Poor friar that he was, he could not afford the great art-prizes of his day, so he bought paintings by masters of the 14th and 15th centuries which he was able to buy cheaply because they were out of favour. His collection was renowned in his day because it showed the step by step progression of art, from the Greeks to the early Venetians, the Florentines, Titian, Raphael, Caravaggio and Veronese. Like Balzac's Cousin Pons, he made up for want of money by untiring ferreting, by a wonderful eye for quality, and by boldness in gathering prizes of high quality without regard to current fashions. Sadly after his death his collection was lost, probably going back to the *rigattieri* — Italian dealers in old clothes and junk — from whom he had found so much of his collection. Russian-born Greek collector George Costakis amassed the largest private collection of Soviet avant-garde art, buying work officially out of favour.

## Collecting

There is the story of Bostonian Mrs Jack Gardner whose collecting through Bernard Berenson established the delightful Isabella Gardner Museum. Though widowed with wealth enough to build her collection, she was eventually priced out of buying by far richer Americans. Always concerned with price, she secured in 1899 what many think the finest painting in the United States, Titian's *The Rape of Europa*, for no more than US$100,000 and, at that, she saved money by wiring to Bernard Berenson her consent to buy in a single word, YEUP, which meant 'Yes, Europa'.

The British publication *Art Sales Index* estimated total turnover on the international art market during 1988–89 at £1.7 billion, a rise of 80 per cent over 1987–88. *Art Sales Index* reported that despite the fact that 194 works sold for more than £1 million (contributing some £560 million to the total), 80 per cent of works sold for less than £10,000 and 70 per cent sold for less than £5,000. In 1988 Sotheby's, New York auctioned five lots for over US$10 million each and 134 more for over US$1 million. Through three days in November, Sotheby's auctioned Impressionist and Modern paintings worth US$200 million. They also sold 190,000 lots for under US$10,000. Of the 200,000-plus lots sold at Sotheby's, New York each year, *more than half sell for under US$5,000* and *one quarter sell for US$1,000 or less*. In Australia, although record prices are usually taken as an indicator of market buoyancy, it is the mid-range buyers, purchasing from income, who underpin the market. Also underpinning any true collecting is the need and activity of upgrading works, of raking the rubbish for the pearls. True and great collectors buy, sell, exchange and trade-up, often many times over until they hold most-desired works of the highest quality. Californian collector Norton Simon sold many of his Impressionist and Modern Masters in the late 1960s to build up relatively inexpensively his museum's staggering collection of Old Masters. In most cases, unless one is trying to be comprehensive, leanness is a virtue in a collection; three superb items are better than thirty worthy but second-rate examples.

Establish the level you can afford and enjoy the opportunities. Look at the alternatives to what is beyond your reach. Many choices exist beyond major master-pieces by big-name artists that are beyond the reach of most. Consider how markets develop in response to activity. The starring roles occupied by paintings of the Impressionist and Modern Masters have boosted the markets of contemporary art and Old Masters. Conversely it was not difficult to predict the recently stimulated interest in drawings and prints.

Once collected mainly by a small scholarly elite, drawings have now found a wider audience and greater acceptance. Drawings were somewhat undervalued because of the relatively small number of people who collected them. Traditionally an old-fashioned collecting area, drawings always attracted a more intellectual type of buyer than other fields. However, spiralling prices for paintings and, to a lesser degree, for prints, have contributed to focusing the attention of new collectors on works on paper. And although prices have been increasing steadily, the market for drawings is comparatively sane and steady measured alongside the dizzyingly spiralling market for paintings and even prints.

Some consider drawings the last affordable area in the art market, the only remaining field that provides opportunity to acquire fine examples at less than astronomical prices. As with all generalisations, this is both true and not true. By definition, drawings are unique works of art on paper. Drawings encompass finished watercolours and gouaches as well as pencil sketches and studies. Drawings that are the most expensive have 'wall power', meaning that they are most like paintings. Usually drawings by artists whose paintings go for the highest prices are most in demand. Impressionist drawings, being so colourful, become substitute paintings for some collectors. Those who are unwilling or unable to spend US$3-4 million for a Degas painting will spend US$300–500,000 for a Degas drawing. While Master drawings may seem inexpensive in relation to paintings, they are hardly cheap. A Cubist charcoal drawing by Picasso in the John R.Gaines collection sold at Sotheby's in New York in November 1986 for US$1.65 million, and the average price of a lot at Sotheby's in November 1988 was close to US$100,000. Pierre Auguste Renoir's *Jeunes Filles au Piano* of 1892, a pastel on paper measuring 45 ½ x 35 inches (116 x 98 cm) offered at Sotheby's New York sale during November 1989 was estimated at US$20 million. Wallpower leads to crazy prices.

Similarly with prints. The market for Modern Master prints is at an unprecedented high, fuelled by the demand for an ever-dwindling supply of great work by 19th and 20th century masters. Prices which would have been unheard of just a few years ago have now become commonplace. Last season's expensive print has become this month's bargain. Prices for prints have been on the rise for the past seven years. The past two years have seen prices for many prints pushed upwards by 50 to 100 per cent. Picasso's *Le Repas Frugal*, a 1904 etching from the *Saltimbanques* suite, which sold for US$18,000 ten years ago, has risen steadily, selling at Sotheby's in November 1984 for US$32,500, in May 1986 for US$82,250, and in November 1987 for US$110,000. It is easy to forget that, historically, prints used to be very inexpensive. A Toulouse-Lautrec print sold for around $3.00 in modern currency when it was first published. Prints were meant to be easily afforded by the public. Fine prints to be collected are those in which the artist has entrusted his deepest feelings, as distinct from prints that result more or less from replication, which are to be avoided.

Whereas cash resources are the sinews of all collecting, buying with unlimited funds is no guarantee of buying well, nor with fun. Whereas financial clout may make it easier to find fine objects, collecting with limited funds disciplines the eye like nothing else does. The unmonied collector must rely on extra research to learn which fields and artists are important and overlooked, as well as have patience to wait until worthwhile objects become available, plus have courage to buy on the strength of personal opinion and connoisseurship. Connoisseurship is being able to assess quality and authenticity. Connoisseurship is the ability to distinguish fine objects from the vast array of mediocre ones, particularly in the lower price ranges. It is the ability to tell what is 'right' in the art of the past and to distinguish (before others) the Old Masters of the future. Often referred to as a 'good eye', connoisseurship is backed up by knowledge, supported by good visual memory, and is independent enough to form individual judgments and fresh observations. Developing an eye requires looking at things first hand, which takes time and is energy-consuming, plus the courage to recognise and revise an incorrect opinion. This takes patience and self discipline.

There are several ways to refine your eye. A good eye is an informed and exercised eye, that has looked long and hard. Looking at work should in a way be a matter of natural reflex. By keeping an open mind, shutting off the aesthetic principles and baggage we all carry around with us that precondition our likes and dislikes, and by absorbing the larger view, we can exceed our expectations, receive surprises, and further develop our 'eye'.

When looking at work at museums, consider the objects and try to identify them before referring to their labels. Concentrate on the best pieces. These are usually the key prototypes from which others have followed so they educate both your feel for quality and your chronological framework into which to fit objects. Discipline your looking. It is better to concentrate on six paintings properly looked at and well-remembered later, than to glance at sixty which later you are unable to recall or, worse, have muddled in your memory. Take every opportunity to handle objects. Auction rooms allow you to do this. Auction rooms really put your learning to the test. Museums display work chronologically or by logical groupings according to school or style. Auction rooms do not necessarily present works in logical groupings. Everything is lumped together, the good with the bad, the damaged, and the mistakenly catalogued. John L. Marion, chairman and chief auctioneer at Sotheby's, New York, regards the auction house as 'an open university of art and antiques with a revolving curriculum, a hands-on approach to learning and a faculty of experts.'

Handle any object as closely as you can; this gives you a closer feel for it. And assess what you think it is before referring to what the catalogue tells you it is. Art experts continually play this game of matching judgment. Catalogues are not infallible, and incorrect attributions do occur. A fabled instance occurred at Sotheby's 1977 Mentmore sale where London dealer David Carritt (a former director of Christie's) bought a moderately sized painting of an indeterminate mythological subject obscured by layers of dirt and dark old varnish. The painting was catalogued by Sotheby's as *The Toilet of Venus* by Carl van Loo, (a pleasing decorative painter of the mid-18th century not much sought after today). Carritt thought otherwise. He bought Lot 2422 for £8,000. A year later the cleaned painting, a rare early work by Fragonard, *Psyche Showing Her Sisters Her Gifts From Cupid*, was presented to London's National Gallery for an undisclosed valuation, thought to be about US$l million. Carritt had suspected something under the dirt and varnish. He had remembered the lost but recorded painting of Fragonard's youth, and his astute guess was confirmed when the heavy film of dirt and varnish had been cleaned off. Differences in opinion can result in unusual buying opportunities for the expert with the sharpest eye.

Small museums and private visits — arranged usually by clubs and societies — to collections generally not on view to the public offer further opportunity to develop visual memory and an 'eye' for quality. As in the saleroom, the unpredictable mixture of styles, objects and quality you may see in these collections surprise, as much as seeing something new and perhaps less well-known can surprise.

Being able to 'see' and recognise distinctions of style and chronology is helped by an understanding of the techniques of production and raw materials used by artists. Printmaking offers a good example. An understanding of the different processes by which prints are made assists the eye to qualify between, say, the sharp-edge line made not by etching (which involves biting into a plate with acid) but by engraving (which involves incising into a plate with a sharp edged tool). Knowing what properties different processes offer artists and what can be done using the different processes puts into perspective the achievements, and failures, of artists using them. A basic knowledge of art history is also an essential tool. Both historical and technological knowledge assist any assessment of a work and the quality of a work. Art history allows you to locate the work within a broader perspective. Is it an innovative piece, ahead of its time and therefore important, or does it imitate earlier models? Is it a unique example from a particular artist, or one of many works the artist made, or perhaps a sketch? This not only helps you identify the work and its quality. It can also have bearing on the value of the work.

A hierarchy of price is determined among different types of works, particularly in the case of works on paper. Multiples produced in an edition, such as lithographs and etchings are almost always less expensive than one-of-a-kind works (a drawing or watercolour) by the same artist. Usually small works cost less than large works; and damaged works, even if expertly restored, are less expensive than those in perfect condition. A signed work always commands more than an unsigned work. Medium or condition aside, subject and period can also affect value. Work out of the ordinary to that for which a particular artist is renowned or an atypical example from, say, early in an artist's career may cost less, despite being of great interest if only for its curiosity value. Similarly, whereas work by an artist enjoying great vogue may be expensive, work by the artist's less well-known contemporaries overlooked by fashion may often be had for reasonable prices. Every era sees artists of great popularity (often expensive) who later fall into obscurity. Compare the cases of Bouguereau (1825–1905) and Paul Cézanne (1839–1906). Adolphe-William Bouguereau, the archetypical Acamedician and bête noire of the avant-garde, achieved glittering success in his lifetime. Accepted for the Salon in 1849, Grand Prix de Rome in 1850, Academician in 1859, the ribbon of the Legion d'Honneur in 1859, Commander in 1885, and Grand Officer in 1903 — such was his glittering career with enormous financial rewards. Today he is regarded as one of the slickest of the French 19th century academicians. Cézanne, only a little younger than Bouguereau, never enjoyed the same sort of success. He vainly sent a picture to the Salon every year for many years, to be always coldly rejected. Yet today Cézanne is the pre-eminent Old Master of the modern age, whose impact on art itself can hardly be over-estimated.[9]

Look at what people are *not* collecting, because areas that have been over-looked by fashion offer rich seams. Overlooked or unpopular fields are always sources of good buys for those collectors who find charm in what others fail to see or regard as unappealing. However, this will call for an open mind and eyes open to new ideas and perceptions.

Once you have chosen which field you will focus on and specialise in collecting, develop your connoisseurship of this field. Begin by relying on the knowledge and advice of sellers who themselves specialise. Other experts, such as museum curators, may offer a more scholarly perspective to further illuminate you. Museums sometimes do offer access to undisplayed works — for example, in their print room and to works in storage. Museums hold 'consultation days' when curators give advice and expert opinions on objects members of the public bring to them. Museums conduct education programs offering lectures, films and tours.[10] Authorities exist in every field, whose studies of the field are respected world-wide. Museum libraries can assist you with reading lists to begin with. Your own reading will lead you to further discovery. However, there is no substitute for *seeing* as many works as possible. The collector's most useful tool is a large mental repertory of images and an exercised visual memory. Art is a visual medium. After reading all about it, the final judgment is really visual confrontation.

As in everything, ultimately you rely on your own judgment. A collector's primary obligation is to evaluate. Your looking, listening and reading will develop your ability to evaluate. You become your own expert. A collection is ultimately more coherent and interesting when chosen by one set of eyes.

Authenticity can affect price, so should therefore be of primary concern. Authenticity documents who executed the work, when, and variations (if any) from the artist's usual working habits. Buying from established, reputable sources minimises the risk of problems that arise if a work is counterfeit or simply misattributed. Reliable dealers willingly give certificates authenticating work. These are usually permanently fixed on the reverse or support of the work to protect their authentication being misapplied to another item. With reliable dealers, their bill of sale, detailing the work, is sufficient authentication. Your best protection is to buy from the most reliable sources, for they are interested in maintaining their reputation for integrity.

Developing your 'eye' also offers protection. Experts instinctively know when a work is 'right' or otherwise. They draw on their memory for details. They 'know' an artist — his style, taste, the way he composed and used colours. Most importantly, they know an artist's facture, or 'handwriting' ie. the way he applied paint, his brushstrokes. Knowing an artist's signature and how and when he signed his works is also important. This can date an undated work, especially in the case of artists who sign their works differently through different periods of their work. Catalogues authenticate works but not all works are catalogued. Not all artists are the subject of exhaustive *catalogues-raisonne*, the detailed, illustrated listing of all known works by a particular artist. Records of a work's provenance and exhibition history are important. A strong ownership record throughout the life of the object gives confidence in the authenticity of the object.

However, it is an art-world adage that all fakes have impressive provenances. No single test is foolproof. Each adds to the sum of knowledge about the object. Even experts seek a 'second opinion' on works they are unsure about, such as an outside expert opinion from an art historian with exhaustive knowledge of the field able to confirm a work's authenticity from stylistic evidence, or that of a conservator able to examine art scientifically to determine its true age and possible authorship.

Under scientific analysis, the materials comprising the work are examined to identify whether their age is consistent with the purported age of the object, as well as whether the technique used in applying the materials is consistent with the usual working methods of the purported creator. A work supposed to have been painted in the 16th century will not be painted on machine-woven canvas. Pigments will be evaluated to determine whether they are consistent with the purported age of the work, or are of recent manufacture. X-rays or ultraviolet light reveals new painting on old canvas, overpainting, or changed signatures.

Always ask before buying what condition a work is in and look to what extent it has been restored. Physical condition is important, affecting the beauty, durability and therefore price of a work, but it is not an absolute. A certain amount of wear and tear is considered normal with older works. Almost every painting over a hundred years old has had some touching-up by a restorer. It is agreed that a certain amount of restoration is desirable to allow viewers to experience a 'whole' work without being distracted by damaged areas, and is even necessary to preserve the physical integrity of the work and prevent future deterioration.

'Restoration' that violates the artist's intention, or that may do physical damage to the work, is not acceptable. Restoration is detectable. Crackle pattern should be visible in paint. You can see where crackles have been filled in if they disappear or their pattern changes abruptly. Because exactly the same materials and brushstrokes will not be used in restoration, restored works reveal variations in surface texture and tonality. Restored areas under ultraviolet light show up as dark spots.

Ultraviolet light also reveals a white glow that occurs if a painting is restored with a paint that is a lead compound. Works on paper should be looked at unframed so that possible tears, folds, discolouration and repairs can be analysed. Despite the opportunities for selection under scientific analysis, many still believe foremost in scrutiny by connoisseurship. They maintain that no machinery or scientific analysis replaces the expert's eye.

These are some of the points to check against your initial attraction to a work in order to protect yourself from buying badly and making what could be costly mistakes. Use commonsense to temper your cupidity and you will be better equipped to make an intelligent decision about whether to buy a work or not. And feel happier that you have bought well!

# 2

# THE ART MARKET: AUCTIONS

*'It's a rummy business'*

J.M.W. Turner on being asked to make a statement about art at a Royal Academy dinner

## A Dollar and a Dream

An auction is a competition in which the auctioneer puts goods up for sale and the buyers compete against each other until there is a winner. Auctions have a very long history. Certainly they were known to the Romans, who used them for a wide variety of public and private sales, including slaves and military booty.

The most commonly practised type of art auction is the English Auction, typified by Sotheby Parke Bernet Inc. and Christie, Manson and Woods International, Inc. The starting point is a low price, with bidders trying to increase their bids until the hammer falls to the last responsive bid. The auction is designed to extract the highest price obtainable from a group of persons concentrated in, or connected by telephone to, one location. Theoretically this should be the ideal way to buy or sell a work of art. The buyer is assured he is paying only the smallest necessary increment over what a rival purchaser would be willing to pay; the seller that he is receiving the best price anyone present is willing to pay. Pre-sale estimates are often listed in catalogues. The lower of the two estimates given for any work is usually in excess of any reserve, which gives prospective purchasers an indication whether they may bid on the work.

Major sales are anticipated events in the international art calendar. The two largest auction houses, Sotheby's and Christie's, annually stage their main sales of Impressionist and Modern works in New York during one week in May and one week in November. In Australia Sotheby's and Christie's stage their main sales through March through November. A much awaited event in the Australian auction calendar is Leonard Joel's sale in November, coinciding with Melbourne Cup Race festivities.

Major auction houses staging important specialist sales attract significant work which is either offered as a highlight of the sale; or, if the work comes from an important collection the sale will be devoted to that collection, like the Trout Collection sale held by Christie's in Australia in June 1989. This sale, on the premises at Everton House, Brisbane, and attended by nearly 3000 people, brought in a total well beyond expectations of A$7 million, with a run of high prices not only for paintings by Australian Impressionists. There was no shortage on bids. Most lots sold well above their estimates with the highest price being paid for John Peter Russell's 1900 painting *Belle-Ile* which sold for A$700,000 against an estimate of A$300,000–A$400,000. Rupert Bunny's 1895 portrait of his wife *Jeanne Morel*, which was highly publicised before the sale, reached A$500,000 against an estimate of A$350,000–A$450,000. The star of the furniture section was a Steinway & Sons concert grand piano made in 1982 which was estimated at A$15,000–A$25,000 and sold for A$64,000. The sale was the third largest house sale ever conducted by Christie's, and the most successful auction in Christie's 223-year history anywhere in the world.

Australia's art auction turnover in 1987–88 was the world's eighth highest, according to Richard Hislop's invaluable annual *Art Sales Index*.[2] Generally Australian sales are less specialised than in the Northern hemisphere. Sotheby's sales of tribal art have been regarded more as a reflection of the personal interest Sotheby's Australian manager, Robert Bleakley, holds in tribal art, than an indication of the degree to which the market for tribal art exists and is catered for by Sotheby's. Specialised sales are rare. Australian sales are more bazaar-like than those of their more specialised major Northern Hemisphere counterparts. Australian sales tend to be oversized. They risk offering many uninspiring works in a big majority of the lots on offer. Leonard Joel's in Melbourne offer on average a staggering fifteen hundred lots. In a single sale Australian buyers can choose from a wide-ranging feast of offerings. They include Australian paintings, European paintings, prints and drawings — even decorative arts and books. From among so much on offer the sharp-eyed collector can often spot an opportunity but should also be wary of the pitfalls of buying at auction, which can be fraught with dangers.

## Perils of Auctions

Buying at auction is particularly hazardous for the unsophisticated first-time buyer who may be short on connoisseurship. Auctions carry an air of mystery and suspense. They call for participants to act with an immediacy not generally necessary for other ways of negotiation. The pace and urgency of bidding can precipitate split-second bidding above the price you have budgeted for. It is always wise to set a limit before the sale begins. Even professional dealers budget limits beyond which they will not bid for desired items.

Without the steely nerves and resolve more experienced buyers develop, unwary first buyers can easily bid beyond their limit. It is also easy to forget in the urgent climate of the saleroom that other opportunities will arise which may be grabbed with more consideration than the saleroom allows. It is all too easy to focus on the most publicised high-priced 'blue chip' material overshadowed by publicity hype, and forget that equally good work by other artists can be had reasonably. For every bargain at auction, prices are paid that exceeded any rational expectation. Of course not every lot goes through the roof. It can be smart to buy against fashion. If you do a lot of homework, examine all the lots carefully, decide what you're going to bid on and how much you want to spend, auctions are a game that can be played with a lot of enjoyment.

Auctions are a game of matching wits, grit and financial resources. The game places emphasis on the individual artwork in its most extreme guise — as commodity. Art on the block is stripped of aesthetic dignity. Each item acquires a false aura of uniqueness at auction. It is easy to overlook just what kind of an object it is. Each sale at auction, given the split-second momentary nature of the process, is endowed with a last chance edge. All of a sudden you and someone else decide 'I've got to have it'. All a person needs to play is the most democratic of institutions: M-O-N-E-Y. The auction is the great equaliser. At that moment, in the heat of the bidding, who is to care if similar other work is available, and for less? Why risk this chance when if you have the 'readies': the item can be yours right then and there if you pay enough.

Though the new collector may find auction houses seem more casual and less intimidating than the hushed establishments of big-name dealers, auctions are not for the faint-hearted. The difference between auction houses and galleries has often been likened to the difference between a big department store and a smaller speciality shop. You can't put the object at auction on hold for a week. New buyers who feel the anonymity of buying at auction offers them protection from being pressured into buying something they don't want, would be wise to beware of pressures which operate at auction.

Be prepared, when bidding at auction. You can bid yourself, or by leaving a written bid, or by telephone or through an agent. Once you have decided to try for several lots, establish how fast the auctioneer proceeds so you can anticipate when your lot is likely to come up and be ready to bid for it. Although the average is 80 to 100 lots an hour, there can be a vast difference in the pace of auctions and indeed between lots. Position yourself in good time in a place clearly visible to the auctioneer and concentrate.

Before bidding, auctioneers require buyers to register for and bid with 'paddles' bearing numbers that refer to the client's name, address, and credit rating in some instances. On the fall of the hammer the auctioneer takes your paddle number. This establishes that your bid has been accepted, and depending on the conditions of sale detailed in the catalogue, this is usually taken by the auctioneer as the contract of sale. The entry of the buyer's name and the amount of his bid then noted in the sale book by the auctioneer is final and binding on all parties. Sometimes the auctioneer notices a bid just as the hammer falls, in which case he will call out 'On the hammer', and continue the bidding. The 'hammer price' is the price at which a lot is knocked down to the buyer. Commission bids or order bids can be made by post or telephone, or left with the auctioneer by buyers who ask the auctioneer to accept and execute bids on their behalf. Commission bids must always be confirmed in writing or by telex with reference being made to each sale through the code name and sale number printed on the catalogue. Almost 40 per cent of all lots at Sotheby's, New York are purchased via absentee, or order, bids. When the auctioneer uses the phrase 'Against you all' this means that the lot has gone to a commission bid and not to anyone who has been bidding in the saleroom.

The auctioneer has the discretion whether to accept bids or not. He also calls the size of increments between bids which are usually in the region of 10 per cent. It pays to bid clearly and be sure you are clearly visible to the auctioneer. The auctioneer will ask 'Are you bidding?' if you are being too obscure or timorous. Most bidding misunderstanding relates to what is described as 'in line' bidding when two or more people are directly in line with the auctioneer's eye and all of them may be convinced that the auctioneer is taking their bid. When this happens the auctioneer will usually re-offer the lot, so that bidding can continue. If you prefer, you can ask a dealer for assistance and can leave your bid with a dealer who is probably more experienced than you and who can sometimes get goods more cheaply by being able to bid more effectively. There is more to bidding than lifting your hand. Experienced bidders can tell when to bid quickly to frighten off a rival, and when to bid slowly to tire a rival. They will know when they are being 'run up' by someone else who is not a serious bidder and can shake off competition. For this service dealers will charge a commission of 5 to 10 per cent of the hammer price.

## How Do You Know When a Price Is Right?

Ultimately value is the price a buyer is prepared to pay. Auctions offer buyer and seller alike the sense that in an open market they are probably getting a fair deal. In a characteristic situation the owner does not know the value of what he is selling, and the buyer does not know what he ought to pay. A successful bidder appears to pay only slightly more than another potential buyer — that is, the under-bidder — is willing to part with, giving the buyer a sense of security about the appropriateness of the price he pays.

All that the fall of the hammer establishes is that on a particular day a certain buyer was prepared to pay a particular price for an object. A month previously he and the under-bidder might have been willing to bid twice as much. A month later neither might have been willing to bid at all, for general reasons such as economic uncertainty, or for reasons entirely personal to themselves. Most objects sold at auction do fall within a predictable price range, but every day there are extraordinary surprises when things sell for much more than expected, or for much less.

Commercial wisdom has it that auction prices fall between wholesale (what a dealer would pay) and retail (what a dealer would sell at). Prices are always particular to each item and circumstance, so auction prices can greatly exceed what the same or comparable objects would fetch at a gallery. Auction levels can often exceed dealers' prices. All that is needed are two competing bidders to push prices. Today, with more private collectors competing against dealers for auction house offerings, fewer 'bargains' are to be found. Many dealers find objects they may have wanted bid up to levels beyond what they feel they can pay, given their need to onsell at still higher prices.

Auction prices cannot always be assumed to truly represent fair market value. You can pay too much for what you get. You can never be certain what is lifting prices, and prices, in turn, can exceed expected levels. You may be bidding against someone trying to raise the level of the market, like dealers who may be bidding to push up the price that somebody will pay for work by an artist in whom the dealer has an interest, then dropping out of the bidding when an appropriate price level is reached. You may also be bidding against the owner's reserve, which may reflect a reasonable market level or may represent the owner's (perhaps extravagant) wishful thinking. You may be bidding against consignors bidding for their own items in order to 'puff up' the price and thus increase the bids of independent persons.

Values beyond the saleroom do not automatically follow auction prices. Only when a pattern of record prices paid at auction continues will values elsewhere generally follow. Otherwise the single high price paid can be regarded as a 'lucky accident', more of a reflection of a hasty buyer's split-second decision than a measure of the market value of the artist's work. The moral is that you have to be guided by your own sense of appropriate market values. This means that you have to know the market and develop your eye for quality.

There is less magic at arriving at fairly accurate estimates of the price of an object than is commonly held. Price guides are regularly published. These and visits to sales will develop a feel for price. Price guides are compiled from recent auction sales and so broadly reflect the state of the market at a given time. They cannot be used as infallible gospels due to the variety of objects. And there is always the exception: the work of outstanding rarity or quality with no existing yardstick against which it can be judged. As with everything, the price can be disappointing or exceed all reasonable expectations. Because no two objects are exactly the same, prices and values vary being particular to each object and other factors which all affect prices — such as the object's condition, provenance, and exhibition history. To ride the market properly you need to be informed about the movement of prices in your field. The astute collector can make good specific assessments on his own rather than follow the wisdom or misjudgments of others. One of the best ways of doing this is to spend six months or so viewing every available sale, but buying little or nothing. When anything interests you, make a note of it in the catalogue, giving details of particularly attractive features and any imperfections, and then put your own estimate on it, preferably without consulting any list issued by the auctioneers.

Then, if you are able, go to the sale itself and see what work which interests you sells for. If you are to be any good as a collector you should be fairly accurate in your estimates, and you will certainly know whether you are in fact going to be able to afford your chosen field.

The vendor consigning to auction, generally has two concerns. First, that the price the consigned work brings will meet at least minimum expectations. Second, that no conspiracy on the part of potential purchasers (a 'ring') will prevent the vendor from realising the highest possible price. The 'reserve' system traditionally erases these concerns. The reserve is a price secretly agreed upon between the consignor and the auctioneer below which no purchaser other than the consignor will be able to buy the consigned work. When bidding fails to reach reserve the consignor becomes the successful bidder. The work is 'bought in'. Bought-in works can be omitted from post-auction printed reports of realised prices. In Australia, unlike in New York, the auctioneer is not required to disclose that a lot is unsold. The only indication of a failed sale is the auctioneer's failure to call out a buying number when the final bid is a 'buy-in' bid by the auction house on behalf of the vendor.

Critics dislike what they regard as a charade under which the auctioneer receives and repeats bids for amounts below reserve. They argue that secret reserves are a sham and bidding should begin at the reserve price. Auctioneers defend the reserve system arguing that by starting the bidding below the reserve price and allowing it to build, they add to the drama and speculative excitement of auction's competitive bidding — which is believed to bring better prices, thereby benefitting the seller. Auctioneers also argue that the reserve price is a defence against 'rings' or 'pooling' or rigging as it is known in the United States. These occur when potential purchasers (such as informally organised groups of dealers) agree not to bid against each other in order to buy goods at the lowest possible price. They depress prices by withholding bids by agreement. One dealer will bid for the items to be later auctioned or 'knocked-out' among the ring. The increment realised by the seller in the knockout over what he paid at the immediately preceeding auction is divided among the other members of the ring who bid unsuccessfully at the knockout. The final purchaser has the work at no more than what he would have paid anyway, and ring members are compensated for their co-operation. Ring-bidding is a criminal offence and only works at sales when outsiders don't top the low bid at which the ring hopes to get the work for its knockout. Auctioneers are powerless to prevent pooling. Sending work to major auction houses for well-publicised sales at which many prospective purchasers may bid can guard against rings.

## Hype

The auction market plays on hype-potential, which multiplies prices, and can double or triple the highest price anybody thought a given item might go for. Of course the auctioneer's job is to match willing sellers and willing buyers, which is why the publicity offices of the auction houses ensure that specialists and collectors the world over know what is for sale and when. However, hype boosts demand and prices when neither aesthetics nor variety exist to make objects intrinsically desirable. Witness the hype-fed hysteria which fuelled prices paid for Andy Warhol's US$65 cookie jars selling in all for nearly US$250,000, skyrocketing way beyond expectations, on wind of the hype surrounding the sale of the personal collection of 'the Pope of Pop' (as Warhol called himself) after his unexpected death at fifty-eight. The Sotheby's Andy Warhol sale and travelling show was a 10-day, 17-session extravaganza from which all but 78 of the 2,629 lots sold for a total of US$25,333,368.[3] Values were cockeyed by Sotheby's marketing skills promoting the Warhol mystique, best exemplified by the 20th century Egyptian Revival chair in which Warhol once photographed fashion-guru Diana Vreeland. Considered by some as a 'piece of junk', the chair far exceeded its US$4–6,000 estimate to sell after a fierce battle in the saleroom for US$170,500 to a telephone bidder. It pays to look hard at work on offer! Like the Warhol chair, the supposed star of the sale may not be quite the dream item that the heavy hype it was given might suggest. Objects elevated by jazzed-up promotion, novelties that titillate, a well-known collector's personal prestige — all can shoot-up prices. Quality is anybody's guess. The big question is: what is the magic imponderable that makes for staying power?

Not one Warhol was offered within his collection. If there was a theme to his collection, it was Warhol's ego. Many works were dedicated to him and, like so many of the other objects he owned, simply because they were objects Warhol owned they seemed to spiral in price. Name and fame appeals to buyers. When name and fame becomes the main issue, distinctions between works of unequal merit are dropped. This symmetrically demonstrates that beauty combined with rarity is no guarantee for success. Hype-potential can boost even objects that verge on the edge of mediocrity. Prices can be multiplied by playing up a name in slogan form (whether it be the name of an artist, or of the sitter he portrayed, or of the monument with which the work is associated). For some buyers the possession of a work by a 'name' artist is a social necessity. Fully recognising this, auction houses play up hype-potential developing high visibility before sales, publicising the glamour of provenance, stirring much media attention through touring exhibitions of major items, and assorted publications, and televising previews. The Warhol sale was a textbook marketing exercise of unqualified success.

Another 'celebrity' sale which realised prices beyond expectations was held in September 1988 when worldwide interest centred on the auction of approximately 2000 lots comprising the collection of British rock star Elton John.[4] Assembled over twenty years, Elton John's collection ranged from fine jewellery, Art Nouveau glass and decorative sculpture of the 1920s and 1930s, to pop memorabilia. Much of this 'pop'-oriented material contained little intrinsic value yet attracted the general public. Prices fetched many times expectations. The four-day sale totalled £4.8 million, with almost every lot sold.

Another marketing coup was achieved by Sotheby's selling James Rosenquist's Pop fresco, *F.111*. Taxi-owner collector Robert Scull had bought the eighty-nine foot long neon-coloured social-political portrait of the F.111, made to be hung continuously on four walls, for US$40,000 in 1965. The painting was bought for US$2.09 million by Citibank's Arts Advisory Service on 11 November, 1986, after the catalogue mentioned the painting could *not* be seen at the viewing, *nor* would it be available to the buyer after the sale, due to its inclusion in an exhibition at the National Museum of American Art in Washington. This conferred cultural heritage status on the work, and made the work desirable — as reflected by the price paid for it.

## Auctions vs Dealers

Buyers often find they have been lured by hype surrounding auctions. As experienced buyers are well aware, few bargains are to be bought at auction. 'Saleroom fever' grips buyers into paying more than they personally budgeted for, or paying more than ever previously paid for similar items, or even more than the item may be worth.

Ironically, in their bid to promote themselves and the escalating prices paid at auction, auction houses have assisted dealers in the sense that many buyers and sellers now prefer trading through dealers. Inexperienced buyers commonly believe they can save themselves dealers' mark-ups by buying at auction, failing to perceive dealers' mark-ups offer buyers facilities and a range of services auction houses infrequently match. Major dealers are noted for their discriminating stock and their interest in supporting the value of their stock. This offers buyer and seller assured quality control. Principally, the buyer is offered the benefit of the dealer's judgment, research and knowledge of a piece, without the pressure salerooms exert. For the seller, auctions do not necessarily sustain price levels and do not have the same interest to protect a market as dealers have.

Dealers are one of the last bastions where serious connoisseurship meets commercialism. There are private dealers who do not have a publicly accessible gallery space, and choose to deal selectively with individual clients, most usually by appointment and often from their homes. Such private dealers are principally secondary dealers handling secondary sales. There are dealers who have publicly accessible galleries, who may also handle secondary work but will also publicly present first sales. Their accessibility distinguishes them. They offer buyers the chance to gain information and to develop familiarity with artists' work which auctions cannot do with auction sales deadlines. Auctions only show you part of the picture of an artist's work. Auctions take what they can get to sell whereas dealers present particular points of view in working with artists they are interested in. Auc-

## The Art Market: Auctions

tions follow taste. They sell what is fashionable. They may extend but do not create taste. Auctions cannot really develop any aesthetic shaping to their sales unlike dealers who present buyers with a variety of interests not represented in the auction market. In addition to offering more personal services and a more selective range of stock, dealers also offer greater assurance of confidentiality in art-related transactions conducted discreetly and without publicity. Transactions at galleries or with private dealers are less likely to attract media notice that is unwelcome to some collectors. Many collectors do not like to operate in public or to a time schedule. They prefer to buy or sell quietly, as and when it suits them. Important collectors who don't want people to know what they have bought and don't want to compete with someone else to buy things, prefer to pay a little more for the privacy and discretion galleries offer them.

The close contacts dealers maintain with museums and important collectors often enable them to negotiate a better price when placing a work privately than would be fetched at auction. Dealers' patient negotiations and agreement on terms of payment may result in more favourable prices to the seller than can be obtained at auction. Museum purchases at auctions are relatively few.

Museums often find it difficult to buy at auctions because their staff and trustees need time to consider potential acquisitions and raise the required funds.

Ironically, as more and more money washes through the art market alarm bells are ringing loudly through institutional arts organisations for the future of the arts. All major national and state museums and galleries and state-subsidised arts institutions in the United Kingdom and Australia are struggling to survive. US institutions are doubly hard-hit because Federal or State aid is minimal, at nine per cent. Recent changes to US tax allowances for donations has withdrawn considerable support from institutions and had a chilling effect on gifts. A recent study by America's Association of Museum Directors reported the value of donations between 1986 and 1988 had declined by 63 per cent or US$161 million.[5] Thus American museums which harvested incredible collections from benefactor collectors as the Cone sisters, Maurice Wertheim, Walter Arensberg, Arthur Sackler, Francois De Menil and countless others, are witnessing the rich inheritances museums might otherwise expect to receive now drying up. Would-be donors now see less attraction in giving to museums. This has drawn out works for sale within an increasingly liquid market, further fuelling higher prices (including Van Gogh's *Irises* which had been intended for Westbrook College, where it had been on permanent loan for many years).

Dealers support prices, setting fair market values on work by artists they represent and whose work they handle. When such works appear in the saleroom, dealers often support price levels to protect prices from dropping too low and to try to develop a new level of prices in the field. Auctions indicate and can set market levels though differences between dealers' prices and auction prices are common, never being in equal balance or perfect sync. Auctioneers regard auctions as rein-forcement of dealers' prices. But prices at auction vary widely. The impact of auc-tion results on prices is a subject of much reflection for dealers handling stock by artists appearing frequently at auction. A specific sale of a specific item can be a spe-cific event. When a price goes up or down it does not mean very much until the same thing happens two or three times in a row — then the auction barometer cannot be ignored.

Record prices are paid when the work has the right ingredients. This was illus-trated at Joels' 1989 sale when Jesse Traill's appealing oil *The Tea Garden* fetched a thumping A$135,000 against an estimate of A$45,000 to A$60,000. Here price result-ed from fashion for a particular subject matter rather than for a particular artist. Traill is best known for her etchings of the Australian bush. Admittedly the painting was a good size at 69 x 123 cm, but Traill's previous auction record was only A$900! This painting was an obvious special exception to the rule for her prices. One remarkable picture does not automatically change the market.

## How to Buy and How to Sell at Auction

Buying and selling at auction are distinctly different activities, each with different conditions, obligations, opportunities and pitfalls. When buying, first identify which sales will interest you. Hundreds of sales are held each year, either concentrating on a particular collecting area or offering further distinctions like one sale featuring works of a higher price and quality, while another containing more run-of-the-mill offerings. Auction sales will be defined by various categories, so the higher quality sale will be entitled 'Fine' (or "Important") Old-Master Paintings' while the catalogue for the more ordinary sale will be simply titled 'Old Master Paintings'. Smaller auction houses offer fewer specialised sales and broader specialities. They often hold 'estate sales' which offer all the auctionable property of the deceased, including furniture, silver and fine art. A 'specialised' sale at a smaller auction house may be a sale of all paintings recently consigned to the house from various sources, regardless of the period or countries of origin of the work offered. More important pieces in sales are often noted in auction catalogues as 'The Proper-ty of a Gentleman' (or similar but unnamed variations). This explains that the piece does not belong to a dealer and is 'fresh', meaning it has probably not come onto the market for some years. When a name is used, the name becomes part of the prove-nance or history of the piece.

Auction schedules are published in advertisements in newspapers and maga-zines, and auction house newsletters. Catalogues available before each sale can be bought singly or by subscription. They can be studied freely at the auction house days before the auction. Catalogue subscribers receive price lists after the sale. Cata-logues are an interesting barometer of taste and fashion and also a sure guide to auction house prosperity. From utilitarian documents with few illustrations and plain paper covers designed to provide a necessary minimum of facts, they have steadily grown larger and shinier in recent years, with coloured covers, lavish colour reproductions, and the same amount of information.

Properly used, catalogues can save you a lot of trouble. Remember: catalogues are the working documents of the saleroom staff and auctioneer when conducting the sale, so knowledgeable and professional catalogue entries are crucial for the auctioneer. Catalogues vary enormously in quality and accuracy. Explanations of cataloguing practices by each auctioneer are noted in their catalogues and should be compulsory reading for all buyers. Only by reading catalogues and comparing the descriptions with objects themselves will you learn to interpret the phraseology and get a 'feel' for a catalogue and an auctioneer's skills. This will enable you to accurately read the auctioneers' catalogues and develop the ability to know when to be suspicious of a catalogue entry. Does the description sound unlikely, for example? Is the object being over-described to make it sound better than it really is? Does a vaguely worded entry perhaps conceal the cataloguer's innocence? Can the object described represent an opportunity — a good buy?

You will need to recognise the different cataloguing conventions auctioneers use to describe works, and to appreciate the subtle differences each description makes. Though conventions vary with auctioneers, the following cataloguing conventions, which Christie's print at the front of their catalogues, are fairly standard and are worthwhile understanding.

A work catalogued with the name(s) or recognised designation of an artist, without any qualification, is declared to be a work by the artist. In other cases, for the paintings that cannot with certainty be attributed to specific artists the following expressions, with the following meanings, are used:

'*Attributed to ...*' means probably a work by the artist in whole or in part.

'*Studio of ...*', '*Workshop of ...*' states the work was executed in the studio or workshop of the artist, possibly under his supervision, but usually executed, in part at least, by an assistant.

'*Circle of ...*' means a work of the period of the artist and showing his influence.

'*Follower of ...*' notes a work executed in the artist's style but not necessarily by a pupil (implying the unknown artist imitated the Master's style but may have had no direct contact with the Master).

'*Manner of ...*' declares a work executed in the artist's style, but of a later date.

'*After ...*' is a copy (of any date) of a work by the artist.

'*Signed ...*', '*Dated ...*', '*Inscribed ...*' details that the work has been signed/dated/inscribed by the artist. The addition of a question mark indicates an element of doubt.

'*With signature ...*', '*With date ...*', '*With inscription ...*' indicate that the signature/date/inscription is by a hand other than that of the artist.

Measurements given usually represent, in the case of paintings, maximum stretcher or panel size. Height precedes width.

Do some works sell better at auction? An auction is a great public forum and generally work must have broad public appeal to do well at auction. Off-beat works for which it is difficult to find potential buyers can sometimes be good candidates for auction. The wide distribution of auction catalogues and pre-sale publicity increases the likelihood that interested collectors can be found for such unusual works. Sellers who have no idea what their possessions are worth are attracted to auction because objects offered to a wide public in open competition usually find a proper, though not necessarily the highest, market level.

Auctions appeal to sellers wanting to liquidate a mass of merchandise quickly (like collectors wanting to dispose of many of their holdings or fiduciaries needing to clear a large estate with small items). A public sale offers unquestionable safety for administrators of estates who don't want the responsibility of deciding what objects are worth. Additionally, auctions usually give them the assurance that work will be sold on a particular day, unless it is bought in for failure to reach its reserve. And many vendors quite rightly fear those rainy-day, poorly attended sales.

Many vendors prefer the discretion of the private sale through a dealer as a work exposed and unsold at auction can acquire the kiss of death. Some works sell better at galleries than at auction. Some works can be sold in the private retail market to great advantage for both buyer and seller at a price the auction house might be afraid to forecast. Impressionist paintings are generally 20 per cent lower at auction than at galleries. Tough, difficult work for which there is a limited audience sells for a better price at a gallery specialising in that type of work. Any object in a rarefied field needing specialised expertise to identify it will always sell better privately. Work that is not familiar does not perform well at auction. Dealers handling unfamiliar, more difficult work allow potential purchasers the time and attention needed to 'see' these works. Only dealers can offer careful education and undistracted viewing. The mass merchandising approach and frenetic atmosphere of auction houses prevent this.

Another trap many unwary new buyers fall into is that they fail to account for the buyer's premium many auctioneers charge — usually 10 per cent of the hammer price — plus other state and local sales taxes and handling charges that may have to be paid. Payment is usually required within several days to a week after the auction sale, and goods not paid for or removed within the specified time are stored at the buyer's risk and expense. Interest is often payable on the purchase price if unpaid beyond the time set aside by the auctioneer after the sale for collection and payment. Selling costs, too, need to be borne in mind. Insurance, handling charges (including freight and packing), special advertising and cataloguing charges, particularly for colour photographs, are billed by auctioneers to vendors. Added to the commission auctioneers take, these charges eat into the vendor's nett receipt on sales.

After-auction sales occur of work that was bought in. Offers from the highest bidder are entertained. At Sotheby Parke Bernet after-auction prices are usually lower than the last public bid (a bid below the price at which the work was bought in by the auctioneer for the consignor). At Christie's after-auction prices usually equal the last bid. Sometimes the auction house can negotiate a higher price than was achieved at the sale. In 1986–87 Christie's US sales totalled US$307.7 million with US$52.6 million in private sales. Private treaty sales are made in the United Kingdom on behalf of the nation in lieu of taxes for which Christie's receives a fee, not a commission. Of Sotheby's total sales for 1986–87 of US$704 million, US$25 million in private sales were made, with US$22.5 million made in the United Kingdom and internationally, and US$2.5 million in the United States. This represented, in all, less than two per cent of the year's total sales, was made mostly in jewellery, and all in items that did not go through the auction process.[6]

Consignors of unsold work are justifiably concerned that it may be difficult to sell a work privately once already publicly 'burned' — art world slang for what may be a dimunition in the market value of a work tainted by the stigma of being exposed especially if unsold at a public auction. Occasionally the successful bidder is 'burned' at auction. Auction houses limit their liability to buyers. Some flatly refuse to guarantee the authenticity of anything they sell. Most auctioneers have extensive conditions of sale which constitute the terms of the contract for sale, which is a contract between the buyer and the seller — not the auctioneer. The auctioneer is an agent of the seller, and so the conditions of sale will be weighed in favour of the auctioneer and the seller. When selling, the consignor relies on the auctioneer to decide if the item is auctionable, and if so, how best to offer the item: in what auction (whether a major or minor sale), and in the company of what other items. The consignor looks to the auctioneer to suggest estimated prices (which are to be revealed) and the reserve price (which is kept secret). The consignor looks to the auctioneer to collect the proceeds from the highest bidder. The auctioneer is regarded as the 'expert' who will support a claim of authenticity if the work is questioned. The auctioneer looks to the consignor to stand behind a claim of title of ownership.

Bearing in mind that the auctioneer deals with tens of thousands of consignments annually, what obligations does the auction house have to the consignor? This question is important when large sums of money are involved and the consignor is relying on the auctioneer's market expertise. Purchased lots are at the buyer's risk in all respects from the time of collection or upon the time limit set for collection from the date of sale. This is usually two days after the sale. The seller indemnifies the auctioneer and the buyer against all claims made or proceedings brought by persons entitled or purporting to be entitled to the lot, and the seller shall reimburse the auctioneer on demand for all payments, costs, expenses or any other loss or damage whatsoever made, incurred or suffered as a result of any breach by the seller through such a claim. If a lot fails to reach its reserve, the seller pays the auctioneer the unsold commission at the published rates calculated on the last bid for the lot plus expenses. In Australia in the case of lots failing to reach their reserve, a charge of 5 per cent may be made on the last bid for the lot where the bid is less than A$1,000 and 2.5 per cent on the last bid of all other lots. If lots are withdrawn once the catalogue including the lot has been printed, a charge of 10 per cent of the reserve together with any expenses, is payable. If there is no reserve, a charge of 10 per cent of the figure at which the lot has been valued for insurance, as determined by the auctioneer, together with any expenses, is payable.

Whereas the seller is concerned with getting the best price (from a method of sale in which the price to be obtained is beyond his control), the purchaser (who has complete command over the price he is prepared to pay) is anxious about other questions. Authenticity is the purchaser's main concern. What can you do if something about the work you have bought — the authorship, history, condition or title — turns out to be other than described? Traditionally, auction houses argue that they sell only as agents for the seller. Also, unlike dealers, they handle too great a volume of work to offer exhaustive examination and investigation of every lot presented. Auctioneers argue that the generally lower prices at auction compared to what a conventional art dealer may charge allow buyers compensation for the risks that may be involved in buying at auction. Auctioneers' conditions of sale disclaim warrantees or representations with respect to their catalogue statements or otherwise, about authorship, history or condition. Any remedies a purchaser may have are against the consignor, who (though often described in the catalogue as a 'gentleman') is generally unknown to the purchaser. For the buyer at auction, it is very much a case of 'buyer beware'. There are many limitations on the liability of the auctioneer to the purchaser, and auction catalogues specifically note that bidding at auction indicates acceptance of these conditions. They apply whether the buyer is aware of them or not. They are clearly stated in each sale catalogue. 'Conditions of Sale' often accompany a limited warranty that spells out exactly what the auction house guarantees. As it happens, this is not much.

Sotheby's (in New York, first in September 1973) and Christie's (when it entered the New York market in 1977) withdrew from denial of responsibility to offer a limited warranty. Henceforth, on lots sold in its New York salesroom, Sotheby's guarantee for five years the authorship of any work executed after 1869, and that the work is not counterfeit in the case of work executed before 1870. More recently purchasers have been granted a five-year period to return a work and rescind the purchase if able to prove to the auction house's satisfaction that the work bought was a 'deliberate forgery', but only as confined to the scholarly and scientific expertise prevailing at the time of the original sale. In this case the sale is rescinded and the original purchase price refunded. This applies only to representation about the authorship of the work, not a work's history, literature or condition — responsibility for which is still disclaimed. Christie's and Sotheby's in Australia give no warranty unless within five years of the date of the sale a buyer satisfies the auctioneer by a written opinion of an expert valuer acceptable to the auctioneer that a lot bought at auction is a forgery. However, the lot has to be returned to the auctioneer in the same condition as it was at the date of sale and there can be no third party to the lot. The auctioneer will refund to the buyer any amount paid in respect of the lot, but not if the catalogue description at the date of auction was in accordance with the then generally accepted opinion of scholars or experts, or fairly indicated a conflict of such opinion, or if it could be established that the lot was a forgery only by means of a scientific process not generally accepted for use until after publication of the catalogue or by means of a process which at the date of the auction was unreasonably expensive or impractical, or likely to have caused damage to the lot. Intending bidders must satisfy themselves by close inspection or otherwise as to the nature of the lot or lots offered for sale and must accept lots with all faults, patent or latent (if any).

Auctioneers generate income by charging a fixed commission to either or both the buyer and vendor on successful completion of a sale. This is normally around 10 per cent on both sides, although in the case of high value items the seller may negotiate a lower commission rate. In 1975 in London, first Christie's, then Sotheby's introduced a 10 per cent premium, which buyers pay on the hammer price. Buyer's premium was introduced in the United States by Christie's in 1977, and by Sotheby's in 1979. Whereas a substantial painting or collection of paintings can form the basis of a significant reduction in the consignor's commission, every purchaser paid the same rate of commission. Protests by English and American art dealers against buyer's premium, and their efforts to force the two major auction houses to withdraw buyer's premium have, to date, been unsuccessful. A suit brought in 1979 by the Society of London Art Dealers and the British Antique Dealers Association caused Christie's to reduce its premium in London to eight per cent. The art community objected that on accepting payments from the purchaser the auctioneer's duty to the consignor would be compromised. Whereas the consignor lost the benefit of the best price not raised, the auctioneer still received buyer's commission. The Art Dealers Association of America claimed it was unfair for an auction house, acting as the consignor's agent, to charge and accept payment from a buyer 'to whom the agent is rendering no services'. In Australia auction houses can viably cut vendor commission from 15 to 10 per cent (or less in Victoria) because they charge a buyer's premium which is illegal in New South Wales. Ten per cent of the hammer price is taken on sales in Victoria and 17 ½ per cent on sales in New South Wales.

Sotheby's, New York, have recently come under criticism for acting as principal in the case of sales they have handled in which they have facilitated finance for the buyer against a purchase and for the vendor against sales, secured by works of art to be sold by Sotheby's. Sotheby's have considerably expanded business through their Financial Services program which provides financing loaned at the ratio of 1:2 secured by works of art to auction buyers and sellers. A purchaser loan could provide bridge financing for up to 70 per cent of the purchase price of a work. An asset-based lender, Sotheby's establish a one-year credit facility for clients who can draw on the facility to finance purchases at Sotheby's sales anywhere in the world. Loans are generally repayable over one year in equal quarterly instalments. Loans may not exceed 120 per cent of the low pre-sale estimate of the acquisition. Minimum credit facility is £75,000 and the minimum loan that may be drawn on the facility is £20,000. Consignors are offered an advance of up to 50 per cent of the low auction estimate of anticipated sales. Advance payments of auction proceeds are secured by works of art to be sold by Sotheby's. Consignor advance is offered from £16,000 and is repaid, together with interest, out of the sale proceeds. Sotheby's also offer asset management loans (art equity), lending up to 50 per cent of the asset value of works of art not scheduled to be sold. This is basically a simple loan secured by works of art. The minimum loan is £150,000. Sotheby's regard this service, the equivalent of high-end private banking service, as instrumental in obtaining major collections and sales. Sotheby's financial services program for the first nine months of 1989 represented 6.48 per cent of Sotheby's overall profit. Financing purchases has been used, Sotheby's claims, only six times on a lot over US$1 million, once on a lot over US$5 million (for *Irises*), with about 15 to 20 people with lines of credit.

Long-rumoured speculation was confirmed in 1989 that corporate entrepreneur Alan Bond financed his US$53.9 million (£30.2 million) purchase of Van Gogh's *Irises* through such a loan from Sotheby's. Taking into account interest, insurance charges and auction commission, it has been estimated Bond would have to sell the painting for as much as US$70 million in order to break even. Whereas Bond's buy was a big boost to the art market after the 1987 stock market crash, Sotheby's (and, no doubt, Christie's) must have been concerned by the prospect of the world's most expensive painting returning to the market quickly — a factor which could prove as destabilising for the market as the record price paid for the work in the first instance. It is generally inadvisable to sell any high-priced work of art in a hurry. Generally pictures should be kept off the market for a minimum of three to five years. Even in the market's recent bullish mood any hint of a forced sale by a big art investor might raise fears that there are other investors who have also been paying prices they cannot live with.

In late March 1990, the Getty Museum (unmatched in financial power with an endowment of about US$3.2 billion and required by law to spend only 4.25 per cent of that amount annually — about US$136 million — on its seven operating programs, of which the museum is one) announced it had acquired *Irises* which the museum evaluated as perhaps the best-preserved Van Gogh in existence. There has been no disclosure about the price negotiated between the Museum, the beleagured Alan Bond who was rumoured to be asking US$65 million for the painting, and

## The Art Market: Auctions

Sotheby's which was apparently eager to broker a deal for the painting and recoup some of its losses from the way it helped Mr Bond finance the purchase of the painting in 1987. It is rumoured that the deal involved not only cash but shares of stocks owned by the Getty Trust. The value of the package at the time of the sale was estimated to be between US$52 million and US$55 million.

The desire of auction houses for bigger shares of the market poses risks. Ironically, significant financial power such as is enjoyed by Sotheby's does not precondition successful auctions and can backfire. Sotheby's willingness to finance and guarantee a minimum sale price for some works can lead to unprofitable results.

Take the case of a Monet landscape offered at Sotheby's, New York (11 November, 1988). The picture was bought in at US$3 million against a totally unrealistic US$3.5–4.5 million estimate. The guaranteed price was fully paid to the owner. The picture remained with Sotheby's months later. At the end of June 1989 Sotheby's had loans for US$158 million outstanding. About one third of these loans were advances to sellers secured on the objects they were about to sell. In 1986 Sotheby's total loan portfolio stood at a mere US$35 million. In October 1989, Sotheby's sold paintings owned by Mr John Dorrance, the heir to the Campbell's Soup fortune, for a total of US$123 million. That was just above the US$120 million that Sotheby's is supposed to have guaranteed that it would pay the sellers. Sotheby's had its work cut out to make even that, despite enthusiastic bidding from a Japanese dealer who bought eight paintings for US$24 million. Sixteen of the best Impressionist pictures in the collection (including works by Manet, Degas, Van Gogh and Monet) sold for less than Sotheby's lowest estimate of what they would fetch. Normally a seller would put a reserve price on a picture at, or close to, the auctioneer's lowest estimate. If the bidding did not reach that price the picture would be withdrawn from the sale. Only one picture in the Dorrance sale was withdrawn. Still smarting from the bad deal with Alan Bond over *Irises*, Sotheby's became entangled in another troublesome financial tale in late 1989 when Japanese dealer Shigeki Kameyama found himself unable to pay the record price he paid at auction for William de Kooning's *Interchange* (US$20.7 million, Sotheby's New York November 1989). Neither Kameyama nor Sotheby's could find another buyer who would match the record price. Sotheby's needing to pay the consignors of the de Kooning had to clear Kameyama's debt through selling a consignment from Kameyama of a fairly large number of paintings.

This practice also raises criticism on ethical grounds, if it is given that auctioneers are not — or rather should not be — dealers. The reasons are not difficult to see. By acting only as an agent for the vendor, having no ownership of the goods sold, the auctioneer has no conflict of interest. But if he becomes a dealer as well as an auctioneer, and holds objects for his own account in order to sell them at auction with the intention of making a profit, this very partial interest makes it very difficult — some would say impossible  — to maintain the standard of impartial advice that has traditionally marked the best auctioneers. Furthermore, if the auctioneer through misjudgment makes losses and not profits on his dealings, his objectivity towards all vendors, reserves, commission bids and his whole role as an auctioneer, may be prejudiced. A healthy market depends on dealers and auctioneers playing their respective but separate roles. It is certainly in the interest of collectors that they do so, since the collector requires overall variety, choice, reliability and a free flow of objects and good advice. Monopolies do not create such conditions, nor do mistrust and bureaucratic regulations.

Blistered by the criticism it received following the 1987 sales of *Irises*, Sotheby's announced in January 1990 that it was abandoning its practice of providing buyers at auction, with loans secured by the artwork to be purchased. When Bond's financial empire collapsed and he was unable to repay his loan, after two extensions, the world warned that the price of *Irises* (regarded in the wake of the 1987 stock market crash as a benchmark and an affirmation of the strength of the art market, and contributing to a continued boom in the paintings market) was not real. Sotheby's was accused of inflating the market and creating artificially high prices. Sotheby's had lent Alan Bond half the US$54 million price, using the value of the painting as collateral. Sotheby's announced they are not going to take a work of art as collateral until it is paid for and owned for 90 days or more.

## Mega-Star Business

The world's two leading auction houses, Christie's International and Sotheby's Holdings, often referred to as 'Christobys', sold between them US$54 billion of art in the 1988–89 season. Christie's sales jumped 63 per cent to US$1.78 billion, while Sotheby's maintained its lead over its rival with a 48 per cent leap over the 1987–88 season sales of US$1.55 billion (excluding private treaty sales) to US$2.3 billion. For the year ended 31 July 1989, the market share between the world's big two auction houses divided at £723 million for American-owned Sotheby's as against £542 million for British-owned Christie's, or 57:43 per cent. Between them the two auction houses sold more than 400 pieces of art which broke the US$1 million barrier, including 20 pieces which fetched more than US$10 million each. Only two seasons previously Sotheby's auction sales for the 1986–87 season surpassed US$1 billion for the first time for any auction house. At that point, sales were US$1.3 billion for the entire season, the same total achieved in the spending orgy of the first six months of 1989.

Christie's and Sotheby's have been fierce market rivals for decades.[7] Their competition has sharpened as prices have risen and the turnover of both cash and art has increased. Though their identity remains on the auction floor they have diversified into real estate, publishing, tourism — even education.

The recent boom in prices of major works of art is flowing through to share

### The Art Market: Auctions

prices of the auction houses. Instead of buying into art or an art-investment plan, it is possible to buy shares in firms that deal in art such as Christie's. Christie's share price has almost doubled since the start of 1989 to around £3 a share, while Sotheby's, which was floated in May 1988 at £4.50 a share, has traded at £14.50. In addition to the prospect of surging profits, Christie's share price has been buoyed by takeover speculation. A number of international investors have taken strategic stakes in Christie's. Interestingly the biggest beneficiary of Christie's soaring share prices was Australian collector Robert Holmes à Court, who was the auctioneer's largest single shareholder. Holmes à Court sold his 7.3 per cent interest in September 1989 for a profit of more than £10 million to a Japanese finance company chairman, Mr Yasumichi Marishita of Aichi Finance, who is, like Holmes à Court, an active art buyer, estimated to have spent more than US$80 million at auctions through 1988–89.

Christie's is a frequent target of takeover speculation with bid-inspired shares estimated at a minimum of £5 per share required to take control. This would place a value of £760–850 million on the 223 year-old British company. Stockbrokers have had a tough time making accurate profit forecasts for the auction houses over the past couple of years because they underestimated the strength of the art market. Both auction houses are trading on high historical price/earnings ratios, fuelling investors' expectations of big jumps in profitability.

Although it accounts for less than one per cent of its worldwide sales, Christie's views Australia as a promising market. It has opened new salerooms and offices in Darling Street, South Yarra, in Melbourne, and is expanding its premises in Double Bay in Sydney. The house has been operating in Australia since 1969. In August 1989 the house announced the formation of a new company, Christie's Australia Pty Ltd, to be chaired by Qantas chairman Jim Leslie. Long-time Christie's executive Roger McIlroy was appointed managing director with the objective of a wider push into the Pacific Basin region. Christie's sales in Australia had jumped 165 per cent to A$13.9 million for the 1988–89 season. This included the record A$7million Trout Collection sale. A previous Australian sales record of A$5.7 million had been set by Sotheby's at their November 1988 auction. Sotheby's turnover through 1988–89 was A$22 million, which it claims is two-thirds of the auction market. The latest issue of Ted Craig's *Australian Art Auctions Record*, covering July 1981 through July 1989, records 14,000 pictures sold with the total value of the market put at A$77 million.

The removal of the European Common Market barriers in 1992 should see the French house of Drouot emerge as a major competitor to the two mega-star world rivals. So much of what now passes through London and New York is sourced from the Continent. France is seen as the last unemptied warehouse of fine art. The French enjoy vast untapped art resources and an enormous public of well-informed art lovers who buy for their private enjoyment.

*Collecting Art*

It is often said that bigger prices are fetched at Hotel Drouot Auctions than in London for secondary works. Nett sales in Paris totalled FF 2.87 billion (US$500 million) in 1988, up by over 30 per cent over the previous year. Ader Picard Tajan supplanted Philips as the world's third largest auction house — a position that Philips had held for at least a decade — by generating US$240 million in sales in 1989. Certainly Paris is the place to go for little-known works by great masters, and Drouot — the world's third largest auction salesroom — has been referred to as the attic of France. A curious mix of treasure house and street fair, Paris's Hotel Drouot is the hunting ground par-excellence for those seeking privately owned rarities that have been out of sight for decades. The truly great event at Drouot in 1988 was the sale in November of Rumanian Dada artist and poet Tristan Tzara's (1896–1963) collection. The cross-section of what could be bought in Paris is shown in the publication *DROUOT, L'art et Les encheres en France*. The offerings are breathtaking. To the annoyance of foreign groups, French restrictive laws dating from 1804 keep auctioneering off-limits to anyone else, even after 1993. Unable to operate as an auction house in France, Christie's and Sotheby's are developing their European operations from other bases — particularly from Switzerland.

While the European market is regarded to be of enormous potential, there is no doubt that America constitutes the largest, most active, and most lucrative market. Hislop's *Art Sales Index* shows the values for picture sales around the world for the year ended 31 July 1989 at America £802 million (45.6 per cent); Britain £557 million (31.9 per cent); France £198 million (11.3 per cent). If Sotheby's and Christie's alone are measured, then 59.9 per cent of pictures by value were sold in the United States as against 40.1 per cent in Britain. In the 'Nineties, America will be selling and reselling the gigantic acquisitions of the previous two decades and will do most business in the burgeoning Contemporary Art market. The 1988–89 season saw dramatic growth in the Contemporary Art market in both the United States and Europe. In the United States, Sotheby's Contemporary Art totals alone were US$195 million, compared to US$64 million in 1987–88, reflecting a 205 per cent increase over the same period.

For the present, Impressionist and Modern paintings in the international market remain the star stocks. They increasingly dominate the art market as a whole, in terms of the sheer value of work sold. This market has reached unparalleled heights. Some observers considered that the price of US$39.9 million paid for Van Gogh's *Sunflowers* in March 1987 might have been an aberration. But Van Gogh's *Irises* sold for US$53.9 million not long after the October 1987 slump in financial markets, thus demonstrating that prices for Impressionist paintings had indeed reached new and substantially higher levels.These sales encouraged excellent works onto the market for subsequent sales. Buyers (60 per cent of whom were European or European-based) paid record eye-popping prices throughout the 1988 Spring sales in New York and the end-of-season Summer sales in London. Monet's *Dans la Prairie* fetched a record £14.3 million, Degas' *Petite Danseuse de Quatorze Ans* sold for £10.12 million and Cézanne's *La Cote du Calet, a Pontoise* achieved a new record for the artist at US$9.2 million. It is estimated that from 60 to 65 per cent of Impressionist and Modern Masters passed to European-based buyers.

On 27 June, 1989 at Sotheby's sale in London, of 79 lots, 34 went to European buyers, 9 to Americans and 2 to South America. In value, Europe accounted for 56 per cent of the £35.495 million (US$56.8 million) in sales, Japan for 22 per cent, the United States for 21 per cent, and 1 per cent from South America. Japanese buyers again proved an important force in the market at all levels. Minor artists such as Marie Laurencin and Raoul Dufy, who appeal to Japanese tastes, brought prices well above expectations. In December 1988 a Tokyo sale of 40 Bernard Buffet paintings totalled US$5.5 million. Market strength continued through mid-1989. Through Spring 1989 in New York, 89 Impressionist and Modern works each fetched US$1 million (£600,000) or more. On the evening of 9 May, Sotheby's, New York, established a new auction landmark when an Impressionist and Modern sale realised US$205 million (£123.4 million), more than any comparable sale in auction history and the first time that the US$200 million mark had been reached in a single season.

In the Northern Hemisphere the art market season runs from the beginning of September until the end of July, with little mainstream activity in August. Throughout the season high geared trade applied equally to dealers, galleries and auction houses. By Summer 1989 there had been 250 antiques and works of art auctioned in various countries for US$1 million or more. The art auction boom has been fuelled mostly by the huge appetite for Impressionist and Modern works by artists such as Picasso and Van Gogh, but also extends to Old Masters, oriental works and jewellery.

With prices for Impressionist and Modern pictures spiralling, the upward shift in price levels also marked the market for Old Master paintings. The several active markets for this sector (including London, New York, Monaco, and Paris) ensure the strength of this sector. European dealers and collectors have long been active within Old Master paintings. Now, however, many more private collectors in the United States are entering the field and bidding aggressively. The subsequent increase in competition is driving prices even higher. The market remains selective, with top prices achieved for the best quality paintings and for those which are in good condition. As is usually the case, 'fresh' paintings which have not been on the market for a number of years attract more attention and yield higher prices than those which have been offered more recently. Demand for poorer quality or second-rate works is patchy. An auction record for an Old Master was set at Christie's in New York in June 1989 when an unsigned portrait by Jacopo da Carruci (1494–1556), known under his *nom de peinture* as Pontormo (where he was born), was sold for US$35.2 million, setting a world record for any Old Master. This was universally regarded as a bargain by Old Master specialists, dealers and auction house personnel. Certainly it is one of the great portraits of 16th century France, and some regard this price as a portent of a future Old Master boom, where more and more pictures will enter that sacred Valhalla of eight-digit prices.

The 1537 oil, *Portrait of Duke Cosimo 1 de Medici*, despite the utter lack of resemblance that the Halberdier bears to documented portraits of Cosimo, was sold by the estate of Chauncy D. Stillman, a New York investor, and bought by the Getty Museum in Malibu, California. For the past twenty years the painting had been on view as a 'permanent loan' to the Frick Museum. With Christie's the painting went on a grand tour to Tokyo, London and Munich before the sale in New York. Such promotion obviously boosted the glamourous 'image' of the work. *The Halberdier* was regarded as possibly the last great Mannerist portrait to come on the market. In this sale price matched rarity, importance and beauty.

The previous record holder for the most expensive Old Master painting sold at auction is Andrea Mantegna's *Adoration of the Magi*, sold at Christie's in London in 1985 for US$10.45 million and now also at the Getty. As 'greatness' is too often defined as 'most expensive', perhaps a better comparison to consider is Peter Paul Ruben's *Samson and Delilah*, bought by the National Gallery, London, at Christie's, London, in 1980 for a mere US$5.82 million. Just as *The Halberdier* represents a supreme achievement by Pontormo, this Rubens is an outstanding representation of the major characteristics of Rubens' art. Both these paintings are great paintings, not just expensive. What is considered a high price for a great Old Master, of course, may only be a usual price for a routine Impressionist or Modern work. Few Old Masters have the instant name-recognition or easy appeal of Impressionist and Modern work. As paintings, Old Master paintings can be generally more demanding on the viewer. As is true of the market for 19th century pictures, the safe subjects and popular schools are the easiest to sell, and it is in these areas — of still lifes (preferably of flowers and fruit), Dutch landscapes and genre paintings, and 19th century Italian *vedute* — that the market is at its strongest.

The highest auction price achieved for a work by a living Australian artist is A$825,000 paid for Sir Sidney Nolan's *First Class Marksman* of 1946, sold by Sotheby's in Melbourne in August 1989. The painting belongs to the original Ned Kelly series and was the only one to remain in private hands. The record was previously held by Arthur Boyd's *Melbourne Burning*, sold by Sotheby's in July 1985 for A$313,500. Most works in Australian sales fetch from A$5,000 to A$50,000. 'High profile' pictures valued in excess of A$200,000 prove rarer and more difficult to sell at auction. The A$1 million barrier was first broken by the sale by a dealer of Arthur Streeton's 'dinkum Aussie' landscape *Golden Summers* to West Australian Bill Hughes. Another dealer secured a then record A$1.3 million shortly after for Arthur Streeton's *Hawkesbury River NSW 1896*.[8] Queensland Art Gallery paid A$1,250,000 for the Melbourne Club's Rupert Bunny *The Bathers* through dealer Joseph Brown in

1987–88. This is a European painting, painted in grand Edwardian manner, spiced with a subtle hint of *fin-de-siecle* decadence. The record Australian auction price for an Australian artist is for Rupert Bunny's 230 x 240 cm oil on canvas *Une Nuit de Canicule* which sold in November 1988 at Leonard Joels for A$1,250,000. This was almost surpassed in April 1989 at Sotheby's when John Glover's *The Bath of Diana* was auctioned for a record price for this artist of A$1.76 million (despite predictions that the painting would be bought in at A$700,000, and despite a legal dispute surrounding the painting foreshadowed before the sale by the afternoon press for money claimed from the vendor). However, the bid fell foul of the Heritage Act. [9]

The overdrive of the international auction market is a far cry from the auction rooms of not very long ago, when they were the refuge of a tiny group of professionals where once all you needed was a dollar and a dream. Not long after the Second World War the art market assumed its completely international character. Auction rooms in the 1980s era of lascivious greed double as 'gambling rooms, vanity parade and surrogate stock market, with overtones of bullring, prize ring, cockfight, dogfight and manfight' as described by *The New York Times* critic John Russell, where 'every last instinct of greed and cupidity and ostentation was let loose and money is the measure of all'. [10] Only history will tell, perhaps 50 years from now, what the real value of the work sold should be, and will show the falling meteorites that were once shooting stars. Meanwhile, whatever reservations, if any, may be felt about auctions, they attract visitors, generate visual awareness, publish catalogues, and give us something to gossip about.

# 3

# THE ART MARKET: DEALERS

*'I wanted to be an art businessman or a business artist.*
*Being good in business is the most fascinating kind of art.'*

Andy Warhol, *The Observer*, 1986

*'I collect money, not art.'*

Frank Lloyd, *The Legacy of Mark Rothko*, New York , 1978

*'I am interested in people who move Art History along, who*
*make the advances; there is something profoundly moving about*
*man's urge and capacity to create. To me that's the way, that's*
*the reason why art is truly international. I believe that the*
*most inspiring thing about a society is the man of culture it*
*produces, the artist is a civilising force in our lives.'*

Marian Goodman, Laura de Coppet and Alan Jones, *The Art Dealers*, 1984

## Dealing with Dealers

Unlike auctioneers, dealers are exclusively responsible for the primary market (of first sales). Many are also active within the secondary market (of second and subsequent sales). The secondary market comprises both dealers and the open market of the auctions. A dealer is a commercial art merchant who maintains a gallery where work is displayed for sale, who purchases art at wholesale to resell at retail and/or carries merchandise on consignment, and, in general, keeps works of art as stock in trade. As we will see, dealers differ in their focus and their *modus operandi*.

A private dealer, for all practical purposes, is one who does not have a publicly accessible gallery space, and who chooses to deal selectively with individual clients. Many operate without galleries, often from their own homes, and can be seen only by appointment. Many hold one show a year with a catalogue circulated to clients. The word 'private' conjures up images of secrecy and exclusivity, of privileged information, of something that stands apart from accepted institutions and is, somehow, a step above them. Many private dealers claim that being 'private' influences the kind of people who come to them. They claim their clients are more selective and

45

they are only approached by people who are looking seriously to acquire, or academics wanting to study a particular object. Their capital is devoted to inventory rather than the maintenance and administrative costs publicly accessible galleries have. Some who begin as private dealers open their gallery to the public. Lifestyle seems to be a major force in determining whether a dealer goes public, plus economic concerns. Private dealers open publicly accessible galleries to work with more clients, to have more space and the opportunity to present more exhibitions a year.

Many dealers will buy work outright at auctions or at a negotiated price. Others will take work on consignment, to sell it for an agreed price less an agreed commission. As the first is a quick transaction, any profit margin is clearly to be enjoyed by the dealer. In the case of consigned sales, the vendor can hope to nett between 70 and 75 per cent of the value of the work sold. This technique is most effective in the case of more highly priced work, or work that is unusual, so therefore more difficult to clear through auction. The dealer earns his 25 to 30 per cent commission by placing the work through his network of contacts, of clients and collectors whom he knows hold interest in the work on offer.

Transactions like these are often made by dealers through their specialisation in work by particular artists or periods. Dealers offer the vendor a ready market which the dealers have been responsible for developing. A dealer's expertise in an artist's work can often add to the value of the work on offer, for example when the dealer brings to the work additional information about it which the dealer has researched. Unlike auction houses, most dealers charge no handling charges and include their costs incurred in conducting the sale within their commission rate. Most price records paid for artists' works have been achieved through this technique, rather than under the glare of media cameras at public auction sales. This is because, in contrast to auction houses, dealers generally offer more personal and confidential service. Business at auction is conducted openly, and prices are publicly arrived at. Whereas auction houses handle volume, dealers are more selective about what they handle. They are distinguished by their choice. Their inventory is usually of a higher and certainly of a more selective quality than that of auction houses. Dealers decide to sell work which they take a personal interest in. They screen their offerings more carefully than can be done in the high-volume auction business. Likewise, dealers take a more personal interest in their clients, preferring to work with clients who share their interest in work they handle.

Collectors wishing to remain private willingly pay for the privilege of discretion that private dealers and galleries offer. Collectors will ask dealers to bid at auction on their behalf. This gives collectors the anonymity some desire. They pay the dealer an agreed negotiated fee or small percentage of the value paid for the work. Many collectors rely closely on the advice of particular dealers whose eye and expertise they trust. They ask dealers to 'second opinion' work they may be considering buying. Dealers customarily reserve their best offerings for valued established customers. Having first call on work by an artist whose work is very much in demand and hard to come by is a privilege and advantage dealers accord their best collectors. Collectors are assured by dealers with whom they work closely that they will be alerted before others of work on offer. The dealer acts as agent for the collector, as both buyer and seller. When buying, the collector benefits from the dealer's personal attention to locating suitable work. Dealers are in the business of matching work to collectors. Dealers know where to get work and when it is available. The dealer secures work through the network he has developed, assisted by his visual memory and by his records, and most importantly the goodwill the dealer has developed during his practice. Extensive and international dealer networks are invaluable to the collector both when buying and selling.

Dealer networks can be especially important for Australian collectors. Australia is far away from the main centres of supply in Europe and the United States. Collectors without the time to browse or attend innumerable small auctions in which many gems are to be found rely on dealers with whom they work closely.

Collectors are central to the existence of dealers. If you are a collector, dealers have a vested interest in your custom, both as buyer and seller. All work you buy may potentially be future work dealers may sell for you. Dealers will tell you which work they specialise in. You will also see which work they specialise in by looking through their stock room. Not only do dealers have more capacity and good reason to specialise, but those who are most successful are those who specialise most. They don't 'sell' work, they allow people to acquire it. By far the largest quantities of Old Master drawings as well as the greatest are to be found even today at the hands of dealers. Between dealers like Kurt Meissner in Zurich, David Tiunick and Eugene Thaw in New York, Paul Prouté in Paris and Baskett & Day in London, many times over more Old Master drawings are sold than ever appear in the auction rooms. Auctioneers acknowledge the importance of dealers in the market for Old Master paintings, a field in which there are still very few (some 20 to 25 really serious) private collectors. A lot of very fine paintings make only £25–£35,000 and most are bought by dealers.[1]

## Buying and Selling with Dealers

Most serious collectors acknowledge the guiding influence of dealers in developing their eye and their judgment. Many dealers and collectors develop close personal friendships. Yet many new collectors, on entering galleries, feel vulnerable and timid. As awesome and intimidating as galleries may be to you, you need not be fearful. Dealers and their galleries offer a rare service to new collectors. Through attending their changing exhibitions and on looking at the different works of art exhibited, you can, without being pushed for a sale, freely learn a lot about art. Galleries open to the public rarely charge admission fees (except in the scarce instance of an admission charge for a 'benefit' exhibition, held to raise funds for a charitable purpose, usually consisting of works that are not for sale and on loan to the gallery for the exhibition). Unless you ask for help or information when you walk into galleries you will probably be discreetly left to study the works on display in peace and solitude. Certainly private 'By Appointment' galleries can be more intimidating. To visit these galleries you must arrange a specific time to meet with the dealer who will want to know what specific types of work interests you so these can be brought out from stock for you to view, creating a sense of obligation that can sometimes be uneasy.

Galleries offer you the opportunity to view works first-hand. This is particularly important in the field of contemporary art. By presenting artists' works over a period of time, galleries offer collectors the chance to measure artists' works. Looking at work gives new collectors the chance to develop their 'eye' and judgment. Once their eye has developed after digesting exhibitions, observed over time at galleries, many collectors revise their initial, often hasty and ill-informed, hence incorrect, unfavourable impressions of work.

Dealers are knowledgeable alternatives to the auction houses. From numerous sources dealers secure works of art that reflect very individual vision and taste. Whereas auction houses follow fashion and taste, dealers often innovate taste and set fashion.

Galleries will post you advance notices of their exhibitions. Most will be pleased to offer you a preview of work you are interested in before exhibitions open. Catalogues they publish and accompanying price lists offer information about work on offer and market values. More lavishly illustrated catalogues, that are expensive to produce, are available by subscription, but often much of the material that galleries publish is freely available. Catalogues and price lists will give you details of the work on exhibition. Usually the artist's name, title of the work, and often the medium of the work, its date, and size with height given before width, are all provided. Catalogues also often feature artists' biographical details, and may additionally offer artists' or critics' notes on the work on exhibition. Prices may be posted alongside the works, or will be printed on catalogues or price lists. These are either freely available, often for sale if they are illustrated, or available at the reception desk. Sometimes prices are not publicised and you will have to ask the gallery attendant for prices. Recent legislation in New York insists on prices being publicly posted, contrary to previous gallery custom there of keeping prices invisible. Such coyness is rare among galleries in Australia, where prices are generally publicly listed and distributed.

You will sometimes see small red spots affixed to the wall next to certain works. These mark works that have sold. Often half red circles (sometimes circles of another colour) are affixed to the wall next to works which are reserved, on hold while under consideration by a potential buyer and as yet unsold. Unlike auctions, galleries allow buyers the luxury of being able to consider their purchase over time.

The best galleries are those whose staff are helpful and eager to answer your questions. If you feel intimidated by a gallery's hushed, dignified atmosphere and nervous that its often well-known proprietor or informed staff will be condescending, look at your first meeting from their point of view. Dealers need new collectors. A dealer's business remains vital and continues to grow only through carefully nurturing new collectors who will rely on and trust the dealer's judgment. The dealer stands to gain much and lose little by being helpful to those who show a serious interest in the work he sells.

The new collector is most likely to feel disadvantaged (and not unexpectedly to lose interest) if dealing with less scrupulous galleries which may try to cash in on someone's lack of knowledge by passing off commercial rubbish or, worse, fakes or reproductions as valuable originals. The new collector can justifiably fear unscrupulous dealers who may unfortunately consider the uninformed new buyer as an easy mark, to conveniently pass on inferior and/or overpriced works to.

The art trade is a highly unregulated business where it pays to observe the rule 'Buyer Beware'. Virtually anyone can open a gallery, selling worthless reproductions or mass-produced paintings for as much as the uninformed buyer is willing to pay. Fortunately it is easy enough to distinguish the sellers of worthless rubbish from the serious dealers by the quality of their offerings and the reputation they have earned among art professionals. New collectors should rely on the advice and expertise of dealers who are reputed for quality and integrity. The problem for new collectors is learning who such respected dealers are.

Veteran, experienced collectors can identify the galleries they consider most worthwhile, as far as their personal collecting interests are concerned. Museums can help you. They are often able to recommend to new collectors the names of reputable dealers catering to specific fields of interest. Museum exhibitions which include work selected by museum staff borrowed from dealers can indicate to you which dealers are highly regarded. Museums acknowledge dealer/lenders on the wall labels and in exhibition catalogues. Reading reviews gives you a feel for which galleries are most seriously regarded by critics. Editorial coverage in journals can give you an idea about which galleries exhibit highly regarded work. Gallery advertisements in newspapers and magazines give little guidance. Advertising space is sold regardless of quality or professional reputation. The same applies to commercial art fairs with the exception of juried invitational expositions. Some of the more established dealers have made it easier for collectors to identify them by grouping together in professional associations which advertise and issue members directories listing members' names, addresses and specialities. These associations usually include only galleries with substantial track records that purport to uphold high professional standards.

The Australian Commercial Galleries Association is a body which has as members leading private galleries in Australia. Only those galleries whose main business is to act as the representatives of living Australian artists are eligible to join the Association. It includes galleries nationwide offering a wide variety of work. The Association was founded in 1976 and meets several times a year. It acts as a forum where members can discuss matters of mutual interest. It operates to further the interests of private galleries and artists. Members advertise regularly together in their local papers. The association publishes a catalogue detailing member galleries, and their fields of interest. Another guide of a similar kind is the list published by the Department of Home Affairs which lists all fine art valuers approved under the Taxation Incentive Scheme with details of valuers' approved areas of expertise.[2]

Membership in an association does not guarantee a dealer's integrity. Marlborough Gallery in New York was a member of the Art Dealers Association of America from 1968. The gallery caused a scandal when unconscionable practices in its handling of the estate of Mark Rothko were revealed and it was heavily fined in court in late 1975.[3] Conversely, lack of membership in an association should not cause you to avoid a gallery. There are respected dealers who are too new to have the track record required for association membership. Other long established, highly reputed galleries choose not to join. Gallery Associations lists offer you a starting point for further investigation.

If you live away from the main centres, particularly Australia's 'art capitals' of Melbourne and Sydney, or further afield, London or New York, it is helpful to develop relationships with selected dealers who have distinguished reputations in the field of your interest. Once you've identified yourself through personal meetings, or by telephone, and long-distance purchases, if you are serious the dealer will find work for you and help you develop your interest. Dealers will send you their catalogues and notices of their shows. They'll alert you to particular items that might interest you. They will send you photographs or colour transparencies of work on offer with related descriptive material from which long distance sales are made.

Dealers specialise in particular artists. Their individual style and the style of their gallery will be instantly apparent to you on entering the gallery. You can draw many conclusions from simply entering a dealer's premises. Look around. The dealer who cares for his pieces usually looks after his clients as well. Assess the location, arrangement, stock and atmosphere of a gallery carefully. These express the personality of their owners. Seek out active or busy galleries that have a look of permanence, that move their stock, take an interest in their clients and welcome new ones. There are always things to discuss in a gallery. You can ask about works, periods, artists, materials, or anything that interests you, and the real enthusiast will be sure to take you up. If you get no response, don't bother. You'll easily recognise the caring professional, enthusiastic dealer.

Beware of dealers selling 'schlock' art, work with commercial decorative appeal but little artistic merit the likes of which are usually sold from glossy premises in expensive retail centres especially in tourist areas that cater to people on vacation. Never buy for decoration. Any work worth its salt has too strong an identity to accommodate such single-minded demands as to 'add a dash of colour'.

Be prepared to develop your eye and rely on dealers to assist you to do this. Having learned who the dealers are, how do you identify which ones are most worthy of your trust? Most serious dealers will stress the artistic merits of work preferring not to flaunt their investment merits. A dealer's return policy may indicate the extent to which he believes in and stands by the quality and desirability of what he sells.

Dealers are often sympathetic to collectors who may be poor in funds but are rich in sensitivity. If you have the eye to see and enjoy, dealers will help and inform you. Dealers themselves have often begun with limited resources and know about collecting on a tight budget and so are often the best sources of leads about doing so. Dealers are surrogate collectors. But you have to interest them in your case to get their help. Others who share your passion for fine things will find your interest hard to resist. Young artists particularly appreciate the attentive collector. Collecting on a tight budget can be a beneficial discipline which helps to focus direction. This makes it easier to chase leads, sales and work. If you are an unmonied collector you will quickly develop your connoisseurship, for you will have to be able to distinguish fine objects from the vast array of mediocre ones in the lower price ranges. If you are flexible, persistent, patient (able to wait until worthwhile but affordable objects come onto the market), knowledgeable, and often lucky, you can build a fine collection on a modest budget. American collectors Dorothy and Herbert Vogel amassed a first-rate collection of minimalist and conceptual art — some 1,500 works of art on public civil-service salaries. Combining her income as a New York City librarian with his postal worker's pension they could never spend more than a few hundred dollars but their hunger for art and more information about what was happening on the contemporary art scene impressed dealers and artists who were often generous to them. Their 'art fever' and burning curiosity gave them a hard bargaining power without their asking for it.

You need time and temerity, plus expertise based on a sense of history, to obtain a top work advantageously. You can certainly make worthwhile acquisitions paying less than a king's ransom, and buying not just out-of-fashion oddities. A sense of history, wherein the entire spectrum of art becomes a continuing experience and not just an episodic one, is vital to comparatively judge individual works. With a sense of history the whole world of human creativity is open for the taking.

Basically dealers help people to see. Dealers must possess the artists' instinct to catch on to important changes in art before anyone else. Most dealers also share artists' interests in the idea behind the work itself. Just as the artist must have a deep belief in the art he makes, without a continuing true belief in an artist's work, there is not much a dealer can do for an artist. Both share the same motto coined by dealer

Andre Emmerich: *'Credo ergo exposito'* ('I believe therefore I show').[4] The dealer stands between artist and collector. The demands these two have of each other, each wanting something from the other, define the space within which every dealer works.

> **❛A wonderful artist should charge highly for his art . . .**
> **no money is too much for it.❜**
>
> Albrecht Durer, *Outline of a General Treatise on Painting*, (c.1510)

## The Business of Art

Dealers, engaged in the business of transacting between those who make art and those who collect it, have always existed. True art collecting first originated in the Greek world in the later fourth or the third century B.C. Art merchants like the Greek Damasippus, whom Cicero refers to in his letters, sold Greek Old Masters to Roman multi-millionaires of the first century B.C. Damasippus was the Roman version of Lord Duveen. He handled the movement of art from Greece to Rome, including commemorative sculpture which Cicero resold. We also have the names of several Chinese dealers from as early as the Tang dynasty, and Western traffickers in classical works of art were active at least as early as the opening decades of the 15th century. In the humanist 16th century, as the artist became thought of not merely as artisan but as creator, dealers like Jacopo Strada, and Florentine Giovanni Battista della Palla (who in 1529 sent a *Hercules* by Michelangelo to Francis I) served as go-between for artist and patron.

Seventeenth century academies ensured the prominence of the commercial middleman in every artist's career. The Academie Royale de la Peinture, founded in 1645, forbade members to engage personally in the commerce of their own works (contributing to the notion that art should be above the market and is vulgarised by being associated with it). The history of Antoine Watteau (1648–1721) and his dealer Gersaint illustrates the role of the intermediary. The role of the dealer was elevated from merchant to a new type of patron by the Frenchman Paul Durand-Ruel (1831–1922).[5] Son of a paper and art supply dealer, Durand-Ruel began to sell the work of his customers who included the then still unknown or little appreciated masters Corot, Millet, Courbet and Eugene Boudin. Durand-Ruel combined and established the roles that the practice of art dealing includes: publicist, banker, merchant, patron, critic, advisor and parent-figure to artist, and advisor to collector too. Durand-Ruel was interesting for the way he looked beyond the commercial practice of dealing, to the role of the dealer as taste or opinion maker. 'A genuine picture dealer,' Durand-Ruel wrote in his memoirs, 'should be at the same time an enlightened patron, ready if necessary to sacrifice his immediate interest to his artistic conviction and preferring a fight against speculators to an association with them.' Durand-Ruel certainly demonstrated Robert Wraight's description of a really successful dealer as 'a man who combines something of the psychologist, the stockbroker, the impresario, the public relations man and the detective, with a touch of aesthetic sensibility and some knowledge of artists' methods of working. He has insight into the buyers' mentality; the ability to anticipate price trends and the power to create them; a sense of showmanship in presenting his wares and an understanding of the value of publicity.[6]

Emile Zola, in his novel *L'Oeuvre*, modelled his character Naudet on Durand-Ruel. He was pictured as 'a dealer who for some years had been revolutionising the picture trade'. Another French dealer who did much to develop the practice of dealing was Daniel-Henry Kahnweiler. Kahnweiler set up business in 1906 and 'contracted' with the many great artists he represented (among them Braque, Derain, Vlaminck, Miro, Leger). He justified his role by eliminating material cares from his artists' lives.[7] Another French dealer who did so much to nurture early Modernists in the face of popular disapproving taste was Pere Tanguy (1825–1894). In the shop of this aging colour-grinder and art-supplies merchant were exhibited paintings by Pissaro, Emile Bernard, Renoir, Monet, Van Gogh, Gauguin, Seurat, and Cézanne — whom Durand-Ruel had passed over. After Pere Tanguy's death in 1893, new artists found support from the legendary Ambroise Vollard (1865–1939) ), who represented some of the most exciting artists of the time.[8] Following the lead of such dealers their galleries and those of others like them became a home for artists' innovations and a showcase for the vanguard. In that tradition of support, today's conscientious contemporary dealers will take time and trouble to encourage and look after their artists so that their work can have the best opportunity to flourish.

Every dealer is different, and the stunning variety of their styles and personalities can be as distinctive as the difference between the work they handle. Their origins and professional beginnings can be as varied as their differing styles and fields of interest. There is no qualifying examination for art dealers. The only functional requirement in their profession is a space with four relatively clean walls and a telephone. Many began as collectors, like Leo Castelli who opened his first New York gallery in 1957 at fifty. Others begin selling art supplies. Some come from schools, as former teachers. Some were once framers. Some were writers, like Sidney Janis (1896–1989), who had written several books — including the first book on American Surrealism — before he opened his New York gallery in 1948. Some were once artists themselves, like Tony Shafrazi who graduated from London's Royal College of Art in 1963 before opening his gallery in New York's Soho in 1981, from where he spearheaded interest in artists like Keith Haring whose drawings with white chalk on empty advertising spaces in subway stations all over Manhattan spawned graffiti artists whose work became part of urban culture around the world. A few were born into the trade like Rene Gimpel, Lord Duveen, and third-generation dealer Andre Emmerich. Indeed, selling fine art is something of a hereditary condition for many French dealers. Families like the Kraemers and Fabres have been dealing for several generations. Since the Franco-Prussian War, the Kraemers have dealt in 18th century furniture, and Fabres' *fils* share a similar history selling 17th and 18th century furniture and *objets d'art* from their Paris gallery in Rue Balzac.

The only characteristic all dealers share is the individual conviction each one has in their infallible judgment as to which artists are worthy of acclaim. Dealers commonly share a passion for art which sustains them through the commercial vicissitudes of the unpredictable and volatile art market. In many respects, the risks dealers take — particularly those in the frontline of contemporary art — are little different to the risks artists themselves take. The dealer needs the dedication and certainty artists must have, plus solid business sense and the skill to anticipate and promote the direction of individual artists and the general public alike.

Because, at its beginning, the art dealer has no intrinsic market, dealing is the last bastion of pure capitalism. The business of art is business. Dealers act on their interests. Like Ambrose Vollard, who became sole representative of Cézanne and Gauguin, who later handled works by Renoir, Degas, Van Gogh, Matisse, Maillol, Rouault, and who gave Picasso his first one-man show in 1901, the art dealer needs both idealism and cunning. Vollard's example as speculator is legendary. He would watch, wait, then sell, at prices set by the artificial scarcity he had created.

Speculation has always been a feature of art. Vasari relates how a Madonna commissioned by Francois I of France from Andrea del Sarto fetched for the merchants four times as much as they had paid for it. Vasari also tells how Perugino was paid 100 florins for a painting of Saint Sebastian by Bernardino de Rossi who resold the work at considerable profit for 400 ducats.[10]

While Pissaro complained about Durand-Ruel behaving like a modern speculator and loathed being part of such a 'degenerate business' as the art market, like most artists Pissaro concurred with Vincent Van Gogh who wrote to his brother Theo (an art dealer himself, employed by the important gallery of Boussod & Valadon which specialised in high priced Salon 'Masters'): 'The crux of the matter, you see, is that my work depends on the sale of my paintings.' The myth of the artist as *reveur*, uncaring about money, is a nonsense and an insult. Artists don't fail because of financial success. Raphael (1483–1520), together with Da Vinci and Michelangelo, was one of the great creators of the High Renaissance when he died at the age of thirty-seven. The favourite of popes and intimate of cardinals and princes, Raphael left a fortune estimated at sixteen thousand florins comprising a house at Urbino, a palace and vineyards and land in and near Rome — all acquired during a working life of barely two decades, a life, more over, spent in great luxury and splendour. Michelangelo's (1475–1564) earnings were so great that he single-handedly restored his decayed family to a high place in Florence.

Both Raphael and Michelangelo were courted by popes and princes, and both had intimate friends close to the highest levels of the Italian world of their time. With Titian they enjoyed the prominent social position that leading artists have been able to claim in the Western world ever since their time. Titian (1487–1526) was the greatest of Venetian painters, and in some senses the founder of modern painting. His career was remarkable for the way he used his genius in unsentimental and determined commercial manner to become both wealthy and a great artist who had the world at his feet. His correspondence is full of blunt reminders of money due. He was the epitome of a grand Renaissance artist yet he persistently refused to use his brush unless on commission or if advantageous to him. Vasari relates how Sodoma (1477–1549) said that 'his brush danced according to the tune of money.' Peter Paul Rubens (1577–1640) was the northern counterpart of the very rich Italian artists. A great genius of universal fame, Rubens was a shrewd businessman who never reduced the high fees he set on his paintings.[10]

Creativity and financial security or well-being are directly related, though usually overlooked. As Vasari wrote of those artists besides the 'most famous masters', who have to face 'famine rather than fame': 'If there were just renumeration in this our age they would, without doubt, produce great and better works than the ancients. '[11] Financial restrictions inhibit the work artists produce. Economic inhibitions depress the amount of work made and impact the quality of work, by limiting what artists are able to do.[12]

## Consultants

Not long ago buying contemporary art meant buying youth and promise with enthusiastic energy and faith. Buying art today is like buying art futures. Like the walls of the traders and brokers in Oliver Stone's film *Wall Street*, power offices and penthouses are heavy with art, and the art world is heavy with brokers and traders, many of whom style themselves 'art consultants'.

Fortunately the sharemarket's shake-out of very high corporate fliers, quickly hungry for the lustre ownership of art adds (as badges of success), among whom these consultants (many themselves *arrivistes*) found a ready market, has resulted in greater selectivity. Art advisors come from many sources, but the best are those with an intimate and lengthy involvement in the art world whether as dealers, critics, curators or historians.

If you lack self-confidence or do not have a trained eye, some consider you can improve your investment collecting odds by consulting an advisor. But to do this, you should still have at least enough knowledge to determine whether your advisor is competent. 'If you want to make money on art,' says New York dealer Richard Feigen, 'you should give a 10 per cent commission to someone who knows what he's doing, leave him alone and not ask him to buy what you like.' Many dealers have an aversion to giving investment advice. With them, your best chance at getting their help is to approach the subject obliquely: ask which works they think will maintain their value over the years and which artists they think may be currently under-valued.

A good dealer meets all the criteria for a good investment advisor except he may have an obvious interest in selling his own goods. The same sort of criticism may be levelled at investment programs that are connected with auction houses like Sotheby Parke Bernet, New York, serving as advisor for New York's Citibank's art-investment program and offering through its financial services department art equity loans against sales.

Art consultants usually work with several clients who may want simply to 'decorate and furnish' rather than develop a carefully acquired knowledge of art, which good consultants advise their clients on. Private curators may be engaged by one collector, to be responsible for the upkeep of the collection and perhaps oversee the future development of the collection, though this is often managed in response to the direction given by the collector.[13] Whereas distinguished art historians are available for consultation, most museum officials feel that hiring themselves out as personal advisors may cause conflicting interest with the collecting interests of their museums.

Financial arrangements among advisors and consultants vary. Some work on commission — usually for about 10 per cent of the price of the works bought on their advice. Some work on a retainer or for a flat fee, particularly when collectors are wary of being recommended only expensive works. It is not unknown for 'secret commissions' to be paid to consultants from dealers whose works the consultants recommend and sell to collectors. Many collectors regard buying an advisor is as difficult as buying a work of art. 'Art consultants' abound, who have few qualifications, other than art-history studies and a claim to understanding the mysteries of 'good taste'. Buyers who demand and get personal care from every kind of professional are increasingly choosing dealers as their advisors. As they choose their doctor or their lawyer, they only want the best art professional because it makes an enormous difference if you choose a good advisor. Major dealers with their depth of expertise and extensive networks offer these buyers the best opportunities and advice.

## Art Fairs

A growing venue for the promotion and sale of art are specialty art fairs of which there are many held internationally. The two 'big ones' are the Basle Art Fair and Chicago's International Art Exposition. Twenty years old, Basle's contemporary art exposition is the world's largest and the most important event in Europe for contemporary and modern art, where over 300 exhibitors participate every June. Ten years old, Chicago's Art Exposition is held every May on Navy Pier, with over 200 exhibitors, where sales over five days in 1989 were conservatively estimated to be in excess of US$75 million. Standards are high at both fairs, with exhibitors only gaining entry by invitation following peer group assessment.

The year's calendar features other fairs worldwide whose composition is less wholly international. Location can influence Fair emphasis. London hosts ART/London at Grand Hall, Olympia, in March where largely British Art is featured (among 150 dealers from 20 countries participating in 1989). Every September Paris hosts the crowd-pulling FIAC at the Grand Palais. Well over half to three quarters of the exhibitors are French.

The pace of fine and decorative art shows around the world is feverish. These fairs, which have sprung up and gathered force in all corners of the world, can be weekly flea markets, seasonal antiques and fine arts shows, and annual and biannual gatherings of the best dealers on the international scene. The best of these shows are those whose exhibitors are vetted by their peers and so are more selective in their quality. These shows offer confidence to collectors and to the legion, less-serious decorators and shoppers who lack the expertise to make judgments of authenticity on their own. Lasting from a few hours to two days, sometimes a week, and in a few cases almost two weeks, they are a considerable source of revenue for host cities, attracting large numbers of out-of-town visitors. They are also a highpoint of cultural activity for the local community. Remarkable works are brought by dealers to the fairs for the exposure. Fairs attract an increasing attendance of curious and determined collectors on all levels. They demonstrate the internationalisation of the art market as well as the developing of collectors and a collecting base never before equalled in sheer numbers.

Interestingly, New York had long resisted an art fair. New York dealers used to consider that one day's offering in Manhattan, in terms of what was available and could be seen there, was akin to a day's offering at any Art Fair. Nonetheless the prestigious Art Dealers' Association of America (ADAA) staged their own art fair in February, 1989, in the cavernous Park Avenue Armory building. Called 'The Art Show', it was an outstanding success. In four days over US$30 million worth of art was sold by 57 dealers. The following week the Armory featured the 'Works on Paper' Fair with 91 specialised dealers of prints, drawings and photography exhibiting. Some dealers exhibited at both these events.

The Grosvenor House Antiques Fair is regarded as the major event of the London summer season. This is the flagship show of the British Antiques Dealers Association. It is widely hailed as the world's most magnificent antiques show, rivalled only by the Paris Biennale. Sales in 1989 are estimated to exceed £50 million (US$80 million). Devoted to English antiques dealers, Grosvenor House's 1989 exhibitors reads like a *Who's Who* of dealers or each area of antique, fine and decorative arts.

London also hosted the ten year-old Burlington House Fair which in 1989 merged with the Grosvenor House Fair. Other speciality fairs in London, among them Silver & Jewellery, World of Watercolours and the International Ceramics Fair & Seminar, are all thriving, because these fairs focus on lower-priced items, and people — in the face of sky-high auction prices —are starved for affordable things to buy. Within the international proliferation of art fairs, the European Fine Art Fair in the historic city of Maastricht, The Netherlands, held each March, is quickly emerging as one of the finest art and antiques events in Europe. With over 100 fine and decorative arts dealers exhibiting, Maastricht demonstrates that business is global, and the only criterion that matters is that objects of high quality are shown.

The Australian Commercial Galleries Association launched the very successful Australian Contemporary Art Fair in July 1988. The first fair was an unqualified success with work by over 300 artists exhibited and sales exceeding A$750,000. This fair will be held every two years in Melbourne's Exhibition Building. The Fair's catalogue is a useful guide to Australia's foremost galleries and the artists they represent. Australia's International Master Print Fair was launched in Sydney in July 1989. Held over four days, all exhibitors were delighted with the success of the Fair, which is to be held each year. The Fair offered viewers a good cross-section of the variety existing within the Print Market. Work to be seen included modern master prints, Botanical and Architectural prints, Belle-Epoque prints and posters, contemporary Australian prints, as well as Australian historical and master modern prints (such as Margaret Preston's coloured wood blocks), late 19th century Erotica, and 20th century posters. This fair offered the new collector as good an introduction as can be offered to the diverse field of prints. Sales are estimated to have exceeded over A$500,000.

Fairs are perfect as a training ground for the new collector. Fairs give the new collector the opportunity to freely look at and to question dealers about the objects on display. Fairs are equally ideal for art professionals where experienced collectors and dealers trade stock. Fairs are becoming a major aspect of some dealers' business. Through Fairs, dealers have the opportunity to introduce themselves to a wider and international collecting base. Five Australian galleries recognised this and exhibited in December 1989 at the International Contemporary Art Fair in Los Angeles. The international flavour of the 1989 European Fine Art Fair in Maastricht, meanwhile, has been heralded as the taste of an art world to come. Transnational dealer linkages in every field are strongly in evidence, and offer challenges to the mass concentration of art available for sale from the two mega-power auction giants, Sotheby's and Christie's.

# 4

# THE CONTEMPORARY MARKET

*❛ The material of vital concern, the **sine qua non**, for the artist is
to exhibit; for it happens after some looking at a thing, that one
becomes familiar with what was surprising, or, if you will,
shocking. Little by little it becomes understood and accepted
— time itself is always imperceptibly at work upon a
picture, refining and softening its original harshness.❜*

Edouard Manet[1]

## The Unique Contemporary Market

The contemporary art market is principally the market of primary sales, where first transactions of work occur. Subsequent re-sales of a work occur in the secondary market through dealers and at auction sales on the open market. Until very recently, communication between artist and auctioneer has been limited to the rare occasion when verification of authenticity has been required. Contemporary departments of British auction houses have operated under the protective wing of established Impressionist or even Modern British departments. In contrast to New York, and, to a lesser extent, Paris, London salerooms were hardly aware there was a market for contemporary art with potential to develop, until 1983 when Sotheby's made a tentative stab at it. Annual returns from Contemporary sales at Sotheby's and Christie's in London and New York testify to people buying more contemporary art and paying more for it. Previously works that had been bought within the safe confines of a dealer's gallery frequently found difficulty in selling on the open market. In New York, on the other hand, contemporary art has always met with strong support.

Contemporary art sales in London were a high risk area for buyer and seller alike, highlighting a difference between the American and European markets. Whereas New York led with more sales of contemporary art, in England since 1985 individual prices have been accelerating in line with overall totals, indicating that the European market is coming of age. Christie's annual turnover in London from two contemporary sales per annum rose in 1985 by an increase of over 400 per cent. In New York the same number of sales over the same period has seen an increase in turnover from £6,357,000 to £15,607,000. Sotheby's figures tell the same story. Between 1984 and 1988, Sotheby's turnover figures for contemporary art multiplied by nearly ten times to US$125 million. In November 1988, auction prices for contemporary art took a quantum leap forward as a broad base of collectors showed a willingness to pay new kinds of prices for contemporary art, especially for American works from the 1950s and 1960s. This hike in demand and prices stems, in part, from the feeling that, while one is hard-pressed to acquire a major painting by an Impressionist or Modern artist, one can still acquire great contemporary works at prices less expensive than comparable prices for Impressionist and Modern masters. Also, contemporary masterpieces come onto the market usually fresh to the market, generally in excellent condition, and not as shopped around and well worn as in other areas.

Many dealers find the contemporary market most exhilarating. They like feeling they have their finger on the pulse of new art and art in the making. They enjoy being closely involved with artists and their works, as they are made. Many collectors share the exhilaration this close contact offers. Some become good friends with artists whose work interests them. Collectors feel that having the opportunity to talk to artists and learn first-hand why the artist chose to make the work, offers them additional insight into the work. They also appreciate the sense of opportunity active contemporary collectors have at having first choice of work on offer. They can visit artists' studios and observe work in the making. So they have often seen the work before any one else (other than, of course, the artist and the artist's dealer). They can select, buy and own the work before anyone else.[2]

Obviously such opportunities are enjoyed by informed collectors who are confident of their own 'eye' and judgment, collectors with faith in their own instinct. Contemporary art offers some of the best opportunities for making brilliant discoveries but also foolish mistakes, and no field makes greater demands on a collector's time, imagination and sensitivity. For the collector, contemporary art differs from all other fields of art collecting, because it involves the living artist making new work that will probably provoke your preconceptions about art.

Collecting contemporary art challenges. It is more challenging than buying with the comfort which history offers. Buying work by an historical artist is comparatively safe. Collectors who buy an artist's works early in their careers while the artist is little-known, require more personal commitment to the work, plus faith in the dealer who may help them to pick out work by artists who are lesser known or even relatively unknown (in the historical sense). Collecting new artists requires a spirit of adventure. Collecting contemporary art involves ground rules and traditions which are different to those in other areas of collecting.

The activity of judging a work is more critical with contemporary art. Art history, and examples learnt from the thoroughly sifted study of earlier art, offers a relatively safe and comfortable platform from which to exercise judgment. Contemporary art offers no such ease, and is likely to radically alter perceptions learnt from the comfort of the past. By definition, contemporary art is the cutting edge of art, where new directions and perceptions are forged. Contemporary art mirrors artists' traits for compulsive innovation, their distaste for doing just what has been done before because of each artist's drive to be in some degree original. Changes in contemporary art, often novel, can affront and therefore be confusing and awkward to assess. This is the thrill of contemporary art. It is a living barometer of change — registered visually, but also conceptually and philosophically. Artists free us from habit. Through them we can set out in search of the extraordinary. While exciting and stimulating, this can also be discomforting. The history of art attests to the cool reception usually received by new movements and artists, who changed perceptions and introduced new relationships with reality which we now take for granted, and whom we now revere.

History is fortunately also peppered with collectors and dealers of foresight who were patrons of the New. Dealers are among the first to register an early impression of each shock-wave. As the French dealer Daniel-Henry Kahnweiler said: 'My greatest pleasure was to applaud a piece of music I liked in the face of lesser adversaries.' The support dealers offered unconventional artists in Paris at the turn of the century was vital to encourage experimentation and counteract the dead hand of official Salon taste.

One of the interesting aspects of art today is the rapidity with which changes are accepted and adopted by collectors avid to ride on the latest 'wave', and by the media keen to follow the fortunes or otherwise of each new art 'star'. Today there is an expanding community of cultural and monetary interests that centres on the artists of our time.

Even among experienced observers, though, opinions on the latest artists, movements and styles are constantly debated and revised, and, because the final returns are not in yet, collectors of contemporary art must rely on their own vision and judgment to a much greater degree than collectors in safer, more thoroughly sifted fields. They must also work hard just to keep up with the latest developments in the fluid, far-flung contemporary art scene by visiting museums, galleries, artists' studios and 'alternative spaces' (exhibition areas, often publicly funded, that frequently display new, unfamiliar art); by talking to dealers, collectors and artists who are in contact with promising new talent, and by reading the books, museum catalogues, art magazines and newspaper columns that try to put the latest developments in perspective. The bewildering diversity of the contemporary art scene, while adding to the field's excitement, greatly complicates the collector's task of distinguishing mere facility from greatness, of distinguishing the really good work from the imitative, and recognising the exceptionally good, with its oddness of originality, from amidst the ordinarily good. Within the contemporary art scene there is such a web of sub and sub-sub styles and continual change that even critics can only follow particular fractions of the activity. No critic can reasonably span the whole complex scene. Consensus, however, does develop about artists and their work, and collectors of contemporary art should become part of the group of people who are aware of that consensus.

## Selecting Talent on the Cutting Edge of Contemporary Art

Few people feature on the pages of the history of the selection of talent. Renoir reminded Paul Durand-Ruel (1831–1922), the dealer whose name and ultimate fortune became inseparably linked to the Impressionists, in a letter of 1881, that Paris contained barely fifteen *amateurs* (collectors) capable of appreciating a work of art that hadn't been shown at the conservative establishment Salon.[4] Here Renoir used the word 'amateur' in the French sense of a collector as one who loves art. Without Ambroise Vollard, Pere Tanguy, and a handful of others whose discernment supported the vanguard throughout the early history of modern art, many artists would have received no support.[5] Lack of support inhibits creativity, as Vincent Van Gogh wrote: 'Not selling, when one has not other resources, one is faced with the impossibility of making any progress, while such progress would go on by itself if the opposite were true.'

An early Australian dealer in the modern sense (of being a support to artists as well as a merchant of their work) was John Young who, in 1925, began Macquarie Galleries.[6] Like all good dealers his enthusiasm and zeal for his artist peers converted collectors to share his faith in Australian artists and their creative ability. Sydney-based entrepreneur and oenologist Rudy Komon (1902–1982) similarly imprinted collectors with his infectious sympathy for then little-appreciated painters like Fred Williams and John Brack.[7] Komon, who opened his Paddington gallery in 1959, combined his enthusiasm with then novel business practices like advances against future sales, which supported his artists. These paid him generous dividends later in his career after collectors caught his enthusiasm for particular artists who had been singled out by his 'eye' and support for their qualities. As Andre Emmerich says, 'Art dealers are like surfboard riders. You can't make a wave. If there aren't any waves out there, you're dead. But the good surfboard rider can sense which of the waves coming in will be the good ones, the ones that will last. Successful art dealers have a feeling for hitting the right wave.'[8] Visionary dealers lead collectors with an open mind and an open eye to new horizons. For the artist, deprived of the support of patrons struggling against popular taste, mass production and advertising, officially sponsored mannered art, and the caprice of fashion, the art dealer replaces the cultivated patron of earlier times. The dealer concerned with living art has to search for true values, as yet unrecognised, and to stake his own fate on them; and new artists have to find dealers who are ready to promote their work and battle for their reputations. Not all dealers want to exercise such critical judgment nor are interested in taking such chances, which often involves accumulating unsaleable merchandise and trusting that the future will vindicate their judgment. Such committed dealers are not mere speculators but are genuinely interested in art who — guided by instinct, love, and deep understanding — possess true discernment.

## Commercial Galleries

Contemporary art is most frequently exhibited at commercial galleries. Commercial galleries exhibit the present, and often the future. They offer a program of ideas. Commercial galleries have taken the role museums are unable to fulfil. The bureaucracy of museums and the expenses involved in their administration have prevented many museums from continually representing much contemporary activity. To keep up with what's going on in art, you have to go to the commercial galleries.

So much activity by an artist has gone on before the artist's work enters museums. Much of that activity occurs in commercial galleries where the artist's work has been exhibited often long before it is presented or acquired by museums. When Picasso told Gertrude Stein that he was to exhibit at the Museum of Modern Art, she said 'No museum can be modern'. Contemporary art becomes 'institutionalised' once brought into or endorsed by a museum. By nature museums are more selective about what they acquire and exhibit. They have to be selective by virtue of their role as storehouse of objects, apart from the very limited opportunities they have to present contemporary art due to inadequate funds or exhibiting facilities. Australian art museums are repositories of art of all kinds and histories. Their broad cover of the history of art includes Aboriginal art (much of which is still housed in museums as the legacy of once being considered of anthropological interest only); Asian art; the Decorative Arts; and Prints, Drawings and Paintings from European and Australian schools dating from the 17th century on. Without specialising as museums of contemporary art, and with such wide collections, institutional art galleries are not able to focus more on contemporary art. Their cover of contemporary art, beyond acquisitions, is limited to survey exhibitions scanning a period (like *Field to Figuration*, Australian Art 1960–1986, from the collection of the National Gallery of Victoria); or a theme like *Perspecta*, the Biennale of Australian Contemporary Art.[9] Staged by the Art Gallery of New South Wales, *Perspecta* has been universally hailed because the exhibition provides a regular opportunity to survey work by Australia's younger, and lesser-known but vital contemporary artists and the issues their work is involved with. Catalogues to these survey exhibitions provide valuable documentation of contemporary artists and useful guides for the collector to refer to for information that is otherwise not readily accessible beyond that offered by the commercial galleries representing these artists. Documentation by commercial galleries of work by the artists they represent provides invaluable information on the contemporary art scene.

Unlike curators, who are art-historians by training and involved with historical associations, commercial galleries are involved with the present and concerned with the creative impact of artists *here and now*. Art education's emphasis on the 'historical' is ironic. The imposing values of history are the opposite of what art is about, given you believe art to be about creativity and experimentation. As Joseph Beuys said: 'Art equals creativity.' Art, then, is about the unpredictability of ideas as they emerge cumulatively from a body of work.[10]

Commercial galleries act as more than brokers engaged in commercial exchange, selling artists' works. Significantly, galleries are educators. Many dealers will agree that much of their time is involved in activities other than 'selling art'. Activity in a gallery occurs in the 'back room' where dealers and their staff are attending to distributing information about their artists and their work. This includes arranging loans to museum shows, arranging exhibitions elsewhere, assembling photographic material for articles or books to be published on artists. Of course, these activities all help to sell the artist. They also reflect the sophistication of dealers who support and promote artists beyond more than purely the 'sales pitch'. These dealers are invaluable agents of cultural activity. It is just as difficult to appreciate a Raphael or Rembrandt as it is to appreciate Matisse and Picasso, or lesser-known 'new' artists. The first thing to do is *look*. By being publicly accessible, galleries offer the chance to look, endlessly.

In a way, galleries are dealers' own funded contemporary museums where dealers alone decide whose work to show and how it will be shown. As the best artists teach us to see, the best dealers lead the public to the artists. Good dealers fulfil the role defined of critics by Picasso, as 'building a bridge people can walk over to join the artists'. Their group exhibitions present different works, each of which can illustrate differences or seeming similarities, and can generate discussion and further investigation and discovery. As Leo Castelli says, 'I consider it the gallery's obligation to function as a sort of museum, to show the most important works of art while at the same time providing a reliable base where artists can count on support and exposure. Sales will hopefully come as a consequence.[11]

Within the contemporary market there are two kinds of dealers: those who, like Kahnweiler, discover artists when they are beginning their career (Kahnweiler discovered Picasso and Braque, among others) and those who, like Knoedlers, deal with established artists and their estates.[12]

The best place to purchase work of some merit is at an established gallery. In Australia there are over 400 galleries exhibiting works by living artists.[13] Of these, about thirty regularly show work of some significance. Frequent visits to these galleries stimulate the confidence of new collectors, helping them in time to make their first acquisition.

Because contemporary art is untested by time, and in continuing production, the investor may regard buying contemporary art, without time to properly digest it, as a speculative gamble. Yet the financial risk for a collector who buys the work of 'new' artists is small, particularly if bought from an established gallery investing its faith, energies and time in that artist's work. The gallery has a vested interest in realising the success of that artist and this is in the collector's interest. The gallery's interest is the collector's assurance.

No 'new' artist simply 'splashes' onto the scene. Usually the gallery introducing or giving the 'new' artist their first exhibition does so after knowing and observing that artist and his or her work for some time. In the 'hot-house' atmosphere of the contemporary scene, in which fashion and publicity can generate hype-inflated prices and quick reputations, real and lasting recognition seldom comes to an artist from a single showing of a few canvases. It is not the quality of his publicity which must stand the test of time, but the quality of his creative ability. His talent can only be truly evaluated upon aesthetic progress. This needs time. 'Little-known' artists, if genuinely talented, will over time stand out and be embraced by the gallery system. The artist exhibiting at a certain gallery enters the milieu of that gallery and the environment of the contemporary art scene.

Most first exhibitions by new artists in top galleries feature work that is relatively inexpensive, with paintings often selling under A$4,000 to A$5,000. For this reason — and because the artist frequently receives support from a circle of personal friends keen to 'launch' the artist — these exhibitions will often sell out, establishing demand for more of the artist's work. Some time later the artist and gallery will hold a second exhibition, in which prices are often higher. A collector can resell work, bought from the first exhibition, or donate work and gain the benefits available through the taxation incentive scheme for the arts. Compound interest is additional if you consider the enjoyment the collector has received living with the work during the time between the artist's first and second exhibitions, as well as the satisfaction of knowing that purchase assisted the 'new' artist at a time when the artist needs such support for their work.

Although, of course, every collector of new art dreams of discovering great artists before their works achieve great prices, collecting is about greater and immeasurable returns. An aesthetic response can occur without the collector realising it. Art is provocative and evocative and difficult to ignore. It tugs at the spiritual and mystical, and signposts so much more than the investor or speculator-collector can ever anticipate. In this sense art is alluringly subversive.

Collecting contemporary art means becoming a part of the cultural colloquy of one's own time. In buying art you are investing in the visual arts culture of your local, regional and national culture. Van Gogh argued for the individual artist's need for support in order to continue working creatively. Individual artists continue to need this support. Culture at large similarly responds to stimulus it receives through this support and interaction. Collectors are central to the well-being and survival of a culture's art community and to that culture's creative development. Without them and their faith in their culture, manifested through their buying and collecting of its work, their culture will be impoverished.

Media commentary on skyrocketing prices paid for Australian art over the last couple of years has tended to misrepresent the facts. Though there are contemporary artists benefiting from a rising market, few contemporary artists in Australia are financially independent, able to support themselves from their work or to even work full-time on their art. Large sums paid on the Australian market are mainly for non-contemporary works in secondary sales, with the money going not to the artist-producers but to on-sellers of art works who gain dividends from their capital investments. Australia Council reports give some insight into the financial situation of the practising artist in Australia today. Many artists are living on the poverty line. Average levels of total gross income for artists in 1986–87 were A\$20,500 with average levels of arts-related expenditure of A\$7,400. About one-third of visual artist's incomes was derived from work other than their primary creative activity. On average, in 1986–87 about one-fifth of professional visual artists' incomes were derived from non-arts sources. A recent update of this report showed little progress had been made through 1987–88, with most contemporary artists living on the poverty line, and substantially worse off than five years ago in comparison to the average Australian worker.[14] The point is that financial restrictions inhibit both the amount and the quality of work that artists are able to produce. There is a direct and poignant relationship between economic well-being and vital creativity, for which ultimately a culture which fails to value its artists properly pays dearly.[15]

## Artist-Gallery Relationships

Exceptions are generally to be found among those artists working within the gallery system. Within this system a mutual interdependence exists between artists and galleries. Both benefit from the sale of work. The artist-gallery system is based on, and financed by, sales of artists' work. There are many ways in which artist-dealer relationships are organised. Some negotiate detailed written contracts, others rely on oral assurances or simple letters of intent to define the terms of their association. Because of the degree of commitment, service and risk inherent in representing an artist, representation is regarded as potentially a long-term marriage. A gallery's representation of an artist is usually continuing and not confined to the three or four weeks of the artist's exhibitions. A dealer who brings an artist into his stable makes an implied or, sometimes, contractual commitment to mount regular shows of his work (typically once every two years) and to promote the artist's reputation in every possible way — through publicity (such as press releases and advertisements), discussions with collectors, critics and museum officials, giving assistance to those who may wish to write about or mount museum shows of the artist's work, often helping to assemble works for the show or even arranging for the publication of the catalogue. There are many cases in which the costs of exhibiting and promoting an artist's work result in a financial loss to the dealer. It may be many years before the dealer receives much return from the support given to an artist. Their association is based on faith and respect, from the dealer in the artist's quality and from the artist in the milieu the dealer has established for his gallery. When an artist joins a gallery his reputation becomes associated with the reputation that gallery holds and has built up through all its years of exhibiting work. This is particularly important for 'new' artists whose work will then receive attention it might not otherwise have received, by being represented by a gallery with a considerable reputation. On the strength of the relationship with the gallery, collectors will give time to looking at and considering that 'new' artist's work. The gallery brings to its representation of one artist the reputations of all the other artists it shows, together with the serious art world milieu attendant upon those reputations. An artist's work usually receives a more serious response in a gallery than in the nicest hired space for just this reason — the gallery's reputation. Conversely, a gallery's identity and reputation are based on the artists it shows; a gallery *is* the artists who show there. In market terms, an artist's work is only as good as his dealer's, and a dealer is only as good as his clients.

Representation usually involves territorial exclusivity, the gallery's right to be the artist's sole representative in a city, state, country or world-wide. Representation is principally designed to free the artist from non-artistic concerns and enable the artist to work unencumbered by the minutiae of many routine but necessary practical requirements. In return for its representation of the artist, the gallery expects to receive commission on sales of the artist's work. Some artists prefer to entrust their affairs to a single gallery with which they are comfortable and which is intimately familiar with the artist's works and instructions for it. The gallery then manages the visibility of that work as well as all sales and financial returns which may result.

Financial arrangements vary. Commissions can vary. It may be 50 per cent for young artists, or 40 per cent for established artists, or 25 per cent for one who produces little work very slowly, or 10 per cent in the case of particular works which may be very important, rare, or difficult. Commissions ranging from $33\frac{1}{3}$ to 50 per cent are the norm. There are, of course, commercially operated galleries where artists pay all the expenses — 'vanity galleries' where an artist essentially buys himself a show. Such a situation confers little or no prestige and usually few or no sales. Artists simply hire space and any exhibition services available within that space, which are often minimal. Sometimes these galleries require commission to be paid on sales in addition to expenses and hiring fees. Commission arrangements also vary depending on whether artists receive regular stipends or advances from their galleries. Some galleries may take a larger sales commission in exchange for paying a regular stipend regardless of sales, which assures artists of a regular income. Likewise, commission varies whether the artist consigns work to the gallery or whether the gallery buys-on work from the artist. Some artists do not use the private gallery system, and handle all their affairs and sales themselves. However, the majority of successful, and by that one means 'well-considered' new and established artists belong to the artist-gallery system because they find the support the system offers benefits them financially and professionally. It frees them to focus on their own work without interruption.

For this reason, because they do not like to have their work interrupted, many artists dislike studio visits, unless of course they are made by serious collectors of the artist's work. The simplest way to arrange a studio visit is to contact the artist through his dealer, if he has one. Whether you want to see as much of the artist's work as possible and to learn more about his methods and his ideas about his art, the dealer will tell you whether a studio visit is possible and, if so, he will set up the appointment. Some collectors try to circumvent dealers, and contact artists directly, hoping to purchase directly from the artist, to cut out the dealer, and save a great deal of money in commission. For this reason many artists avoid studio sales. They dislike being exploited, will not undersell their work and expect their galleries to protect their financial interests better than they can themselves. Often when collectors try to make purchases from artists' studios, the artists contact the gallery and the gallery bills the collector. Where artists are contracted, or have such arrangements with galleries all sales are subject to payment of commission. Artists who dislike cheap approaches that may compromise their relationship with their gallery may even charge more than would ordinarily be asked for a work, to allow for the inconvenience and bother such studio visits represent. Whereas the dealer offers the artist protection, the dealer also offers the collector protection in the case of studio visits, including protection from feeling compelled to buy before leaving the studio and from being bribed into a purchase by the artist's personal charm rather than on artistic merit. It is perfectly reasonable for a collector to visit the artist's studio with the artist's dealer, and after looking at the work to be seen, to leave without obligation. Prices and terms can be discussed or negotiated privately with the dealer who would expect the collector to then consider and reflect on possible purchases. Without the dealer the collector may feel compelled to buy.

In the case of those artists who are not affiliated to galleries, you will have to deal with them directly if you are interested in their work. The major contemporary galleries can give exposure only to a small percentage of the thousands of working artists, and most of the artists represented by those galleries are the ones who have already established reputations and certainly some track-record. Because the galleries represent artists continuously their calendars are devoted to the artists they represent. They are unable to help the hundreds of aspiring artists who approach these galleries and submit their portfolios. Even the younger, less well-known galleries who show larger amounts of new work by emerging artists may be unable to help.

Adventurous collectors may wish to take a 'long shot' and seek artists who lack any gallery's patronage and who are at the stage in their careers where they most need the financial and emotional support that an interested buyer can supply. Bear in mind that most of today's little-known artists will always remain little-known. If you do want to find the most promising unaffiliated artist and avoid 'horrible mistakes', start minimising the risks by relying on word-of-mouth advice from dealers, artists and curators who know the scene. They are your best sources of leads on emerging talent. Alternative, non-commercial spaces can also introduce you to artists. Occasionally, a group of unaffiliated artists band together to form their own artist-run gallery. Compared to non-commercial spaces these artist-run and financed galleries present more one-person shows. They obviously vary in quality, and are sometimes very short-lived, relying totally as they do on the energies of the artists behind them — who more often than not return to the preferred quiet of their private studios where they can work without interruption.

Of course, you may find mediocre work in galleries but the chances of your finding tomorrow's hot commodity from among today's commercially untested art are reduced the further afield you go from the mainstream.

All work within the contemporary scene is assessed and filtered in one way or another, if not by dealers then in the case of artists not affiliated to galleries by their peers. Grants are awarded by arts agencies whose expert panels assess the many applications they receive. Further selections are judged for juried exhibitions by critics or curators of distinguished reputation. These exhibitions are preferable to the many non-invitational, non-juried 'open' prize exhibitions staged with few or no criteria for selection or benchmark for quality. You will save your legs, much patience, and probably develop your eye further and better by focusing on the large enough selection of work by artists already preselected by experienced professionals.

## Artists' Rights

When buying contemporary work you should also be aware of your responsibilities to artists' rights, which can also add some complications.[16] Most collectors consider that once they buy an art work, they have the absolute right to do with it what they wish, without being subject to any conditions imposed by a previous owner or creator. It comes as a shock to them to learn that copyright protection is now available to artists and their heirs for the lifetime of the creator plus fifty years (or seventy-five years for works created before 1 January, 1978). Copyright does not automatically pass onto the purchaser of a work, unless copyright is transferred by the artist by written agreement. Reproductions cannot be made without copyright clearance. Where copyright is not assigned by the artist, fees and royalties are negotiated and payable. In New York the Visual Artists and Galleries Association was formed in 1977 to monitor and take action against violations of artists' reproduction rights. Other groups, including SPADEM in France, perform a similar service.[17] Some artists feel that while collectors may not be willing to sign royalty agreements, they can reasonably be expected to agree to other non-economic stipulations that are important to the artist and yet are not likely to impose a significant burden on the collector. Therefore artists sometimes seek assurances that if they want to borrow a major work from a collector for display in an important gallery or museum exhibition, the collector will cooperate. Also receiving increased attention from artists are 'moral rights' (*droit moral*), including the artist's right to protect the physical integrity of his work. The moral rights of artists are protected by law in France, Germany and Italy, and California. Resale royalties (*droit de suite*) are a hotly debated issue. Some artists feel that when a collector resells a work at a profit, the artist (who is responsible for the arts work's value but who may have sold it cheaply at a time when he was struggling for recognition) should share in the windfall. Most collectors, predictably, disagree. They feel that once they have bought a work for a price mutually agreed upon with the artist or his representative, they have absolute title to that property and their financial obligation to the artist ceases. They feel that the collector who risks his money on little-known artists deserves to reap any financial benefits that may occasionally come his way. Dealers generally feel that requirements for payment of resale royalties are difficult or impossible to enforce, and that attempts to impose them would hurt sales of contemporary art. Certainly the difficulties of administration and enforcement have prevented resale royalties from becoming more common. In California, since 1976 the seller is required by law to give the artist 5 per cent of the resale price on paintings, drawings and sculpture which are sold at a profit, provided that the seller resides in the State or the sale occurs there. Works resold for less than US$1,000 are exempt. The law has been largely honoured in the breach, with enforcement left up to artists. Artists can protect their rights only if they keep track of sales and sue offenders for unpaid royalties. France, Germany and Italy provide for payment of resale royalties under certain circumstances.

# 5

# ART AS INVESTMENT

*'Does a tomato cease to be a tomato merely because it is named a work of art? To buy a tomato while realising that it's a work of art that one is buying is participating in a great spectacle. In a spectacle what is false becomes true, provided one enters into the game.'*

Daniel Spoerri, *The Snare-Picture as Picture, Spectacle and Interrogation*, 1962

## High Art and Big Money

No-one could predict the hectic progression of the art market through the 1980s. This was the decade of spiralling super-prices and dizzying social prestige attached to collecting. A decade of record prices, record sales attendance and record success. The art market is no longer a place of traditional values, of discretion and private connoisseurship mainly for the wealthy. Today the art market is the stuff of TV cameras, newspaper headlines and Hollywood films. Now glamour goods bring out the glitz in the gaudy circus of a power auction, where large numbers of sufficiently well-heeled collectors vie ferociously for a limited number of prizes for which they pay previously unbelievable prices in a championship atmosphere of gamesmanship and fierce competition.

When the Van Gogh painting *Sunflowers* was knocked down at auction in 1988 for US$36.3 million, the world gasped: it was the highest price ever paid for a work of art. But, soon after, Van Gogh again claimed title to the world's most expensive artist with US$53.9 million paid for his painting *Irises*. These prices proved to be not so extraordinary with other records following fast. Picasso's *Acrobat et Jeune Arlequin* was easily sold for US$38 million and even living artists saw record prices paid. Jasper John's 1959 painting *False Start* reached US$17.05 million and this record was surpassed in November 1989 when Willem de Kooning's 1955 riotously colourful Abstract Expressionist painting *Interchange* sold for US$20.68 million at Sotheby's, New York. Twelve new records were set at that sale, and at Christie's New York Contemporary sale in late 1989, artist records were set at the rate of more than one for every four pictures sold.[1]

The 'Eighties ended with the two leading auction houses in the world boasting the highest sales ever: in 1988 US$1.144 billion for Christie's, US$1.548 billion for Sotheby's. In 1989 reported nett sales by both auction houses totalled US$5.1 billion, a 60 per cent increase on the previous year. A record for any single auction session was established at Sotheby's New York Impressionist and Modern sale on 15 November, 1989, raising US$269,567,000 with only four paintings out of 75 failing to sell.

The art market, seemingly oblivious to the stock-exchange crisis, embarked on an unprecedented upward cycle. Despite prices soaring, cash-rich investors came to regard 'blue-chip' paintings as safer than gold and huge amounts of money descended upon the art market to escalate prices further. Much of it was new wealth, hitherto not involved in the auction game. The Reagan years saw a time of inordinate accumulation of wealth on the part of a relative few, not unlike the first decades of the 20th century. The art market was flooded with the biggest tranche of new money since the 'Twenties, much of it the wealth of people of limited experience in buying pictures and fine art.

Forces are at work in the art market that have no relation to art. As the number of individuals or corporations capable of spending large amounts of money have increased in an affluent world where the number of 'masterpieces' is finite, there is increasing potential for purchasing a restricted commodity with decreasing supply. Therefore prices must go up. If the material is scarce, the chase becomes terrific.

While the media dwell with relish on this activity, it is interesting to note how record price levels have widened the financial gap separating various categories of art to proportions hitherto unthinkable. Many buyers appear to be generally a one-track minded crowd. They seem to seldom think in comparative terms, appearing to be unaware of what else the same sum of money might buy them. While the spotlights glare on the glamourous works that claim the highest prices in these much-publicised artstakes, there are many masterpieces to be had for 'bargain' prices, at a ratio of 200 to 1 or more. In an international market in 1987–88 which rose 80 per cent to £1.7 billion, 70 per cent of works sold for under US$10,000. Sotheby's financial report noted they sold approximately 190,000 lots in 1988 at under $10,000. If, as it appears, many art buyers do not much exercise comparison, their blinkers create opportunities, which perhaps will always be a feature of the art market. Whether buying in vogue or out of vogue, for speculation or for love of the object, undirectional collecting can be as expensive for the buyer following fashion as true passion can be rewarding for the enterprising buyer. One of the golden rules of buying is to buy against the trend. Old Master dealers on London's Bond Street have recently shown how even they have to meet trends. For these dealers the turn in the market is obvious. With increasing demand drying up their supply of top quality Master works, and as too few works of the sort they deal in are coming onto the market, quality must be hunted in new areas. They are now buying in fields where there is still quality and availability, in which living artists keep on producing — such as prints, where multiples are available.[2]

It is very interesting to reflect on how perceptions and fashions change. In the 1950s modern art was generally considered as rarefied and daring, and buying it was regarded almost as a sign of intellectual snobbism. The 18th century was taken

*Art as Investment*

for good taste. Now the needle has turned 180 degrees. Today modern art of the 20th century is widely embraced worldwide and 18th century formal court painting appears too formal and too subdued to have an instant impression and, beyond the highly decorative, to sell well. It is generally considered that one undervalued area today is 17th and 18th century painting (with the exception of Dutch 17th century paintings which have been the most popular Old Master category among collectors for the past forty years).

The popularity of the Impressionists is a clear example of how the art market is affected by forces that have little relation to art. Certainly Impressionism was a turning point in western history, generally perceived as a revolutionary change that challenged an academic tradition gone stale, investing in the process a new rendering of light and space.[3] More, it was the last great school of European art that rallied under its banner a large number of artists painting many pictures in similar style over twenty years down to around 1890. It was followed by a comparative whirlwind of varied activity as a succession of more short-lived movements, each claiming a handful of followers, marched through the early 20th century. Compared to the differing styles these zig-zagging modern movements produced, Impressionism offered an easily recognisable style. And this was the formula for its success on the market. The fundamental reason Impressionist painting first took off from 1967 to 1972 was because of the ease with which it could be apprehended by a new public of buyer with only the slightest acquaintance with art. Beginners, at anything, tend to go for the obvious. Impressionism offered them not only an easily recognisable style but also artists of highly visible profile (as measured by the amount of published literature on the subject and special exhibitions assembled). And the artists most sought after were those with idiosyncracies that became instantly familiar: the Monet landscape touch, the Renoir feminine look. The obvious star successor to the Impressionists in this conditioned market is Van Gogh. He has transcended celebrity status. He is a myth. The aesthetics of his works are enhanced by the 'glamour' of his poverty and ultimate suicide. The amount of art historical literature covering his works is enormous. His credibility has been endorsed by more museum exhibitions than have been given to other artists. He is the only painter so far honoured with two exhibitions within three years in the same major museum, each dealing with a particular phase of his work: at New York's Metropolitan Museum in 1984 and 1987.[4] All this satisfied buyers' feverish search for credentials. More, Van Gogh's 'trademark' paintings are instantly identifiable. Van Gogh's palette is idiosyncratic and his brushwork is unique. His twitchy strokes render his compositions to swirl, shimmer and gyrate, and drunkenly leap at the viewer. All these factors worked their magic at a four-and-a-half minute sale on 30 March 1988, when Van Gogh's *Sunflowers* sold at Christie's, London. The painting was hammered down for £24.75 million (US$36.3 million), doubling its estimate and tripling the previous record for a painting besides being the first work to sell for more than £10 million. The sale, attended by 1,300 people, was held on Van Gogh's birthday, in honour of which the press office presented a post-sale, birthday cake, decorated with painterly golden sunflowers, to the press corps.

Van Gogh magic worked again in May 1990 when a powerful psychological portrait study of Dr Paul Ferdinand Gachet, the artist's friend and doctor, painted six weeks before Van Gogh suicided, eclipsed *Irises* as the world's most expensive painting (which had hung on loan since 1984 in New York's Metropolitan Museum of Art). Through ten minutes of spirited bidding the troubled and introspective *Portrait of Dr Gachet* sold for US$82.5 million, at least US$15 million more than the most optimistic estimates and US$30 million more than the previous world record.

Look, too, at the painting by Jasper Johns, *False Start*, which briefly held the world record price paid for a work by a living artist. With strong Fauve-inspired colours and a suggestion of collage created by colour denomination painted in block lettering, the painting looked familiar, both by being evocative of earlier trends in the 20th century, and by having the typical broad brushwork of Johns' manner around 1960. Also the glamour of recent history surrounded the painting: *False Start* was painted in 1959 when Johns burst on to the New York scene. For this 'autograph' painting, a record price was paid, not so much for the painting, but for an abstract notion of the 'importance' of the painting and of Jasper Johns, as recorded by noted historical events, like happenings reported in the media, exhibitions in major museums, and articles discussing controversies. A record price was paid because of the mental perception that *False Start* was a 'trademark' painting — immediately recognisable as a Johns, displaying all the trademarks of his style, plus also being of historical importance, belonging to the period when Johns first became prominent. This sale demonstrated the inordinate importance of a 'name' sale. Trademark pictures with the right historical pedigree aside, the imprimatur of a celebrated collector adds weight particularly to contemporary sales, otherwise the most speculative area of the market. *False Start* had belonged to notable 1960s collectors Robert and Ethel Scull, who sold it to Francois de Menil. The eight-digit figure paid for *False Start* in 1988 was so far and away above what anyone had anticipated that with each successive bid, Ethel Scull who attended the sale, found it harder to choke back her tears and finally had to be helped from the salesroom as she was so overcome with emotion.[5]

To go through the roof, any work has to lend itself to glamorous characterisation. If visually identified with a stereotyped image, projected by exhibitions and books, and associated with names and notions that have the ring of history, then the sky is the limit. Look at *Sunflowers*, one of a series of six which Van Gogh executed in Arles between August 1888 and January 1889 to decorate his studio. It is exactly what a painting by Van Gogh should be. With its heavy impasto and intense colours, *Sunflowers* is an accurate document of Van Gogh's increasing insanity. Four of the series are tucked safely away in museums in both Europe and the United States for all to see and none to own; a fifth, owned privately in Japan, was destroyed there during World War II. The *Sunflowers* at Christie's was not the largest version, but was the only one remaining in private hands. Consigned by the estate of Helen Chester Beatty, whose family had owned the painting since the 1930s, the painting was 'fresh' on the market, though not in the best condition. The chrome yellow colour which Van Gogh had struggled to achieve, and which was symbolic of his supposed frenzied state of genius, had deteriorated badly. However the painting was the only one likely to ever become available on the market. The Yasuda Fire and Insurance Company of Tokyo paid what amounted to US$2.42 million per sunflower (four-fifths the total price paid for all the fabulous jewels of the Duchess of Windsor). And because of its price, *Sunflowers* became an icon. It is a very real symbol of the power which is accorded any successful and large accumulation of wealth.

Spiralling prices signal far-reaching changes. One change is the precedence given to abstract notions connected with the work of art over its purely visual aspect. What the mind is told takes over what the eye sees. Anything that is seen to matter in an historical perspective (whether of political or art history) becomes more desirable than other works of comparable and sometimes greater quality. Historicism drastically modifies price scales. Nationally-oriented collecting and regional associations also inflates prices. Additionally, spiralling prices reflect, and have in turn been affected by, the internationalisation and worldwide expansion of buying.

Just as 1987–88 had belonged to Van Gogh, 1988–89 belonged to Picasso. Picasso's cubist *La Cage d'Oiseaux* from the Ganz collection started prices rolling into the eight-figure range when it fired to reach US$15.4 million at Sotheby's. This was the first Picasso to break the US$10 million barrier at auction. One week later *La Maternité* sold for US$24.75 million at Christie's. Shortly after in London, the rose-period 1905 gouache *Acrobat et Jeune Arlequin* made £20.9 million (US$38.5 million). Then in May 1989 at Sotheby's, the dramatic 1901 self-portrait *Yo Picasso* made US$47.9 million (£28.8 million), setting a record for the artist and for any 20th century work of art. Its vendor, Kentucky collector Wendall Cherry, had bought the painting for US$5.83 million in 1981. Though remarkable that the record for a painting by Picasso should have been beaten three times running so quickly in a single season, it is not surprising that the absolute record for 20th century art should be held by Picasso. Picasso's name is familiar even to those who have never set foot in a museum. From the memorable retrospective that broke all attendance records in New York and Paris, to the one-man museum opened in the Hotel Salé in Paris, through the late 1980s, Picasso's image towers far about that of any other 20th century artists, transforming him from a much admired man in modern art circles into a myth for the millions.[6]

Similarly conditioned responses are found with Old Master buyers. Old Master dealer Bruno Meissner laments the imbalance between the popular and the neglected. 'Too many people want only one type of picture,' he has said. 'It is perfectly fine to want a nice still life or a pretty landscape, but too many people limit themselves. It can be challenging to take a fresh look at Old Masters. When you look at modern art or abstract art, you do not assess its decorative qualities first. You look at the power and emotion of the image, and how the colour and composition are rendered. You take all these qualities into consideration. Once a friend of mine objected to a Ter Brugghen I had of a cavalier with a woman seated on his lap because she wasn't pretty. It was very amusing to me, because you would never say that about a Francis Bacon. Can you imagine yourself saying to a dealer of contemporary art, "I don't like that de Kooning — it isn't pretty?" Of course not. It should be the same way with Old Masters.'

Another dealer notes, 'When it comes to Old Masters people get very fussy about what subjects they want to see hanging on their walls. It's all fashion really, and like any fashion, you can't predict it and at times it doesn't make sense. There is often a huge price discrepancy between pictures of comparable quality and subject matter simply because one artist is more desired at the moment than the other.[7]

Through the late 'Eighties Japanese buyers demonstrated that they were following a pattern, buying works considered important investment works, as for example when they bought period pieces from the recent history of the American New York School. A Japanese buyer set a record for Ellsworth Kelly twice within 15 minutes; first bidding US$319,000 for *Block Island*, 1959, then US$352,000 for *Black and White*, 1958. This was the first time the Japanese chased Kelly in a public auction and the attraction of the paintings is obvious. Both are representative of Kelly's style when he splashed onto the scene in the 1950s. *Block Island* enjoyed the credibility of a prestigious museum's approval, having been on view for years at Fort Worth's Kimbell Museum. *Black and White*, suggestive of a geometrised ideogram, has a starkness and bold graphic quality considered appealing to Japanese aesthetics.[8]

Japanese buying of Western art in terms of category or type can be considered as 'yuppie' as possible. It was noted that Kurosawa Ohkawa, the real estate developer who paid US$2.3 million for Willem de Kooning's oil on paper study for *Woman*, 1953, had not heard of De Kooning until a week before the sale.[9] Not perceiving the criteria by which relative merits within an artist's *oeuvre* can be judged, Japanese buyers often underbid what they don't buy, which further contributes to rising prices.

Through the 1980s the art market witnessed the strength of Japanese buyers. Japanese buyers were active at auctions all over the world. Christie's estimate that the Japanese regularly buy 30 per cent of their international sales. Between 1984 and 1987, there was a 500 per cent increase in the value of art works bought by the Japanese in terms of foreign currencies. Japanese purchases in 1988 alone were in excess of £750 million. So large has the trade in art become that it now shows up in

## Art as Investment

the figures for trade between Japan and the European Community. In the first quarter of 1989, purchases of art in Europe accounted for 103 billion yen (US$92.4 billion) in a total Y900 billion of imports to Japan from Europe. It has been noted that Japan's purchase of works of art abroad accounts for 25 per cent of the world's total. At Sotheby's New York sale of important Impressionist and Modern paintings on November 15, 1989, Japanese collectors and dealers took away five of the seven top lots at prices from US$11 million upwards. The Japanese bought 21 per cent of the value of Impressionist and Modern works sold at Sotheby's in 1987.

Japanese buyers aside, European buyers have also been active. Their combined buying, with the strength of their currencies against the US dollar, rendered the international integration of the market dramatically apparent. The art market's accelerating internationalisation was underlined by two initiatives taken by Sotheby's. In 1988 Sotheby's held the first sale ever conducted by a western company in the People's Republic of China.[10] Direct telephone lines to New York and Los Angeles were installed. Bidding was taken in English, French and Chinese. One month later, Sotheby's followed this with a sale in Moscow, again the first of its kind. Though commercially modest affairs, both sales were historically important in terms of their potential implications.

Through the 1980s the motivation behind the art market has changed. The history of the art market has long been a tangled web of long-term neglect and short-term fashion. Percipient investors since the 1930s have known that investors in art unload less in times of trouble than other investments. Through the 1980s prices of paintings rose rapidly. With contemporary art also propelled into the blue-chip category, against the background of intensifying competition in a shrinking world, prices for truly 'unique' works frequently multiplied their high estimates four or five fold. Old Masters rose by about 90 per cent while the more frequently sold Impressionists have jumped 150 per cent. Through 1987–1988 Sotheby's and Christie's sold 405 works for more than US$1 million each. In the first half of 1989, Christie's sold 147 items for more than US$1 million each, compared with 95 in the previous full year.

This activity has encouraged comparison between the art market and the stock market. Though the art market makes works of art into something very like growth stocks, the difference between the art market and the stock market cannot be emphasised too strongly. The fact that the place where stocks are traded and the place where works of art change hands are both called markets provides no valid useful parallels. The art market is a series of several small, fragmented markets influenced by unquantifiable factors such as fashion, degrees of restoration and aesthetic choice. Notable differences exist between the markets for contemporary art and Old Master paintings, and again between the market for prints and drawings in both these fields, and these different markets do not necessarily intersect. Differences between values paid for first-rate prime quality work and lesser work by the same artist demonstrate this. Values are particular to each single item and sale. Technical or quantitative demonstrations of results in the art market feature in the press and in auction-house literature. Though an interesting diversion, these are not a basis for decision-making as they are in the securities markets. Unlike securities, art 'stocks' are unquantifiable, or at least very difficult to quantify because of their unique properties. Works of art are not homogenous. Besides, art has always enjoyed a special spiritual hold enjoyed by all who can afford it, and for that enjoyment, which is totally subjective, buyers will pay what they consider they can afford — even in the case of bargains for the more open-minded, less fashion-conscious, less well-heeled collector. Individual collectors set prices, and prices are only a gauge. For all we hear about the 'commodification' of art, the implicit story is not simply about prices. Prices don't tell us of the love of the hunt, the thrill of the chase, about knowing what is available and getting it against competition, about the collectors' pleasure and excitement in acquiring what they love. The greatest drawback to the cold investment approach is that this often involves no knowledge of the singular qualities of the object. There is no real interest in the objects beyond price alone. And art cannot be valued this way. By merely filling a vault with canvases, the investor will not collect with the same rigorous standards as the collector planning to live with the canvases even for only a few years. Investor-collectors will have less opportunity to improve their eye and knowledge in the most natural way, and thus may be more likely to make unwise investment. One option for the investor-collector is to give a suitable amount of money to a good art dealer and instruct him to spend it wisely. But much like handing the whole decoration and furnishing of one's house over to an interior decorator, the result may be immediately impressive but is ultimately soulless. It is also no fun.

Ideally, collecting what you love should always take precedence over investment. It is all too easy for the investor to acquire second-rate works by first-rank names, while the true collector will be buying the best examples of second-rank artists and craftsmen. Financially there can be little doubt who will do better in the long run.

How differently does the law, particularly tax law, treat the owner of collectibles from the owners of other assets? What will the difference be for the individual who maintains two adjoining safe deposit boxes? One holds certificate for 1000 shares of major stock, the other holds several small Picasso sculptures. For income tax purposes are the annual rental fees of both these boxes deductible? If both the stock and the Picasso sculptures are sold at a loss, will the loss be deductible in both cases? Are there any tax benefits to be gained from the ownership of works of art? Does an art purchaser have similar protection to the purchaser of other investment vehicles? Can collectibles be the investments for limited partnership, as is often used to finance real-estate ventures or theatrical and film productions? What tax benefits, if any, are allowable to the investor engaged in the collection and maintenance of art objects primarily for investment reasons rather than for their own personal pleasure and enjoyment? Can the art investor, like the investor in market stocks, deduct capital losses and ordinary and necessary expenses against income? What are the tax consequences of the disposition of such an object, whether voluntary or involuntary, through sale or gift, death or theft, donations to charitable institutions, or through marital break-up? Such practical questions related to the ownership, acquisition and disposition of works of art, including such legal and tax aspects should be discussed with a personal tax advisor who can map out the tax consequences of art transactions and the best art-related tax strategy for a particular collector. Due to the frequent changes to tax laws, consultation with a tax advisor is essential for the most up-to-date information.

Art as an investment is a misconception that rests on false premises, both aesthetic and financial. First, 'art' is a matter of judgment. The acquisition of a painting is basically the purchase of an object, objectively consisting of a canvas attached to a support to which pigmentation in an oil or water base (ie paint) has been fixed. It may be an object with very little claim to a commonly shared aesthetic value. Not every pigmented canvas object merits characterisation as art, nor is all art 'good' art. The word 'art' is value-neutral. It generally classifies an object fabricated for aesthetic rather than utilitarian purposes, but does not qualify whether the object is a good or bad example of its type. Not every art-like object appreciates in value. Not all objects are resold at nett prices substantially higher than the original investment. Not every painting when resold fetches more inflation-adjusted nett dollars than the initial purchase price. Costs of ownership have to be taken into account: loss of income on the cash investment; possible carrying costs; expenses of insuring the work; costs of framing; conservation, freight; and commissions to be paid when the painting is sold.

Transaction costs in the art market are high. Commission on sales can range from 10 to 50 per cent. As an investment, a work of art must constantly escalate in value simply to keep itself abreast of other forms of investment, yet art can be more illiquid and expensive to trade than some capital market assets. When you want to convert your art investment to cash, the market for the work you own may have weakened temporarily. Besides, art is perishable and requires care. Also, art is not income-producing. The negative yield on art as investment has to be considered. Consider an investor who bought a painting for $10,000 and a Government Bond for $10,000. If neither investment had been sold after twelve months the purchaser would have his painting with no additional cash increment and he would have his bond plus interest earned — funds that could be separately invested. Compound interest does not accrue in art. The statement that 'Art is a good investment' usually means 'Some works of art have been a very profitable speculation'.

Certainly in recent years there has been a fascination with the potential for incremental values in art investment. There have been attempts to index the value of art and to combine art and finance. Many investors have begun to view art as an attractive alternative to stocks and bonds. Compared to the stock market, the art market is more difficult to analyse. Availability of objective data about the art market is limited. Factors that defy quantification such as taste and fashion render any technical analysis of trends very tenuous. Britain's *Art Sales Index Ltd* publishes auction price trends from 1970 on, for over 60,000 artists. However, these give no indication about the quality of the works passed through the auction houses, and they ignore private gallery sales (where often higher prices are paid). Late in 1981 Sotheby Parke Bernet began releasing *The Sotheby Index*, appearing weekly in Barron's newspaper. Attempting to do for art and antiques what the Dow Jones index does for securities, the *Sotheby Art Index* purportedly tracks trends statistically in twelve fields of collectibles, including Old Master paintings, Impressionist paintings, 19th century European paintings, Impressionist and Post-Impressionist paintings, Modern paintings (1900–1950) and American paintings (1800 to pre-World War II). Aggregate figures show how the market as a whole has fared. Because this index is based on auction results, figures remain unchanged until a relevant auction occurs, which can be weeks, even months, apart. To overcome this problem Sotheby Parke Bernet's specialists try to update the index periodically by estimating what particular objects (thought to be typical for each category of art works) would fetch on the market. The statistics sound impressive but are unreliable. The source of most statistical information about the art market are public auction house prices. Auction houses naturally tend to exaggerate their successes and play down their failures, so unsold works are rarely mentioned or are omitted from after-sale price lists. Private transactions, which comprise the bulk of activity within the market, are rarely reported.

In investment terms, the vagaries of the value of art — so difficult to define — are unsettling to responsible portfolio managers. With equities, stock certificates may vary in value but they are all exactly the same. There is no equivalent in the case of art. No two Matisses are the same. No two Ming blue and white pots. Not even two etchings off the same plate are equal, because other factors such as condition and provenance are very significant to the individual value of each piece. Therefore, unless the same work of art is repeatedly sold, indexes of art value are largely worthless.

## The Success of Art as Investment

Through the 1980s art captured public imagination in a new, fetishised way which affected our perception of art. With highly libidinous sums of money paid for art, increasingly many found that all they might remember of an art work was its price. Of course, art and money have always been closely associated. The dynamic money in whatever society — whether of the Pharoahs, the Medicis, or the

Saatchis — focuses th artistic lenses of the culture. Artists, too, have long recognised their work as a commodity. Rembrandt (1606–1669) was one of the first to do so.[11] Salvatore Rosa (1615–1673) made paintings he chose to paint, and then offered to collectors in a modern way, without painting on demand for patrons. But the 1980's avarice for art, which has prompted colossal rises in prices and triggered journalistic fixation on the market with media promotion of the notion of glamour of the US$50 million Van Gogh has, ironically, had a cheapening effect on art. This has produced permanent and inescapable harm to museum experience because we can no longer look at a well-known painting without considering what it cost. Now part of our experience of Van Gogh is how much money his work sells for. As Robert Hughes tellingly puts it: 'Once price was not relevant to the experience of the work. Art investment propaganda and market activities have blurred the distinction that once existed between price and value. The price of the work now became part of its function. It redefined the work, whose new task was simply to sit on the wall and get more expensive.' Sadly, art is cheapened as it becomes more costly. 'By the end of the 1970s, we were getting to the point where everything that could be regarded, however distantly, as a work of art was primarily esteemed not for its ability to communicate meaning, or its use as historical evidence, or its power to generate aesthetic pleasure, but for its convertibility into cash.'[12]

Robert Hughes has pointed out that a succession of exhibitions (*The Treasures of the Vikings, The Gold of the Gorgonzolas*), helped to reinforce the illusion that art was basically a kind of bullion.[13] Much connection has been made between gold and art. The rise in the price of art and the profits to be made from holding it are telling when compared with the classic refuge of gold. Against gold, investment in works of art proved a winner. Through the 1970s and 1980s with the art market's remarkable performance, art has been extremely profitable — bearing in mind the shortcomings of the Sotheby's Index against the *Financial Times'* 30 Share Index and accounting for currency fluctuations. Even in the decade before 1914 prices had not risen so fast nor over such a wide range of categories. Gerald Reitlinger's classic study of the market value of art observed in 1963 that buyers capable of spending large amounts of money have increased in an affluent world where the number of what are called masterpieces is finite; there is increasing potential for purchasing a restricted commodity with decreasing supply. Prices escalate as the material becomes scarce and the chase becomes terrific.

The London *Economist* Intelligence Unit's 1979 (and to date, last) report on *Art As Investment* supported this. Comparing 182 paintings, books and art objects that had been sold at auction twice between 1960 and 1979 against stock performance measured by the Dow Jones and London *Financial Times* industrial shares index, works by the Old Masters in the study surpassed 70 per cent of stocks, and work by the Impressionists outperformed 56 per cent of stocks.[14]

Activity in the art market since 1979, and particularly more recently, since the stockmarket fall of 1987, show very substantial increases in values of select works of art compared to other works of art in general, and compared to other forms of investment. According to Sotheby's Index, art prices had appreciated by almost 20 per cent from 1983 to 1988. This trend has accelerated in an art market that is increasingly becoming more liquid and efficient, fuelled by a growing number of collectors and demand for art as investment, together with improvements in information and financing options.

Naturally many collectors have accounted for the investment potential of art, even wealthy American collectors who bought from the legendary dealer Joseph Duveen (1869–1909). Henry Clay Frick, the Pittsburgh coke and steel industrialist and benefactor of the Frick Museum in New York (who also received art-buying advice from critic Roger Fry and Knoedler and Company), was no exception to collectors' common and frequent concerns about paying large amounts for acquisitions. When Frick paid approximately US$400,000 for Velasquez's *Philip IV of Spain*, on considering that Philip IV had paid Velasquez the modest sum of approximately $600 for the painting, Frick calculated what this would have been worth at 6 per cent interest compounded semi-annually from 1645 to 1910. If the money paid to Velasquez had been invested in a financial instrumentality at a modest interest rate, it would have produced a sum far greater than Frick's US$400,000 purchase price. Frick was consequently delighted to buy the picture for what he considered to be less than nothing.[15]

## Art Funds: Depreciation, Gifts, Bequests and Tax Deductions

The most renowned instance in which art has been acquired as a pension fund asset is in Great Britain, where one of the biggest collectors of antiques and works of art in the past 15 years has been the British Rail Pension Fund. This is the only systematic institutional attempt to invest long-term in works of art acquired specifically for profit. In 1974 the Fund decided to diversify its investment portfolio and invest some £40 million (less than 1 per cent of the total value of the Fund) in 'blue chip' works of art. Sotheby's was retained as the Fund's advisor.[16] The Fund intended that works of art would be held for at least 20 years before returning them to the market for resale. When begun through late 1974, criticism was levelled at British Rail for the wisdom of such investment in 'alternative investments' (like art and antiques) compared to the greater bargains available at the time in the 1974–1975 stock market when the market was acutely depressed with inflation in Britain seeming out of control — at one point reaching 27 per cent. 'The aim,' the Fund said, 'in addition to portfolio diversification, was to obtain sufficient long-term capital appreciation to provide at least a hedge against inflation.'

'Works of art met the criteria,' the Fund said, 'on the grounds that strong growth both in volume and prices had already been demonstrated. The effective fixed supply of works of art coupled with increasing and firmly established international demand offered the reasonable expectation that over the long term prices would continue to appreciate steadily, as has proved to be the case.'

Up to 1980 the Fund bought more than 2,000 items including Old Master paintings and drawings, tribal art, silver, Impressionist paintings, 18th century sculpture and Chinese ceramics. By the end of 1988 the Fund had sold about 1,000 items — something less than half of its purchases — for a total of some US$24 million, three times their original cost. This total represented a less-than-thrilling return of around 11 per cent per annum, or three per cent per annum return on the original investment in real terms, discounting inflation and income foregone in interest or dividends, plus costs to insure, preserve and store the admittedly unique investments held. This return compared unfavourably with the average annual gain of British stocks and bonds over the same period (in which the vast majority of British Rail's pension funds were invested) of about 20 per cent. However, in April 1989 British Rail sold 25 Impressionist and Modern pictures and sculptures at Sotheby's in London, at a sell-out auction that doubled estimates and realised £38.4 million (US$65.58 million). The sale was then the second most profitable of a single collection, surpassed only by Christie's US$85 million sale, in New York, of 28 Impressionist works from the William and Edith Mayer Goetz collection.[17] The British Rail pictures had been bought between 1975 and 1981 for a total of about £3.4 million (US$5.7 million). This represents a 20 per cent return per annum, or a respectable 12 per cent after allowing for inflation, and raises the overall return for the Fund's investments to 15 per cent. Maurice Stonefrost, chief executive of the Pension Fund, declared at a press conference after the sale: 'Impressionist and Modern pictures have been the single best investment I have had on my books.'

One incalculable public benefit from the Fund has been the availability of a third of the Fund's collection (worth two thirds of the collection's total value) on anonymous loan to mostly smaller provincial museums without the capacity to acquire similar items, as well as some favoured foreign institutions like the Detroit Museum. Proportionately the biggest beneficiary has been Doncaster, an English railway town with very little in its museum. This lending policy not only gave the public a chance to enjoy the works but also shifted storage and conservation problems to the museums and obtained free 'insurance' in the form of a government indemnity against theft, loss or damage. For ten years The National Gallery of Scotland enjoyed hanging Pierre-Auguste Renoir's painting *La Promenade*, an 1870 *plein air* portrait of Alfred Sisley and a woman in a park. The painting had been bought in 1976 for £682,000 (then US$1,974.390) and sold in 1989 to the Getty Museum for £10.34 million (US$17.7 million), more than doubling Renoir's record of US$8.8 million set months before at Sotheby's, New York.

On the heels of British Rail's divestment, the Chase Manhattan Bank is developing the Chase Art Fund. This Fund is being developed by Chase Investors Management Corporation, the institutional-money-management arm of Chase Manhattan Corporation. The Bank plans to raise US$300 million from large pension funds to invest in artwork, in a collection designed to provide long-term capital appreciation. This collection will be separate from the Bank's existing corporate collection. The plan calls for attracting minimum investments of US$10 million from as many as 30 major pension funds. The Chase Art Fund will invest in art valued between US$1 million and US$10 million. The Art Fund will probably appeal to pension funds that have total assets of at least US$1 billion, that will commit to invest for a minimum of five years. Unlike the British Rail Pension Fund, which established a controversial partnership with Sotheby's, Chase plans to rely on a 'select team of dealers' who would be paid on a profit-sharing basis according to a formula yet to be determined. Consensus is that working with dealers offers the opportunity to buy at more favourable prices than at auction and to buy on a more discreet basis, plus offering deeper access to and wider scope within the art market.[18]

It is unclear in Australia whether non-producing asset investments like works of art are permitted within Pension Funds, as has been the case in the United States. Whereas the US Department of Labor (which has the principal responsibility of regulating employee pensions plans) concluded in 1977 that the 'total portfolio' concept was permissible for a pension trustee, including non-income producing assets. Congress has taken a contrary position and ruled in 1982 under Section 408 (M) of the Internal Revenue Code, that 'any work of art' cannot be placed in Individual Retirement Accounts.

In Australia, as is now the case in the United States, for the owner of works of art there are few tax benefits or deductions available. The privilege of being able to deduct on a current basis the expenses of managing, conserving and maintaining a collection is clearly allowable to art dealers. Dealers are defined as regular commercial art merchants who maintain a gallery where work is displayed for sale, purchase art at wholesale to resell at retail and/or carry merchandise on consignment, and, in general, keep works of art as stock in trade for income-producing purposes. Such privileges do not apply to the collector whose primary purpose in acquiring works of art is the pleasure they give him in decorating his surroundings. The status of the investor, whose primary purpose in acquiring works of art is to hold them for resale at profit, is less clear.

Capital gains tax is payable under present Federal Government policy on any profitable resale of any items acquired after 19 September 1985. This applies only to real gains after allowance for inflation. Losses (without allowance for inflation) can be offset against gains. The question of depreciation also bears consideration. What is the economic useful life of works of art, if treated as decoration with allowable depreciable deductions? In Canada depreciation can be claimed each year on works of art used in business at 20 per cent of their reduced carrying costs, though only to works produced by Canadian artists.

Viewing Room at Christie's Auctioneers

**Jacopo Carrucci** called **Pontormo**
*Portrait of Duke Cosimo I de Medici*
Oil on panel transferred to canvas
92 x 72 cm

**Andrea Mantegna**
*The Adoration of the Magi*
Tempera and oil on linen laid down on canvas
54.6 x 69.2 cm

**Peter Paul Rubens**
*Samson and Delilah*
Oil on panel
185 x 205 cm

**Vincent Van Gogh**
*Sunflowers* 1853–90
Oil on extended canvas
100.5 x 76.5 cm extended
92 x 73 cm originally

**John Peter Russell**
*Belle Ile* 1900
Oil on canvas
54.5 x 65 cm

**Rupert Bunny**
*Jeanne Morel* c. 1895
Oil on canvas
184.6 x 90 cm

**Sidney Nolan**
*First Class Marksman* 1946
Ripolin enamel on hardboard
90.4 x 121.2 cm

**Arthur Boyd**
*Melbourne Burning* 1946–47
Oil and tempera on canvas
90.2 x 100.5 cm

**Charles Blackman**
*For a Child*
Oil on canvas
127 x 102 cm

## Art as Investment

The problem with depreciation rests in the question of what constitutes the useful life of each work of art and also its salvage value, both of which are difficult to determine precisely. In the United States the prevailing business practice is to classify works of art as furniture and fixtures and depreciate them accordingly. This treatment is generally not questioned by the Internal Revenue Service. When ownership of art is viewed as a form of investment the critical question arises as to how to protect its inherent monetary value against loss through theft, accident, or even deliberate damage. Methods of protection and a comment on insurance as viewed from the perspective of collectors are included in Chapter Six.

Another aspect to consider is the implications of the disposition of works of art through sales, gifts, bequests and exchanges. The most satisfying way to dispose of any work of art is to sell it at a profit which will be either a short-term or long-term capital gain. From a tax viewpoint if it seems likely that the work of art may sell at a loss the object can be gifted. Taxation incentives for the arts were introduced in Australia in 1976.[19]

If you gift items suitable for donation to public institutions, these gifts are deductible to the average amount of two valuations provided by valuers approved as experts in the field to which the object belongs. The institution will give you a list of approved valuers and recommend at least two who are registered to value the class of property you wish to donate. With bequests, the situation is similar to gifts, the estate being entitled to a deduction for the value of the works bequeathed to a museum. What usually becomes an issue in these cases are the valuations provided and claimed. Valuers will give you a valuation certificate. The institution will send the valuation certificates and a Certificate of Donation to the Committee on Taxation Incentives for the Arts, which will validate them at the meeting at which the gift is considered and will return them to you. Attach the originals of the validated valuation certificates and Certificate of Donation to your income tax return, and claim as a tax deduction the average of the valuations. The deduction may be claimed only in respect of the financial year in which the donation was made. The amount of the deduction to be claimed is restricted to the purchase price or the average of at least two valuations, made by approved valuers for the purposes of the Scheme, whichever is the lesser.

Sophisticated financial concerns have recently developed techniques to make art income-producing. Limited partnerships have been formed to pool funds and purchase art for the purpose of realising income and appreciation. Three French banks (Banque de la Cite, Banque de L'Union Occidentale, and B.N.P.) operate in the art market. B.N.P. is developing a collection of French art for resale within seven to eight years for up to 250 co-investors at US$40,000 each. The international art dealing group Artemis, backed by banks — most notably the Banque Bruxelles Lambert — was originally called an 'art investment trust' to appease the prejudices of the founders who preferred the idea of art as investment to art as tradeable beauty.[20]

Sotheby Parke Bernet, New York, serve as advisors for the art-investment program that Citibank, New York, began offering in 1979 for very wealthy clients. Citibank counselled its wealthiest clients to join the 'tangibles' cult and allocate up to 10 per cent of their investment capital for art and antiques. While art used to have high value but low liquidity, financial services now lend money to buy art. As already noted, Sotheby's, New York, is advancing money to bidders. Other efforts to combine art and finance include a so-called Art Master Credit Card to permit purchasers of art to acquire a credit line at galleries and selected retail outlets for the purchase of art and antiques. The 1980s saw the introduction of leveraged art: millions may be borrowed with owned artworks, or the artwork being bought, as collateral.[21]

Paradoxically, the best way to buy art to appreciate is to appreciate art. The only sure way to profit from art is to love it, and to find a category not greatly in demand. Reitlinger made this underlying distinction between speculation and investment. He wrote in 1963:

'It cannot be denied that enormous profits have been made in the past two decades by those who followed fashionable trends, regardless of cost, in order to sell out a few years later, but these are not investors but speculators. The only investors are those who never meant to invest at all. Those who bought some 20 years ago, preferring such things as English 18th century drawings, the "primitives", or English pottery and porcelain, Mughal miniatures, early Japanese porcelain and Chinese blue and white of the early Ming dynasty, may have seen their treasures multiply in value in some cases two or three hundred times over.'

The great international art dealer Rene Gimpel tells in his *Diary of an Art Dealer* the story of Bernard Franch, a French army contractor who spent 30 years collecting 18th century dance cards, which he loved. The American collector J. Pierpoint Morgan paid him US$200,000 for the collection. After Morgan boasted it had taken him 'five minutes to get the collection together', Franch speculated on finding other such Americans. 'Franch built up still other collections of needle cases, boxes, etc., pouring no end of money into objects which today aren't worth a quarter of what he paid for them: the miraculous Morgan sale was the worst transaction of his life.'[22]

Perhaps the moral is that art should not, and certainly cannot satisfactorily, be measured in terms of other investment avenues and indices. Objects of art cannot be valued by reference to standard volumes, weights or regulated prices. Art possesses qualities that make it unique and should be acquired for those qualities alone. If profit results as well, so be it. This should be a bonus, but not the principal concern for the collector.

All genuine art collectors gather their works of art because they love them. How else is one to account for the courageous and discerning collectors who have seen beauty where no others saw it? Aesthetic sense is an essential factor in art collecting. There are many instances of expensive misjudgment due to buying art and hoping for gain or from following fashion. With any investment, buying what everyone says is fashionable is hazardous. Fashionable investments are rarely profitable. Buyers interested in beauty and associative value (such as history) who buy, preserve and sell art with knowledge and care will most surely enjoy its lasting rewards. Take courage. Bolster your conviction and vision about desired objects by knowing the subject. When you buy art solely to make money, you are forfeiting art's chief value — the surprise and delight it gives in changing or heightening how one sees things. Without some personal feeling for the artistic value of what you buy, you have no objective way of evaluating the wisdom and reliability of others' advice. Buying, preserving and selling art with knowledge and care is the surest way to enjoy its lasting rewards, whether you collect for love, money or both.

# 6

# PROTECTING YOUR TREASURES

*'Painting: the art of protecting flat surfaces from the weather
and exposing them to the critic.'*

Ambrose Bierce, *The Devil's Dictionary*, 1906

Whether you believe owning art is for investment or for other forms of appreciation, a critical question all owners of art need to consider is protection against loss through theft, accident, deliberate damage, or age related damage. Artworks need care in their handling if they are to be protected from damaging effects that can reduce their value. Damage diminishes both their aesthetic and monetary value.

Besides wanting to protect your investment, owning a work of art makes you a custodian of a small, irreplaceable part of the world's culture. This entails responsibility to maintain the condition of the work, which must be kept in no worse (and possibly in better) condition than it was when you acquired it. Owning a work of art entails a moral obligation to share works of cultural heritage and (if asked) make them accessible to a wider public through loans to museums (provided adequate protective precautions are taken).

Two factors, basically, cause the deterioration of objects: internal (or inherent) processes and external processes. Because internal processes are set up during manufacture or crafting, very little can be done to reduce their effect. All the materials from which works of art are made are vulnerable to attack from moisture, heat, dust and pollution, light, biological pests, mechanical forces and human interference. Steps have to be taken to protect works of art from these hazards. First you will want to ensure you house the work in an environment best suited to ensure its good health and longevity. Theft and damage from fire, water and other environmental hazards, also have to be guarded against. It is easier, less expensive and preferable to maintain works of art in good order than to try to restore them once damage is done. Many collectors invest time, passion and money in the pursuit of their collectibles. They do not want to see their investment diminished by deterioration or damaged by environmental factors. Yet, through ignorance, laziness and neglect many make it virtually certain that damage will occur. This chapter will, I hope, help collectors avoid putting their collectibles at risk.

*Collecting Art*

## Display and Storage, Framing and Looking After Paper

The best protection you can provide for your works of art is to keep their environment constant. Their worst enemies are wide fluctuations of temperature and humidity. Most works of art are composed of organic materials such as paper, canvas and wood which have different characteristic responses to environmental factors such as fluctuations of temperature and humidity. The organic components of a painting that are moisture-responsive are the support (canvas, wood, paper) and the sizing layer, if it is present. These components react quite markedly with fluctuations in humidity and place the less moisture-responsive design layers (priming, paint, varnish) under considerable stress.

Air temperature has a direct bearing on humidity (humidity is generally expressed relative to the temperature, that is, relative humidity or RH). Many paints are thermoplastic, that is, they soften when heated, and in this state are easily deformed. Conversely, when thermoplastic paints are cooled they become brittle and are easily broken. The interaction of both the organic and inorganic components causes a work of art to expand and contract unevenly.

Thermal shock is the internal strain produced when a change in temperature causes the different materials in an object to expand and contract unevenly. This causes cracking, blistering and flaking. Under excessive humidity some varnishes turn opaque white and 'bloom'. This is an iridescent blanched condition caused by decomposition from excess moisture. Brownish stains from mould growth 'fox' and dot paper. Prolonged exposure to low relative humidity causes desiccation. Loss of moisture results in permanent weakening, embrittlement and often discolouration, warpage (or distortion of wooden parts) and shrinking (especially of vegetable fibres).

Canvas and wood, the most popular support upon which artists paint, are readily affected by moisture. Some unsized fabrics contract on becoming wet, others expand because of a glue size. Fabrics swell when wet, increasing the twist on the thread and resulting in tightening of the fabric. Canvas can become loose and sagging when damp and tight as a drumhead when dried out. Fine cracks called 'crackle' are the fine, uniform network of interconnected cracks over the surface of many old paintings on canvas. These fractures are caused by expansion and contraction of canvas over a period of time in response to changes in atmospheric conditions. These cracks appear on wood panels, either running parallel to the wood grain or forming a cracked pattern. Shrinking of the wood or canvas compresses cracked areas of paint, forcing them to cup and flare.

Ideally, works of art should be housed in a dust-free environment with the temperatures between 20 to 22 degrees Celsius, relative humidity between 50 to 55 per cent and low light levels ranging from 50 lux for works of art on paper to 200 lux for painting. Temperatures can be controlled by air conditioning. Humidity can be measured with a hygrometer and moisture content controlled with dehumidifiers to protect your work from steam, damp, heat.

It is inadvisable to hang art against a building's outside walls, particularly if they are subject to extremes of temperature or get damp. It is also unwise to hang work over heat-vents, radiators or fireplaces. The best level of humidity to maintain is a constant 55 per cent. When over 60 per cent the danger of mould developing on canvases carrying a glue size becomes acute. Prolonged excessive heat and relative low humidity can dry paint film, rendering it brittle. Prolonged excessive humidity softens the glue sizing of canvases and promotes development of mould. Fungi cannot exist unless the relative humidity consistently exceeds 65 per cent. Mould or mildew is a fungus growth which appears on water-soluble surfaces on canvas and paper. Mildew is a whitish coating of discolouration; mould is a growth of minute fungi as a downy or furry coating. Their growth is promoted by prolonged exposures to high temperatures and relative humidity above 65 per cent, and can be eliminated by exposure to ultraviolet rays or to sunlight. Alternatively, the vapours of thymol crystals will eliminate the fungus. Foxing, the brown spots or 'freckles' on paper, is due to the reaction to moisture of iron particles in paper (from rollers used in manufacture).

Strong light, especially that containing ultraviolet — such as direct sunlight and light from most fluorescent tubes — causes varnishes to discolour, some colours, particularly in watercolour, to fade, and weakens paper and canvas. Avoid direct sunlight. As you protect your soft furnishings from the bleaching effects of sunlight, take even more care with your works of art. Always hang a work on paper in the recessed areas of a room. Avoid direct light from fluorescent tubes that have a higher ultraviolet content than light from incandescent bulbs. Most light sources produce heat that can adversely affect a work of art so keep them away from direct sunlight and hot 'spot' lights. Avoid heat from light bulbs on the surface of any work, or you will bake the surface of the painting. A work of art should not be placed where sunlight and indirect light is particularly strong. Turn on lights near a work only when necessary, or use dimming devices to lower light levels, and keep light-sensitive works as far away from light sources as possible. Use an ultraviolet absorbent acrylic sheet (Plexiglass 20, Perspex VE and Perspex VA) to filter some of the damaging effects of light when glazing a picture or building a display case.

Avoid locating works near air vents around which soot and dirt circulate. Airborne dust and dirt can settle on a work partially obscuring it. Dust and grime can become ingrained in paint layers, especially if they have been softened by heat from strong lights or heaters. Dust also contains a large number of airborne mould spores. Decay (loss of strength and colour) occurs through chemical attack by substances in the atmosphere, or foreign matter or bacterial products, and corrosive smoke damage. Gases such as sulphur dioxide, a major component of our polluted city environment, can be absorbed by both organic and inorganic art materials becoming acidic and hastening the chemical deterioration of your valued work. Insects and rodents can also have a serious impact on the stability of a work of art and it is advisable to regularly monitor your collection to prevent wholesale damage from these agents. They leave worm holes (tunnels made by the larvae of insects in vegetable matter) and flyspecks (small spots or pits caused by the corrosive effect of substances in the excrement of insects). Silverfish attack papers and glues. They will eat their way through pictures to get at flour paste and glue sizing and they also enjoy bleached wood-pulp paper. Termites and woodworms will devour virtually anything made of cellulose, including paper. Cockroaches cause damage to leather, paper, fabric and any glues or painting media containing sugar. Never use chemicals in the vicinity of objects; often long-term chemical damage is worse than the potential insect damage. If you must spray, remove the object first and return it only after some time.

Proper framing and mounting is essential protection against environmental hazards. Be warned — improper framing can actually hasten the deterioration of your print, drawing or painting. It is very important to only use framers who insist on archival framing standards. The problem is that so much of what framers do is invisible and damage that results from improper materials and handling will only become visible once significant damage has occurred.

Particular care should be taken in framing works of paper.[1] Works on paper need the protective shield of sealed frames for insulation from changes in atmospheric conditions. Works on paper need to be sealed from airborne dust, pests, and pollution. Framing under glass or acrylic plastic also protects the surfaces of works on paper. Some plexiglass filters out ultraviolet rays. Unfortunately plexiglass also generates static electricity which tends to collect dust. For this reason plexiglass cannot be used on unfixed pastels, charcoal drawings or paintings with flaking or powdering paint.

Cardboard backed onto works on canvas and on paper protects the reverse side from dirt or damage. However, beware the vast majority of cardboards offered for framing made of wood-pulp board, which is acidic and contains a high percentage of unrefined pulp that inevitably disintegrates. Use only pure ragboard that is made of high-grade cellulose obtained from cotton fibres, together with acid-free materials. This includes window and backboard mats and hinging tapes. Material which is not acid-free (even mats with acid-free surfaces but acidic cores) will eventually stain work and, even worse, cause the molecular structure of paper to break down.

The pH of museum board should be neutral (pH7) or slightly alkaline (pH8). Works on paper are matted or mounted, with the backboard of the mount protecting the entire back of the picture extending beyond the border of the work to the paper it is on. Works are hinged to the backboard, while the front 'window' mount which protects the face of the work is cut out of the centre of the mount like a picture window with an opening of an appropriate size to permit the work to be visible.

The edges of the window mount framed under glass or plexiglass protect the glass from touching the face of the work and allow 'airspace' needed between the face of the work and the glass to guard against sweating and mould growth. The work of art on paper is hinged onto the backboard, and the backboard and window mount are hinged together along one edge with gummed cloth tape. Works on paper are best hinged to the backboard of their mats with thin Japanese tissue paper and paste. Starch paste is the best adhesive, made with wheat and rice starch and water. The hinge is a narrow strip cut to whatever length is necessary to support the size and weight of the paper. It is folded in half along its length so that one half can be attached to the back of the paper, and the other half can be attached to the backboard of the mat. Unless the work is very large, two hinges placed near the corners on the top edge are used. The work hangs freely to allow the paper to expand and contract without stress, as environmental conditions vary.

The work of art on paper should be able to be removed from the mounting hinges without tearing or ripping. One should *never* use any pressure-sensitive tapes like Scotch tape or masking tape etc., or synthetic glues and rubber cement, heat-sealing mounting tissue or gummed brown wrapping tape, to attach works to their mounts. These adhesives are not only difficult to remove but they penetrate the paper fibres, causing irreversible staining and embrittlement. Works of art on paper should never be glued or pasted to their mats. The back of any paper should be kept as clean as possible to protect the work. The paper should also never be folded, cut or torn.

Matting of works on paper is done for conservation reasons but also for aesthetic reasons. A well-proportioned mat improves the visual presentation of the image. The sides and top of the mat should be of equal width, preferably not less than 65mm (2½ inches) with the bottom of the mat 5mm (¼ inch) to 10mm (½ inch) wider. If the mat is cut an equal width on all four sides, an optical illusion will make the mat seem narrower at the bottom. A well-proportioned mat reflects the dimensions of the image, with its lower margin slightly greater than the upper margin. The inner edge of the mat should allow a space of at least 3 to 4mm (⅛ inch) around all sides of the image or plate mark (caused by the pressure of the edges of a printing plate on paper). This is important for a print without margins, since, if too little tolerance is allowed the edges of the print may be damaged when the mat is opened and closed. The window cut in the mat should have a bevelled edge. Simple mats are best. A mat which repeats the basic colours in the work can interfere with and often deaden the impact of the work. For example, in the case of a drawing drawn with conté crayon the brick rich colours of conté crayon, would be lost if surrounded with a mount of similar tan or umber tone and would read more clearly if mounted in a contrasting cooler shade like blue or soft grey which offers a visual complement to the warm colour of the drawing. The colour of the mats should not compete with the colour values in the work, but complement and enhance the work's appearance. A toned mat can unify the tonality of the picture but only when carefully balanced. For this reason it is often best to use the simple off-white colour of the all-rag mount or museum board which contributes to the brilliance of colour in the work.

Often double window mounts of different colours are used, with the inner mount under a narrower outer mount. Here, again, colours should not interfere or compete with the work, but enhance and complement it. 'French mats', decorated with colour, ruled lines, perhaps a narrow strip of gold paper, can sometimes be effective. Mats are usually of four-ply 2mm, ($\frac{1}{16}$ inch) thickness which provides adequate depth to allow for minor buckling of the work's surface as well as sufficient air space between the glass and the work when framed. Eight-ply 4mm, ($\frac{1}{8}$ inch) thickness is recommended for pastels, collages and very large works on paper. Avoid non-reflective frosted glass which obscures colours, thereby distorting the work.

The rule to follow, then, is to mount and frame works on paper to archival standard using acid-free materials with mats cut to proportions to suit the work. The object of framing is both to protect the work from environmental hazards and also to present the work for continued enjoyment.

A good frame should support the work physically and aesthetically Physically a painting is framed correctly when firmly held, placed in a true plane, without warp, strain or pressure. The inside or rebate dimensions of the frame should allow a painting to be stretched tighter if the canvas slackens. Securing paintings in their frames with nails should be avoided as hammer blows cause unnecessary shock and vibration to often fragile and brittle paint layers. It is preferable to hold paintings in their frames with small metal brackets screwed to the reverse of the frame. Generally mouldings for small paintings can be proportionately larger than mouldings for bigger paintings. Small paintings need space and can be dramatised by a carefully selected combination of frame mouldings. The larger the painting the less important the insert. Many large contemporary paintings are framed by narrow wooden 'baguette' strips 5mm to 10mm ($\frac{1}{4}$ to $\frac{1}{2}$ inch) wide, hugging the sides of the stretched canvas if they are framed at all. Unless they interfere with the work it is best to retain original frames, in which the work was first framed. These frames belong to the period from which the work derives and were often selected by the artists themselves. Therefore, period frames are always more appropriately sympathetic than later, modern versions. Besides, period frames also often qualify the pedigree of the work. If the work comes from a series of paintings that were all framed the same way, period frames date and locate the work to that series. If the frames have not survived, as is often the case, particularly with 20th century work when less substantial materials were used due to postwar austerities, frames resembling their original or period flavour can be reconstructed by good framers. Frame auctions at Ader Picard Tajan in Paris are routine and Bonham's in London holds four frame sales a year. Good framing will enhance the value of a picture well beyond the cost of the frame.

Just as frames should be sturdy enough to support the work they house for both conservation and aesthetic considerations, similarly objects and sculpture should be mounted on supports which display the work to best advantage and are also sturdy enough to ensure the work does not topple over. More delicate, fragile objects can be boxed for table or wall mounting; or housed in glass cases.

It is a good idea to periodically change the work you have on display. Rotating works of art on display with other items 'resting' in storage conditions that minimize exposure to light, dirt, and fluctuating climate can assist the longevity of the work and also allows you to see work afresh, especially when its relationship with other works of art varies.

Stored works should be stacked, raised off the floor, preferably slid into fixed racks and separated by rigid sheets of strong cardboard or masonite. The ideal way to store paintings is to hang them on sliding screens made of heavy metal mesh. If stacked, avoid too much weight resting on the frames, and watch for damp if stacked against walls. Oil paintings should not be removed from their stretchers unless necessary.

The best way to store unframed works on paper is either in metal storage drawers, plan cabinets, or Solander boxes. These are sturdy, hinged, acid-free boxes specifically made for storing unframed documents and works on paper. Unframed works on paper are best stored matted, with a thin cover of acid-free tissue. Clear cellulose acetate, which is sometimes used, is statically charged and attracts dust and loose particles so is not suitable for storing work of pastel and charcoal, nor for long-term storage. Pastels and charcoal drawings are best stored in their frames. However, if they are removed from their frames, they can be stored in their mounts with a sheet of acid-free card on top of the window mat. The thickness of the window mat protects against contact with the image layer. Avoid heavy pressure and any friction during storage when keeping such works in portfolios. Fixatives can partially solidify the powdery surface of pastels but should be used economically because fixatives can darken colours, especially if used excessively and sprayed from a short distance. Works on paper should be stored where relative humidity is maintained below 65 per cent.

Different types of works of art require different 'housekeeping' procedures. The golden rule to observe in handling any work of art is to take no action which is irreversible. Do-it-yourself cleaning is not recommended.

## Conservation and Restoration

Conservation is the science and art of treating condition defects that need attention, and of preventing further damage from occurring. No matter how conscientious you have been at proper display and storage, chances are that several works of art in your collection will have condition defects that need attention.

You need to be 'condition conscious'. Carefully monitor changes you observe in your works. Corrective action by professional experts should be taken when changes threaten a work's physical integrity. Defects may exist when you buy the work, or occur through accidents or mishandling. When you buy a work carefully examine its condition, preferably noting this in writing, and periodically re-examine the work. You may like to engage a conservator to undertake a condition report to establish the exact condition of a work of art prior to purchase. Examine your paintings under light cast parallel to the surface of the painting. This raking light throws irregularities into sharp relief. Look out for age cracks (cracks in the painted surface through which you can see the canvas), flaking paint (which occurs if age cracks are not treated), surface ripples and bulges (from the canvas being too loosely stretched, or being pushed out from behind by a knot of excess picture wire or debris in the space between the canvas and the bottom of the stretcher). For works on paper look out for fading and discolouration, foxing and brittleness of the paper. Note the condition of the varnish; if it is very discoloured it may be hiding damages to the paint film that are not immediately obvious.

Be very careful with conservation and restoration. Many works have been irreparably ruined by inexpert quack conservators. Avoid working on any artwork as long as it is reasonably sound, not deteriorating, and bears some reasonable resemblance to what we know or can imagine the artist's original intention to have been. Avoid over-restoration. Works on paper are often made to look like a sheet of fresh stationery. Such over-cleaning negates, and does violence to, the history of the work. If a work is heavily over-painted you are buying the restorer not the artist. Restoration should be a palliative for the abuse a work of art may have suffered.

Conservation is the profession concerned with the preservation, restoration and repair of works. The conservator is the doctor, who knows the composition and attributes of the supports and media artists use, is familiar with the technical bases of different media applied to grounds, and understands and respects works of art. You should only allow your works of art to be treated by suitable experienced conservators with recognisable qualifications. A conservator should not only be conversant with the technical and scientific requirements of the item undergoing treatment but have a knowledge of its historical and artistic period. Without an appreciation for art history as well as the work and period of the artist whose work is being cleaned, the conservator may put a slant on a work very different from that which the artist intended. Conservators have to judge the appropriateness of proposed treatment, basically not doing anything that cannot later be undone nor doing anything that modifies the known character of the original. Each work of art possesses unique properties calling for different attention, particularly works on paper and contemporary paintings — many of which are unvarnished and painted on unprimed canvas.

Conservators should compile records and reports on works under their care. Owners of works should receive copies of these: examination records documenting alterations or deterioration observed in the work; a treatment proposal that outlines what the conservator intends to do to correct these defects, and a treatment report that details the materials and methods used by the conservator to correct defects and provide new protection. Photographs should document condition before treatment, during treatment, before filling and inpainting, and condition after treatment.

When looking for a restorer it is best to seek recommendations from qualified professionals most likely to have frequent contact with restorers — like art dealers and museum curators, particularly those in the field to which your artwork belongs. Check with recommended conservators whether they have experience with work from the period or field to which your work belongs. There is no point in asking conservators specialising in 19th century works to restore a contemporary painting. Specialisation is a question of degree, so make sure the conservator you use is experienced. It is wise to find out the names of some previous clients (including museums) and what experience the restorer has had. A fine art conservator should have completed a comprehensive science and art-based course that emphasises practical work followed by a suitable period of work experience in the conservator's chosen field. You are responsible for the work of art you own so you should discuss and approve proposed conservation. Look at the work conservators have done and assess their experience and their philosophy to restoration. Discuss their philosophical approach to rectifying the damaged condition of your work. Are they mindful of long term effects? Do they use materials that are reversible? Are these and the long term condition and health of your work of more concern to them than immediate cosmetic restoration?

Different conservation practices attract debate and controversy. All conservation processes involve an ethical input which should be discussed. Consider, for example, when and how a painting is to be re-lined. Different solutions exist and suit the problems of particular paintings. Choices range between wax-resin lining, glue-paste lining and white-lead lining, each with advantages and shortcomings to suit different circumstances.

Wax-resin helps to re-attach badly flaking paint but can darken colours and change their relationship to each other. Because wax-resin lining is often ironed onto the back of the old canvas it can flatten the picture surface. Wax-resin linings are carried out when circumstances require an impregnating lining to consolidate flaking priming or paint.

Glue-paste lining avoids changing a painting's tonality but contains moisture that may cause future condition problems and is little used in Australia due to the climate. Most relining now involves the removal of glue-paste adhesives. White-lead lining is almost impossible to remove without causing damage besides expanding and contracting to potentially ruin the surface of the painting. It has never been widely used as it is dangerous to both painting and operator. Other lining adhesives and techniques are now available to replace older methods.

The major change in lining over the past few years has been that fewer paintings are subjected to a lining process. Most conservators now recognise the often dramatic and irreversible effects of lining and take other measures to correct structural problems on paintings. Controversy still exists over the removal of discoloured varnishes: when is it necessary to remove a discoloured varnish; should all the old varnish be removed or should a 'patina' be left; once removed, should an old varnish be replaced with a natural or a synthetic resin; should unvarnished paintings be varnished? Custodians and owners need to consider the effect that removing and replacing varnishes have on the value of their paintings.

Conservators are in short supply in Australia, and there are as yet few services and sources of information specific to Australian conditions. The Australian Institute for the Conservation of Cultural Material is about to set up an accreditation board. This will at least establish a standard for commercial conservators, of which there are many with varying degrees of skill, experience and accountability. Conservation information is generally available from conservators employed in State and Federal collecting institutions. The South Australian Ministry of the Arts houses a State Conservation Centre (SCC) which engages preventative conservators. The SCC began in June 1985 as a central resource for South Australia's major cultural institutions. It is also Australia's first comprehensive conservation centre, with five specialist laboratories for Objects, Paper, Textiles, Paintings and a Scientific and Technical Services Branch. Apart from being South Australia's central conservation facility, the Centre publishes information on conservation policy, particularly to meet Australian conditions. It also holds monthly clinic days on the last Wednesday of each month for the general public, and has set up a commercial division.

The National Centre for Cultural Heritage Science Studies at the University of Canberra similarly provides information on the conservation of works of art and culture in a number of fields. The Centre also undertakes practical conservation treatments on a wide range of individual objects including easel paintings, works of art on paper, ethnographic and industrial objects. Staff act as consultants to other institutions and organisations and organise lectures and workshops for interested groups on conservation topics.[2]

## Art Loans

Many collectors, including artists, are unhappy about sending work out on loan for fear of damage. The risks to a work's condition are indeed multiplied when sent out on loan. Notwithstanding the risk, many collectors feel a responsibility to make works they own available to a wider public. Through lending works of art by lesser-known artists to retrospectives or other exhibitions, collectors can help these artists increase their visibility. In some cases self-interested motives can condition a loan. Collectors can enhance the reputation of their collection by lending work to museum exhibitions thereby boosting the market value of works they own. Because of limited acquisition budgets many museums rely on loans from artists, dealers, collectors and galleries to exhibit work, especially in the case of contemporary art. No matter how careful borrowing museums may be, mishaps beyond their control can happen: a reputable shipper could lose a shipment through an accident; a visitor could go berserk in the gallery; a museum staff member could accidentally cause damage when displaying the work. Fortunately such mishaps are rare. No knowledgeable collectors would lend valuable work, nor would museums be able to provide the public with programs of temporary exhibitions and distribute information about artists and their works, unless the lender's interests are protected.

Though infrequent, vandalism unfortunately does occur in museums. Leonardo da Vinci's *The Virgin and Child with St. Anne and John the Baptist*, widely known as 'The Leonardo Cartoon', was badly damaged in July 1988 when a man fired a sawn-off shotgun directly into it at close range as 'a protest against the condition of society'. Before this, the National Gallery cartoon was slightly damaged in 1962 when a man threw a bottle of ink at it, which fortunately affected only the cartoon's perspex shield. However in the more recent attack, the shotgun blast projected many splinters of the cartoon's new protective bullet-resistant glass into the surface of the drawing, tearing away dozens of small fragments and distorting its canvas backing.

Museums naturally downplay such attacks. They are rare, after all. Brokers and insurance companies agree that catastrophic losses through theft or total destruction of an artwork on loan are virtually unheard of. Even minor damage is relatively rare. Most institutions are extremely careful about the packaging, transportation and storage of borrowed art. However, collectors should beware of the increased risk of damage which occurs at any time when a work of art is moved around. This is why proper insurance is a primary concern. There are many questions collectors should ask themselves and the borrowing institution in order to determine the best way to protect their art while it is away from home.

Usually works are lent for particular periods, generally associated with an exhibition the museum is staging, and which may subsequently tour to other museums. In deciding if you will agree to lend, it is wise to consider where your work of art is to be loaned and the venues to which it is to travel. State and larger museums are equipped with stable environmental conditions, conservation facilities and expert experienced professional staff, which smaller galleries may not have. As a lender, it is perfectly reasonable to enquire of museums what protection your work will receive: adequate security, uninvasive lighting, climate control, experienced art handlers. Many collectors consider that lending to small museums puts work at too great a risk. As a collector, your responsibility is to ensure that all due care will be taken to minimise the risks of damage.

There are widely accepted procedures for the management of loans. Loan agreements issued by museums to lenders have been developed to protect lenders against risks. Loan agreements detail the museum's obligation to protect the work loaned. Generally the museum undertakes to insure the borrowed work for the amount specified by the lender. This insurance usually covers all forms of risk except for perils like war, nuclear damage, and so on. You may prefer to maintain your own insurance if you do not want to get involved with someone else in the event of a claim. In that case you will undoubtedly want the claim to be settled on your behalf, and will want to be in control of that claim and settlement. If the lender elects to rely on his own insurance, the museum will be released from any liability in connection with the loan unless the museum is stated as an additional assured or a waiver of subrogation is provided against the museum.

Agreement regarding the degree of liability is crucial. Damages can be recovered if proof exists that the borrower was negligent. The lender has no basis for recovery when the borrower exercised reasonable care. Besides their concern with liability, loan agreements also cover additional conditions regarding the loan: permission for the museum to photograph and publish the work in the catalogue and for publicity for the exhibition; arrangements concerning the framing and presentation of the work in the exhibition; arrangements for any restoration or cleaning considered necessary by the museum; arrangements for the return of the work. Collectors relying on the institution to insure their art should always obtain a certificate of insurance from the institution. This certificate describes the item, lists the value at which it is being insured and names the owner as an additional insured, so that in the event of a loss, payment will be made directly to the collector. The most important thing is to have an up-to-date appraisal, because you want to be insured at today's market value of the loaned work, not the price you bought it at five years ago. Regularly updated appraisals protect you from serious financial loss in the event of an insurance claim.

Keeping reasonably careful records is vital. If you agree to lend a work, a condition report supported with photographs describing the work's condition before it went out on loan will help you, the borrower, and the insurance company, to verify the nature and extent of any damage that may occur during the loan period. Then, too, the collector has proof of the original condition of the work if it is returned with damage the museum failed to notice.

As lender you have the right to negotiate the circumstances of the loan and can ask for provisions in loan agreements to be changed if they do not suit you. Because most damage to artwork occurs in transit, it always pays to ensure that adequate care is taken with packing and shipping. Sometimes handlers can cause a considerable amount of damage, especially if they are not made aware of the specific requirements of a work of art. Travelling frames are advisable if available. It is preferable to use commercial packers and shippers with specialist fine art divisions and fine arts experience.

Often the front and back of the work is cased with sheets of rigid cardboard or polystyrene foam. For longer hauls, and in the case of more fragile material, work should be firmly packed in crates made of timber or rigid plastic. Spaces in crates should be wedged, filled and cushioned by bubble-wrap plastic sheeting, plastic or rubber sponges, blocks of polystyrene foam cut to fit the size of the object, or sections of felt undercarpeting. Paintings can be screwed into travelling frames which are inserted and screwed into crates. Corners should be padded with card or bubble-wrap. Crates should be waterproofed, lined with strong waterproof paper. They should be easy to open and reuse. For this reason screws rather than nails are used to secure the top of the crate. Smaller crates are additionally reinforced by timber edging of slotted cross-strips of timber laid flat on the outer perimeter of the wooden crate to support the crate. Crates should be clearly labelled 'Fragile' and 'This Side Up'. It pays to take special care with proper packing. There is no guarantee your work will be spared the rough treatment all cargo receives, even when you are dealing with specialist carriers. With insurance rates costlier than air freight, any savings on packing and freight should be weighed against increased insurance costs.

You should also consider how you would like your loan to be acknowledged in museum catalogues and in any publicity, and on the identification labels hanging alongside the work. Some collectors, who prefer anonymity, request their loans are acknowledged as coming from a private collection. Some collectors are anxious about publicising their collections, fearing that this causes security risks and can invite thefts. Other collectors enjoy the attention their collection may receive. Because additional value often accrues to a much publicised work or collection, some collectors regard this publicity as an asset to bank on when selling their collection or works from their collection. At any rate, whatever your request, it is best to lodge your request with the museum in writing to avoid misunderstanding and consequent ill-will.

Do museum exhibitions affect the market and values? Though some dismiss museums as followers rather than leaders of the market place, it is widely recognised that an important, publicised exhibition can affect the market. Some see the record price Christie's received for Van Gogh's *Sunflowers* as not unrelated to the Metropolitan Museum's exhibition, *Van Gogh In Saint Remy and Auvers*.[3] 1990 marked the centenary of Van Gogh's death in a rash of exhibitions and merchandising (like the Rijksmuseum's *Vincent Van Gogh* retrospective of 135 paintings, the largest retrospective of Van Gogh's work assembled, and the *Van Gogh 1990 Foundation's* posters by 20 internationally distinguished artists, among the many events throughout the year to celebrate the remarkable achievement of the short-lived painter who painted for only 10 years).

The astounding US$82.5 million hammered down in May 1990 at Christie's, New York for Van Gogh's *Portrait of Dr Gachet*, smashing all records and more than doubling expectations, resulted from the considerable focus on Van Gogh through the year. A museum exhibition can prompt the re-evaluation of previously neglected articles with the most obvious impact on the market. However, a small market will not necessarily be stimulated by a museum exhibition when the art is of an esoteric school or is of minority taste and of specialised interest collected by too small a number of people to be strongly affected even by a critically acclaimed exhibition. Also, bad curating can damage an artist's commercial standing, with market quietness often following a big show if that show was unfavourably received. Generally, though, the impact of museum exhibitions and of loans to these exhibitions can be beneficial. Travelling shows broaden the base of collectorship and widen the pool of collectors. A museum exhibition for a young lesser-known artist validates that artist's work for some collectors. Collectors are impressed by a provenance that includes exhibition in a museum. Having a work listed in a museum exhibition catalogue gives the work a cachet that can be important, and can add considerably to the value of a work when offered for sale.

## Cataloguing and Record-Keeping

Reasonable records should be kept by all collectors. They not only assist with insurance but are also necessary for tax purposes.[4] Additionally, recording information about work may add to its value when it is sold. Because information such as the exhibition history of a work and that of its ownership can affect the value of a work, it is in your interest to collate such information about work you own.

Simple systems are the best and easiest to maintain. Number every item in your collection on a card index or similar list. Place corresponding numbers on the reverse of the work. Record the following details of each work: name of artist (and dates of birth and death); title and date of work; medium (including support, that is the surface upon which a work is executed, such as oil on canvas, ink on paper); where and how it is signed (such as 'initialled L.R.' for lower right), and dated; date of aquisition, price paid, where you bought it from, details of exhibition if relevant (title, and date of the exhibition, catalogue number of the work); provenance (details and history of previous ownership) and earlier history of the work such as where it was exhibited (location, dates and titles of exhibitions and catalogue numbers) and documentation (source and date of publications). The better documented a work is, the easier it may be to sell. The history of the work can be of as much interest as the work itself and can add to the value of the work, especially if such documentation accompanies the work itself. Additionally, many collectors find that recording and researching this documentation leads them along all sorts of paths where they may learn more about the work, the artist, and art in general.

### Protecting Your Treasures

Proper records assist the prompt settlement of any insurance claim. These include comprehensive detailed lists of insured items with photographs of bills of sale, or a professional valuation of each item. Valuations provided by professional valuers are accepted as the basis of any claim so long as copies are lodged with your insurers at the inception of the policy and approved by them.

Items can be valued on different bases which will affect the insurance premiums to be paid and the documentation insurers require. The maximum valuation is the full market price, or replacement cost, of an item — that is, what it would cost to replace it in the 'retail' market. This is the basis of many insurance valuations. Many collectors, however, are satisfied in the event of loss to recover a lesser amount, such as the sum they would realise if they sold the object or collection in the open market. If cover is based on the object's original cost to you, you should give the insurer a copy of the receipt for your purchase. If cover is based on the object's replacement value, the insurer will most probably require a valuation performed by a professional valuer. Whichever valuation basis you choose, whether cost-basis or replacement-basis, it is important to reach a mutually satisfactory 'agreed amount' and valuation for your collection with your insurance broker before taking out a policy. In the event of a claim, you do not want to add a quarrel over valuations with your insurer to the trauma of theft or damage.

If you want your insurance to reflect very recent, if not current, market values then it would be prudent to update your valuations every three years. Because insurance is based on the principle of 'utmost good faith', insurers will insist on your giving them as much detail of any material facts as possible. Details you provide are likely to influence acceptance or evaluation of the risk by underwriters. The insurer's 'Proposal Form' requires careful completion because this document forms the basis of the contract between you and the insurer. Nondisclosure may nullify your insurance. If in any doubt, consult your insurance broker.

## Security

Theft is obviously a major risk to guard against but damage by other factors, including fire and water, should not be underestimated. Not only will risk-management and loss-preventing strategies help reduce your insurance premium but many insurance companies will not offer protection unless collections are protected adequately. With the increasing number of art thefts, particularly in the Northern Hemisphere, protective measures required by insurers have become more stringent. The Stolen Art Alert of the privately funded nonprofit International Foundation for Art Research (IFAR), located in New York, reported roughly 1,300 stolen works in 1979. Today this has increased to more than 30,000 cases on file. Their records of art thefts show an increase worldwide from 1,649 thefts in 1980 to 2,686 thefts in 1987, while recoveries only grew from 207 to 396.[5] Identifiable, well-documented works can be too hot to handle. However, less identifiable works with little documentation are difficult to trace and their recovery rate is low, at about 10 to 15 per cent.

Theories abound about the 'obsessed' thief, passionate about his hoards, as exemplified recently by the theft during 1988 of some 600 objects worth over US$3 million stolen by a German art-history student from storage in several Paris museums, where he worked for his training periods. These museums included the Petit Palais, the Marmottan, the Guimet, the Carnavalet, and the Louvre, as well as two other museums outside Paris, at Rueil-Malmaison and Compiègne. Spurred on by 'love of art', the student told the police, when apprehended, that he had no intention of selling any of the booty. He liked to 'admire all these things, peacefully at home'.[6] However, the art thief will rarely keep the stolen work himself. The stolen piece will eventually find its way back into the stream of legitimate commerce — a worldwide, art-hungry market not given to probing the origins of the artwork it consumes.

With financial stakes now so high, heists have become well-managed and organised activities. Five unmasked gunmen held up nine guards and forty visitors in a daring raid of Paris's famed Marmottan Museum which saw the disappearance of nine Impressionist masterpieces, yet to be found, among them two Renoirs and five Monets valued at US$12.5 million including a Monet *Impression, Sunrise* which gave its name to the Impressionist movement. Investigators believe the paintings are in Japan, probably in the hands of Japan's infamous tattooed mafia, the Yakuza.

The Irish police suspect Dublin's Southside gang in the biggest haul of Old Masters in modern history. On the night of 21 May, 1986, 11 paintings were stolen from Russborough, the elegant 18th century Georgian house of Sir Alfred Beit in County Wicklow with military efficiency. Works stolen included paintings by Goya, Gainsborough, and two by Rubens, to date not recovered. Nineteen works from the collection had been stolen twelve years before in April 1974, including Vermeer's *Lady Writing a Letter with Her Maid*, one of only two Vermeers known to exist outside museums. The thieves demanded a ransom of US$1.2 million and the transfer of four Irish Republican Army members serving life sentences in London, to jails in Northern Ireland. The conditions were not met but the paintings were recovered undamaged a week later. Only about 35 works by the 17th century Dutch Master Jan Vermeer have survived and apart from one owned by the Queen, the Russborough painting is the only one known to be in private hands. The scale of this theft was surpassed when 12 masterpieces were stolen from The Isabella Gardner Museum in Boston in March 1990. In what is believed to be the biggest art theft in history, two thieves dressed as policemen took a dozen works conservatively valued at more than US$200 million, including Jan Vermeer's *The Concert* and paintings by Rembrandt, Degas and Manet, as well as a 3,000 year-old Chinese bronze beaker from the Shang dynasty. The theft prompted an unusual agreement between

## Protecting Your Treasures

Sotheby's and Christie's to underwrite the reward offered of US$1 million for information leading to the recovery of the stolen works. This was the first time that either auction house had helped a museum put up a reward for stolen art.

It is now widely acknowledged that the art, narcotics and arms underworlds overlap. The Marcos 'collection' is a titillating case of politics, drama, and foul-play yet to be unfolded when the Marcos acquisitions are divested. After the Marcoses fled the Philippines early in 1986, the Philippine government established the Philippine Presidential Commission on Good Government (PPCOGG) to find and recover the Marcos assets. Sales to date of recovered assets have netted just over US$2 million, turned over to the Philippine Land Reform program. The bulk of the purloined possessions are yet to be sold, including 27 important works found under the control of Saudi arms dealer and Marcos buddy Adnan Khashoggi.

The British, Italian and French police run trained, full-time 'art squads' devoted to art theft. Unlike other police forces, the Italians put recovery above arrests on their priority list. They fear unique works may be lost forever or virtually destroyed, and many are irreparably altered to be resold on the open market as a different work by the same artist or his school.

The *Carabinieri* in Rome maintain an art theft investigation unit of 100 staff who receive reports of between 20 and 30 new thefts every day. More than 64,000 items are recorded on their computerised files. During the past 20 years, over 200,000 items have been stolen from Italy's museums and archaeological sites and churches, most of them sold abroad in Britain or Switzerland. Between 1969 and 1974, Italy experienced an annual increase in the incidence of art theft of almost 30 per cent. The *Carabinieri's* recovery rate is less than 50 per cent for Italian art, against the French Police's recovery rate of less than 30 per cent and Interpol's recovery rate of less than 10 per cent.

There is no central registry for art where one can make a definite title search prior to transactions. This could give art buyers a complete and reliable source of information on provenance. It could presumably also make it more difficult for thieves to sell stolen objects to innocent buyers. The International Foundation for Art Research (IFAR), is currently in the process of compiling the first comprehensive listing of extant stolen art for its Art Theft Archive. The Archive is the pilot project of IFAR to examine the various means of cataloguing information on stolen art. The two tasks of the Archive are to maintain a thorough inventory of stolen art and to make this information available to law enforcement agencies, art specialists, and transferees of art. It is hoped that the existence of the Archive itself will act as a deterrent to art theft.

When it becomes common knowledge that a transferee may check on the ownership of a given piece of art through a reputable, independent source, stolen art will become virtually unmarketable through legitimate channels of commerce.

Sotheby's is presently working with insurers from Lloyds, with IFAR and other groups, to develop a computerised data-base of stolen art accessible to dealers everywhere. Such a central worldwide computerised data-base will take time to become established. Two new international data-base services to combat art crime were established in 1990. These are London-based LaserNet and the International Art and Antique Loss Register Ltd (IAALR) which will work with IFAR and computerise the IFAR files.

The International Criminal Police Organization (Interpol) — a group of police agencies in 134 countries — has established an Art Program, which computerises and circulates information on stolen and forged art. Because Interpol's main focus is international criminal activity, the Art Program is concerned primarily with art objects believed to have been smuggled across international borders. The Art Program maintains records on stolen objects through a computerised case-tracking system. This system enables Interpol to store and retrieve descriptive data on stolen and forged art objects. However, Interpol is concerned primarily with disseminating information about stolen art rather than in maintaining a comprehensive inventory of art objects.

The United States National Central Bureau (USNCB), Interpol's United States office, receives monthly stolen-property notices through Interpol's headquarters in St. Cloud, France. The USNCB then transmits these notices to those on a select mailing list, including the FBI, the ADAA, IFAR, customs officials, and the police departments of New York, Chicago, and Los Angeles. These notices include descriptions of stolen objects, the date and location of the theft, the stolen object's physical condition, and a photograph, serial number or other identifying characteristic. From the monthly notices, Interpol publishes a list of prominent stolen objects in a biannual poster, 'The Twelve Most Wanted Works of Art'. The criteria for selection of the twelve most wanted works of art include monetary value, historical significance, and cultural significance. These posters feature photographs of stolen objects accompanied by vital information written in French and English. The posters are distributed to law enforcement agencies, art-theft archives, art publications, major museums and police departments in all Interpol member countries.

Less than 8 per cent of all stolen art is recovered, according to Interpol. Meanwhile, as prices for art soar and uncertainty on the world's stock markets make investing in art more attractive than ever, illegal trafficking in art proliferates. IFAR estimates the value of art thefts at US$500 to $750 million. Many stolen works never resurface and title to other stolen works is in limbo. Take, for instance, the Getty Museum's *Aphrodite*. Bought from a reputable London dealer for an undisclosed price, the 5th century B.C. figure was reportedly insured for US$20 million. The Getty Museum was embarrassed, though, when the Italian police traced this work to the *Tombardi*, modern-day night-thieves of age-old graves, who stole the statue from the ancient Greek colony of Morgantina in Sicily. Italian police state this busi-

## Protecting Your Treasures

ness of stealing archaelogical treasures is now controlled by the Mafia and its southern Italian counterparts, the *Camorra* and *'Ndrangheta*, as a way of recycling some of their huge drug profits.

All this has prompted stricter security precautions and higher insurance premiums. Premiums have become so prohibitive for many museums that none of Holland's state art treasures are insured. In December 1988 three early Van Gogh's were stolen from the Kroller-Muller Museum. One was returned slightly damaged in April but ransom of US$2.5 million was demanded for the rest. The Dutch Parliament stepped into the negotiations to demand that no ransom be paid. Money was found elsewhere, but the thieves never came for the pick up. The paintings are still missing.

Australia's most remarkable recent thefts have mostly occurred in Victoria. On New Year's Eve in 1978, 92 paintings were stolen from the home of noted South Yarra dealer, Joseph Brown. All the early Australian masterpieces from his private collection were later recovered. In July 1985 A$3.5 million worth of treasures were taken from the home of Frank and Zlater Kastanek at Narbethong. The haul which was recovered included Raphael's *Holy Family*, valued at A$1 million. There was also the farcical theft of Picasso's A$1.6 million *Weeping Woman* from the National Gallery of Victoria in 1986. Then in July 1988, 24 paintings worth A$1.3 million were stolen from the Toorak home of industrialist Sam Smorgan. The Queensland Art Gallery bought for A$25,000 on the open market in 1986 a double-sided portrait by Sir William Dobell (1899–1970) *Study for a Cypriot*, to later discover this painting had been stolen in 1961 from the National Gallery of Victoria. The thieves had cleverly displayed the lesser-known reverse portrait when they offered the canvas for sale. The painting was returned to the Victorian National Gallery.

Good physical security not only offers you protection but is also regarded by insurers as an essential prerequisite for the issue of a policy. For most insurers, premises must be securely protected by reinforcements like bars, security glass and deadlocks. They must also be alarmed, linked to security companies or the police. You can choose from a bewildering range of sophisticated and simple devices to prevent and detect fire and theft available from assorted services with varying degrees of integrity and expertise. Overly complex security systems can be costly, and difficult to install, maintain and operate. Alarm systems activated when an object is moved are so sensitive they can be activated by inconsequential happenings such as air currents and blowing curtains, changes in temperature, and passing pets or bugs.

Unless insisted upon by insurers, it is really not essential to maintain additional security features beyond the usual sensible precautions basic to home security: sturdy, pick-resistant locks; lighting of rooms through timer switches, particularly in unoccupied homes; relying on the watchful eyes of neighbours while away for extended periods; sufficient external lighting around the house to make it harder for intruders to escape notice. And do not leave the keys in the house! As a general rule, two mortice deadlocks of the highest specification should be fitted to each external door, and window locks should be fitted to all ground-floor and first-floor windows. Examine all doors and window frames to make sure they are at least as strong as the locks. This applies particularly to older properties. Remember that protection should be in effective operation at all times when the house is unoccupied and that vulnerable windows, such as those at basement level and out of sight of passers-by, might benefit from iron bars, internal shutters or a collapsible grille. The basic principle is to protect the perimeter of the property to prevent an easy entry. No thief likes to spend a long time outside a building trying to get in. The loud noises and flashing of local alarms protecting well-lit points of access to a home or building deter and frighten off burglars. If your insurers insist you install a burglar alarm, have one installed by a nationally recognised firm with good local maintenance facilities, and one that gives a complete guarantee. You can store your work off-premises if you will be away for extended periods. Specialised fine arts shippers store work.

Fire sprinklers and smoke detectors can damage work in preventing fires. Fire sprinklers react to heat, but can cause water damage The most efficient extinguishers are dry chemical extinguishers. They leave a powdery residue, but do not damage objects. The owners of works of art can obtain advice from fire prevention companies.

## Insurance

Insurance has to do with the material and financial aspects of art. It is concerned with objects that can be bought and sold and that are exposed to the dangers of destructions, damage or theft.

Insurance is a matter of personal choice. Maximum realistic cover is expensive for works of art, yet shopping for the lowest quotation is not wise. With insurance you get what you pay for. Those who collect mainly for pleasure and take out insurance can lighten their insurance burden prudently in a number of ways.

First, you need to find a suitable broker. It is advisable to deal with brokers who specialise in fine art insurance. Few brokers appreciate or wish to be involved with the specialised field of fine art insurance. Leading auctioneers, dealers or trade associations will recommend brokers. You will need to use an insurance company which does not tend to shy away from art, as many do, through feeling uncomfortable with 'unfixed' assets with such a high value. Special fine art insurance policies may be less expensive than standard homeowner's policies, so you'll need to find brokers offering these. The broker or insurer you need is one who knows a great deal about the objects he is insuring. Not only will he give you the fullest and least expensive cover but you will also get every possible assistance in the settlement of your claims which are, after all, what insurance is all about.

The nature of the cover required defines the kinds of 'risks' to be covered. 'Householder's Comprehensive', or 'All-in' policies cover only certain specified perils such as theft, fire, explosion, water damage, or storm damage. In the event of a claim, the policy holder has to show that the loss or damage has occurred as the direct result of one of these perils or 'risks'. It is not sufficient, for example, to say that something has disappeared and therefore must have been stolen. Actual evidence, even if only circumstantial, is required before a claim will be considered. Insurance companies will ask if the police have been informed, and in the United State a police report from the investigator is required.

It pays to shop around among brokers for the best coverage and rates. Collectors trying to tuck art under their normal household contents policies find this is very expensive, and a policy designed for videos and carpets is clearly unsuitable for art. Such areas as restoration, partial loss, depreciation and appreciation are not catered for and insurers have had problems getting claims paid. Though a 'Householder's' policy may seem to be the simplest method of providing some cover there may be restrictions associated with this policy that work against the collector, such as limitations on claims. Many Homeowner's policies work on a formula basis, whereby the contents of the home are valued at 50 per cent of the house's value regardless of what is in the house. Your insurers may not be willing to accept the added risk of a valuable collection at the same rate of premium. Under many policies there is a $500 limitation on claims for precious metals, which includes silverware and items of numismatic interest, as well as a $500 limitation on jewellery, both new and antique. These limitations make the Homeowner's policy unsuitable for almost any collector. Generally speaking it is better to cover a collection under a separate 'all risks' policy.

When shopping for fine arts insurance, you should look for coverage that is 'multi-risks', insuring all losses except those specifically excluded in the policy, as opposed to the usual 'defined events' policies available in Australia. A 'defined events' policy lists those perils which are covered by insurance such as fire, lightning and theft. The insured's loss has to fall into one of these categories. With a 'multi-risks' policy, most risks are covered, except for a few standard exclusions such as wear and tear, moth or vermin and gradual deterioration. 'Multi-risks' insurance represents the maximum cover you are likely to obtain and is less of a misnomer. It will cover you in addition against accidental breakage and disappearance, but like any other insurance it should be emphasised that it will not cover 'inherent vice', such as progressive deterioration through atmospheric conditions.

Works lent out should be insured 'wall to wall', protecting the work from the moment it is picked up from its normal resting place, until it is safely back again. Separate cover may be required for valuable works.

There are two issues involved when a work of art is damaged: first, the cost of restoration; second, the amount by which the object's total value has been lessened by the damages. Both are covered in a fine arts insurance policy, but the 'depreciation' (as the loss in value is called) cannot be determined until after the restoration work has been done. At that point, the collector should get an independent appraiser or dealer to give a written appraisal of the item's current value. The insurance company may accept this valuation and pay the owner the difference between that and the value at which the piece was insured. Or, the insurance company may feel the loss has been overestimated and may hire another appraiser for a second opinion. If the two estimates differ, the insurance policy provides for binding arbitration by a third party agreed upon by both appraisers.

Once an agreement has been reached about the extent of the depreciation, a document called a 'proof of loss statement' is signed. This lists the amount the insurance company has agreed to pay in compensation for the value lost due to damage. It generally includes the cost of restoration as well, although sometimes the insurance company pays that cost directly to the restorer and this payment is not part of the final settling-up. The insurance company is required by law to make payment within 30 to 60 days of signing the proof of loss statement.

Understand the geographical limitations of your policy and make sure that it is worded in accordance with your probable requirements. Policy covering your residence will not normally cover items sent away to restorers or loaned for exhibitions. If you choose to get coverage for such occasions, the restorer or exhibitor may require a 'waiver of subrogation (abrogation)' from your insurer before he will take the object into his possession. The waiver states that your insurer is covering the object while it is away from your home, and it may not be issued immediately. Many exhibitors and institutions, and a few restorers, carry their own insurance. If you agree to have your property covered under their policy make sure that they list a valuation for your object on your receipt or in a separate letter. This valuation should be acceptable to you. You may also want to stipulate that they will be responsible for repairing any damage to the object and that you have the right to choose or at least approve the restorer. Another important point is to make sure that their policy does not simply cover 'legal liability only'. Transit to and from the exhibition must also be considered, and if there is any doubt whatsoever then consult your brokers, arranging your own cover if necessary on a 'wall to wall' basis. The more specific your requests the more satisfactory your recompense in the cases of loss or damage.

Carefully read the fine print of your policy. Take special note of any warranties, conditions and clauses that you think may present difficulties in the event of a claim. Avoid clauses excluding the breakage of 'brittle articles' which have never been satisfactorily defined; and 'pairs and sets' clauses unsatisfactorily stating that if one article of a pair is lost or broken the insurers will only pay half the value of the pair, despite the fact that a pair of articles can be worth more than twice the sum of the two single items. This clause should be amended to provide payment for the loss of 'set value'. Be mindful, too, of the 'average' clause which says in effect that if you are under-insured any claim will be reduced proportionately. If a collection worth $100,000 is insured for $60,000 then payment will be made for 60 per cent of any claim. Whether your policy contains an 'average' clause or not, you are asked to confirm the sum insured represents the full value and in the event of substantial under-insurance you may find that the company would try to reflect such under-insurance in the claim settlement. The 'average' clause does not apply to specific items insured individually for an agreed value. Pay particular heed to the provisions of warranties in your policy. The most usual warranty is the 'protections maintenance' warranty, which says that all protections provided for your premises must be in full and effective operation whenever the premises are left unattended. It means exactly what it says: namely that every lock must be locked, every window shut and all doors closed. Do not expect any sympathy from your insurers if you forget to lock the door when you depart or if you leave windows open for ventilation. If you have a burglar alarm it must be serviced regularly and checked if it is in good working order before you go out. If, after that the alarm fails to function or the locks do not withstand the attempts of the thieves to enter the house, you will not be penalised.

Premiums obviously vary, depending on the articles covered and on the crime rate in your area. You can insure for less than the full total value of the articles: for example, having prepared a schedule of values you can elect to be your own co-insurer for 25 per cent of the risk, leaving the insurers with the remaining 75 per cent, and you pay only 75 per cent of the basic premium. You can insure on a 'first loss' basis, calculating what you feel would be the maximum value you could lose as the result of one burglary or fire. Thus you might take the view that burglars would be unlikely to take all of your collection and you insure only a certain sum. If they take more than this you have no claim for any loss over the agreed maximum. Also, bear in mind that the chances of total loss by fire are considerable. You can exclude theft risk altogether, but cover in full all other risks such as fire, lightning, water damage, etc. The exclusion of theft risk reduces the premium substantially. You can save on the premium by taking a substantial 'excess' (or 'deduction') in respect of any loss other than by fire. This means that if the 'excess' or 'deduction' were, say, $1,000 you would not receive the first $1,000 of any claim. This is another form of self-insurance, which should reduce the premium slightly.

Should you have to claim upon your insurers, in the event of a major claim they will probably appoint a loss adjuster. A loss adjuster is a professional evaluator, expected to give a fair, independent verdict on any claim though his fees are ultimately paid by the insurers. A mutually acceptable valuation made on a properly understood and agreed basis minimises the potential for disagreement. Should differences arise, report the difference in opinion to your insurance broker, or to the insurance company if you normally deal with them direct. Differences can sometimes arise over depreciation in value following damage which particularly applies to objects which by their very nature are unique and irreplaceable. For example, a damaged picture can be restored in most cases, but if this is the first damage that the painting has ever received there will undoubtedly be the basis for a claim for depreciation in value. If, on the other hand, the picture has been restored extensively in the past, a first-class restoration at the time of the recent damage may not reduce its value. If you request, when you first take out your policy, that a particular restorer should handle your item in the event of damage, you will be assured that the damage will be properly repaired and the loss minimised. Do not undertake restoration work before obtaining your insurer's written approval as to whether damage and restoration affects the ultimate sale value. Firm rules on this cannot be laid down and will always be a matter of opinion. There is no doubt that if the loss in value is substantial, and the article treated as a 'constructive total loss' the insurers take over the salvage. This means that the insurers pay the claim in full, as though the object had been wholly destroyed. They take the damaged article, dispose of it for what it will fetch, and keep the proceeds.

What happens in the case of property which was lost or stolen, and which is subsequently traced? Normally when an insurance company has paid for a loss, ownership is transferred automatically to the insurer, and if the article is recovered the insurer is entitled to sell it for his own account. If you wish to have the stolen property back, you can probably come to an arrangement with the insurance company at the time of settlement that if an article is recovered within a reasonable period of time, say one year, they will give you the opportunity of buying it back for the amount paid on the claim. However, you cannot expect them to extend this time limit indefinitely. If a valuable painting is recovered some five years later the insurers may not be willing to let you have it back for the price they paid for it originally, especially if there has been a substantial rise in the market value in the interim period. It is worthwhile to try to negotiate a clause that allows you to buy back the painting if it is recovered for the amount you received for it, plus interest.

## Valuations

The basis of valuation is one of the most difficult areas of insuring art. 'How do you tell how much it is worth?' is a question frequently asked. Valuations are necessary for insurance companies to substantiate the loss in the event of a claim.

To avoid possible disputes, you should clarify with your insurance company as to how valuations are based. Best cover is a 'valued at' policy, by which the insurance company agrees to accept the appraisals you have given them in advance and to pay you the full amount of those appraisals in the event of a total loss. Obviously appraisals need to be regularly updated. Otherwise, you may find compensation based on an outdated appraisal is in fact less than the full market value at the time of the loss. The difference between the two amounts may be recoverable if the insurance company agrees to pay. Disputes may also arise over payment in the event of a partial loss, where the work is partially damaged but not destroyed.

It is wise to revise your valuations every three years. Valuations are provided and recognised by insurance companies from specialised valuers from auction houses or galleries. In Australia valuers listed by the Department of Home Affairs under the Taxation Incentive Scheme for the Arts are generally recognised by insurance companies.[7] You should receive from valuers a detailed schedule of work, listing identifying characteristics of each work (like size, medium, where signed, date of work). Collections should be photographed, so that work can be readily identified in the event of loss or damage. Such identification can assist recovery in the event of a theft and is also valuable to support your claim in the event of damage. Many collectors report stolen works to police without knowing the exact details of the works concerned — like dimensions — and with no photographs of the work, just a description like 'landscape, you know, trees'. Art-related cases are usually assigned to burglary detectives, most of whom handle residential burglaries, and they could not be expected to recognise or be familiar with the subtle differences between paintings. Your records should be kept off-premises or in a safe deposit box so, in the case of fire, they remain intact. Some valuers will retain copies of their valuations in security files which can be invaluable future reference should your copy be lost. In any insurance claim, the most important document is a detailed, itemised inventory of your possessions and their value. If regularly updated, this record will protect you from serious financial loss in the event of an insurance claim.

Valuations are given for insurance, probate, capital gains, family division for sale of works, or for tax incentive purposes. Valuations are an approximate judgment as to financial worth under normal circumstances. The cornerstone of the valuer's pricing scale is 'current market value'. One statutory definition of this is 'the price which it (the object) might reasonably be expected to fetch if sold on the open market' in normal circumstances. The grey area in this legal definition is to know what 'reasonably' means in the context of markets which are so often volatile, subjective and difficult to predict.

Informal valuations are usually given freely, in anticipation of sale, or as an encouragement for the owner to sell. A wise owner should be level-headed about such a valuation, especially if it is accompanied by any sort of pressure to sell. Avoid this situation by seeking valuations from dealers and auction houses with reliable reputations. Do not be seduced by over-optimistic talk, and finally if you consider the suggested value seems surprisingly high then ask for it to be supported by a cheque or by a firm, written commitment to undertake the sale for not less than a certain price within a certain time limit.

Formal valuations are produced in written form and contain a carefully worded certificate stating the purpose for which they are executed, whether for taxation, legal or insurance purposes. Formal valuations usually carry fees paid on a percentage basis, often on a sliding scale if not on a fixed percentage basis with minimum inclusive charges, plus out-of-pocket charges such as travel expenses. Valuation fees vary and are negotiable. Updated valuations are sometimes provided freely or with a minimal charge to regular clients. As ultimately, insurance is a matter of personal choice. Some collectors decide against insuring their collections, preferring to spend their money on conservation, and security precautions, or even additional acquisitions, than on costly insurance premiums.

# 7

# FAKES, FORGERIES, FRAUD, REPLICAS

*If I like it I say it's mine. If I don't, I say it's a fake.*

Pablo Picasso, *The Sunday Times*, 1965, (When asked how he remembered which paintings were his)

*Only a forger could, in our day, paint in the style of Vermeer (however perfect his technique) because, to paint like Vermeer, the artist would have to forget that he had ever seen a Manet or a Cézanne.*

Arthur Koestler, *The Heel of Achilles*, 1984

Forgeries and fakes have been passed on to unsuspecting buyers since the appreciation of art began. There is nothing new in daily reports which scandalise the art world of buyers having been conned into buying an 'original', for example, by Miro, Picasso or Chagall, at a fly-by-night gallery which is no longer in business the next day. When super-prices prevail widely, the art market has always seen a distasteful trade of seamy opportunism preying on the ignorant, unsuspecting, and the greedy.

An early recorded major fake of western art was made by Andrea del Sarto (1480–1531), who painted an exact copy of Raphael's rendition of the first Medici Pope and his two nephews, owned by Don Ottaviano de Medici and now in the Uffizi. Frederigo of Mantua, one of the earliest true collectors of Renaissance art, who was also Captain General of the Holy See, wanted a Raphael for his collection and applied political pressure on Pope Clement VII in 1524 to give him the painting. A painting by Raphael has always, even then, been considered a prime capital investment. Don Ottaviano de Medici refused to give up the original and instead sent to Mantua the copy he commissioned Andrea del Sarto to paint, which is now in Naples. The copy fooled everyone, even Frederigo's court painter Giulio Romano (1499–1546), fresh from being Raphael's chief pupil and studio assistant and who claimed to have worked on the original in Raphael's studio. Debate raged into the 19th century between art historians over which of the two paintings was the 'real' Raphael.

Towards the close of the 16th century faked paintings by the great masters of the High Renaissance were very common in Rome. Besides 'antiquing' their fakes with smoke, the fakers in Rome regularly secured 'old panels' on which to work, so that the reverse sides of their fakes would look convincing. Before art history became a quasi-scientific discipline, fakers were so numerous, and false attributions were such a routine art-dealer's trick, that successful deceptions were really beyond counting.

Major art forgers are rarely caught, but when nabbed and their talents revealed, they illustrate an extraordinary perversion of talent. Artistic competence and technical proficiency are necessities in the forgery of works of art. Basic methods of art forgery include forging signatures and supporting documentation forging specific original works; utilising the style of a known artist without copying an existing work; completing unfinished works, and pastiche — combining diverse compositional elements from original paintings to produce 'new' compositions which are attributed to the artist.

The first world-wide sensation in the domain of art forgery was caused by the life-sized naturalist terracotta *Benivieni Bust* acquired by the Louvre in 1866 for about 14,000 francs. Given that at the time it was not known *who* had made the Bust, this was a high value compared to about 6,000 francs paid for *The Venus de Milo*, discovered in 1820.

For a while the Bust was regarded as one of the masterpieces of the Florentine Renaissance in the Louvre. A year later it was discovered to be only three years old. It had been made in 1864 by Fiesole sculptor Giovanni Bastianni. He produced imitations of Quattrocento portrait sculpture but did not intend to defraud, and his imitation sculptures were not sold as 'antique originals'. In the case of the Benivieni Bust, Bastianni's work was considered so good, that experts had mistakenly judged his contemporary copy.

Scarcely any forger achieved such fame as an artist in his own right as Alceo Dossena. Known as the 'King of Cremona', mason forger Dossena was a remarkable craftsman and stylist. He made counterfeits acquired by numerous museums, which took Dossena's work to be by Donatello, Simone Martini, Mino da Fiesole, and Giovanni Pisano. Dossena was exploited by Alfredo Fasoli, a Roman goldsmith, and Romano Palesi, an art dealer and well-known dealer in ancient art. They recognised the opportunity to distribute false 'antiques' through Dossena's ability. They employed him in 1916 to execute carvings in the manner of this or that 'Master' for an average monthly income of £80. For many years they sold Dossena's work unchallenged as genuine works of the Antique Medieval and Renaissance periods. Their fraud came to light in 1921 when they offered a 'Sarelli tomb' ascribed to Mino da Fiesole (1430–1484) for six million lira to Henry Clay Frick's daughter, Ellen Frick. Her own investigations revealed Alceo Dossena, who immediately acknowledged he had made the piece for which he had been paid 25,000 lira.

The Dutch painter, Hans Van Meegeren, caused one of the greatest sensations ever made by a forger of works of art. Between 1937 and 1943 he deliberately defrauded the art world with his expert forgeries of paintings by Pieter de Hooch (1629–1684) and Jan Vermeer of Delft (1632–1675). Like Dossena, Van Meegeren was not a copyist but a stylist. He took extracts and details from a number of different originals and combined them in a single work, borrowing a gesture here, a pose there, a colour harmony elsewhere — all from genuine paintings by Vermeer, whose work he studied closely. Van Meegeren developed a process to harden the pigments to a degree consistent with the painting's purported age. He produced the requisite cracks in the painted surface by rolling and baking the finished canvas. His swindles amounted to some £800,000 and convinced notable Dutch painting authority Abraham Bredius, the Dutch Government, and Hermann Goring, who in 1942 bought Van Meegeren's *Christ and the Adulteress* painted in Vermeer's style and bearing his signature. Van Meegeren passed off his handiwork during the War, when it was difficult for art experts to cross national borders to study authenticated Vermeers, many of which were hidden away for safekeeping. His forgeries were so convincing that his confession to painting 'Old Masters' was disbelieved. He painted a 'Vermeer' *Christ Among the Scribes* under observation in prison, to convince his doubters.

Legal fakes (called an 'imagine-art' work) are sold from Zurich by an enterprising Swiss businessman Bruno Schmed. He began 'The International Imaginary Museum' after a friend bought a supposedly authentic Miro painting for 80,000 Swiss francs, which turned out to be worthless. 'Because so many people are cheated like this,' Schmed says, 'I asked myself, why not legalise such fakes?' He sells 'original copies' of great paintings for between 3,000 to 12,000 Swiss francs. Only 10 'copies' are made of any one painting. Each copy is signed in the name of the original artist but their sizes differ from the originals. Bach work is accompanied by an original certificate attesting that it is indeed a 'genuine fake', and each artwork carries a stamp on the back declaring it to be a forgery. Available stock includes about 250 paintings to choose from with Impressionists most in demand. If there is a special request, Schmed will find an artist to create the copy. Schmed contends that his 'interpretations' may actually help to dampen the criminal forgery business. However, many gallerists are wary of such legitimate fakers. With similar and unrelated companies existing elsewhere, gallerists fear this art fakery practice will encourage others to sell forgeries and add to the general art-buying public's confusion — degrading the real artist's work, as well as the public's appreciation of real masterpieces.

Mark Twain observed that modern copies were easier to look at than originals by Old Masters, because copies often substitute a pleasing treatment concentrated on external effects for the uncompromising devotion to inner truth expressed by their models. Missing from forgeries, this strength of integrity is clearly detectable when comparing the forgery to the original. No forger can create a style, but can only imitate it like a mimic. Most fakes hold up for at most a generation because they embody the tastes and prejudices of the times in which they were made. Van Meegeren's forgeries, in hindsight, reveal his own 20th century origins. His subjects have faces and expressions that are curiously modern, sentimental and wooden. They have a dated 1930s look that appealed to viewers at the time but which to modern eyes are obviously wrong. Current forgeries are masked by contemporary prejudices and preconceptions. Looking beyond these helps to unmask forgeries, which look and feel wrong in ways that may not be immediately easily definable.

Forgeries and swindles are perpetrated by the unscrupulous, lured by profit, often encouraged by the gullibility of many buyers and collectors. Every collector who is cheated has only himself to blame. As opportunity makes a thief, lack of knowledge in the potential purchaser attracts the forger and the dishonest dealer.

The scale of the 'Dali scandal' illustrates the ease with which art swindles can be pulled off. There is no knowing how many Dali counterfeits were circulated, so the sums involved can only be guessed at. Prosecutions have only just begun. Countless, worthless, photomechanical reproductions of 'calendar quality' and of little value were passed off to unsuspecting buyers who paid prices ranging from US$1,000 to as much as US$6,500 each for these so-called, but worthless, Dali lithographs. Their 'investment potential' and Dali's personal participation in the creation of the lithographs were part of the sales pitch. Yet these prints were worthless because Dali had no involvement with them, beyond pre-signing unknown quantities of batches of blank paper sheets — each batch containing 175,000 sheets. In some cases even the original, from which the photomechanical reproduction had been taken, had not been done by Dali. Many Australians unfortunately fell victim to this swindle. Though practised world-wide, many of these 'Dali prints' were sold from galleries located in Hawaii's tourist centres of Honolulu, Maui and Oahu, a stopping ground for many Australians en-route home or on vacation. The United States Federal Trade Commission in 1989 charged an art publisher with supplying forged prints mainly to Hawaii for a return vaguely estimated between US$6 million and US$44 million.[1]

As Dossena and the *Benivieni* bust proved, there are many different kinds of bogus works of art. Many 'forgeries' without a forger exist. They are not deliberate swindles. They include copies, extracts, restorations, overpaintings, and free versions, executed without intention to deceive but which may later become forgeries owing to false ascriptions. Artists and students have often 'copied' the Masters before them as exercises to a better understanding of the Masters and knowledge of their painting technique. These are not deliberate forgeries but exercises in learning, though in the wrong hands they can be misread and misrepresented. It may be useful to clarify what the differences are between fakes, forgeries, copies, reproductions, replicas and other terms.

A **fake** is any work deliberately made or altered to pretend to be something older or better than it is. A **forgery** is any work made in fraudulent imitation of something else, created and sold with the intent to deceive. A **copy** is an imitation of the original, which, so long as it does not pretend to be the original, is not a forgery. A **reproduction** is either a copy of a painting or print made by photographic or mechanical means, or an object made in imitation of earlier styles. A **replica** denotes a copy of a work made by the artist himself, and can also mean a facsimile or copy or reproduction. A **facsimile** is an exact copy. A **pastiche** is a work made in the manner of an artist. Art is not a forgery if it doesn't directly copy an existing work, and is not a fake if it doesn't pretend to be anything else.

**Surmoulages** are casts made from moulds taken from an original cast. They are normally reproductions that are slightly smaller and more generalised, lacking the fine lines and crisp details of the original, being usually softer in appearance and less distinct in surface detail. There are legitimate foundries that manufacture reproductions for sale which they stamp and identify as surmoulages. They are often called 'recast' or 'aftercast'. Posthumous casts — bronzes produced after the artist's death — are 'unauthorised' when the artist's heirs or executors have not approved them. Posthumous casts are not generally worth as much as lifetime casts, and unauthorised posthumous casts are considered by many scholars of sculpture to be neither valuable nor ethical. They are really 'commercial souvenirs', which may be difficult to resell. Neither Sotheby's nor Christie's will deal in surmoulages.[2]

This not to say that all works produced with limited artist involvement or even posthumously should be scorned. The final test is the quality of the piece and how it ranks in relation to other works by the artist and his contemporaries. Degas modelled in clay and wax for 40 years yet he had only three of his models cast in plaster and none cast in bronze. He allowed only one of his sculptures, the wax *Little Dancer, 14 Years Old* to be shown in public. All Degas bronzes are posthumous works. A cast of *Little Dancer, 14 Years Old* sold at Christie's, New York, in May 1988 for US$10.175 million — a world record for sculpture of any period.[3]

## Provenance and Attributions

Every work of art has a history. Examination of this history — the provenance of the work — ideally lists all the owners of the work in a continuous chain from the moment the work was created to the present owner. Unfortunately most, especially minor, items are bought, sold, bequested and exchanged without anyone recording the fact, so therefore have no provenance.

Raising provenance is less difficult with contemporary work. Artists are always eager to know who their works have sold to and will willingly authenticate their work in addition to that given to the purchaser by the art dealer who transacted the sale. Catalogues document the exhibition history of the work. Labels on the back of the work indicate which dealers previously had the work, which auction house sold it, which museums exhibited it. Further details can be gained by contacting these dealers, auction houses and museums, and examining their catalogues. Auction houses rarely identify consignors, many of whom wish to remain anonymous. After you buy the work you can ask the auction house for details of the work's previous owner. Sometimes the consignor may be attending the sale and will identify himself to the new buyer.

Fraudulent documents can be manufactured to create convincing but spurious provenance for sham works, hence the importance of attributions. These are expert opinions ascribing an unidentified work to a particular artist or craftsman. There may be no indisputable evidence that a particular artist executed a work but circumstantial and stylistic evidence will render it probable in expert opinion. Of course, opinions change and experts disagree. Misattributions occur when an opinion is proved to be incorrect by the production of factual evidence.

Misattributions can occur in many different ways. A work from an artist's studio, sometimes an exact copy of a work by the artist, can be wrongly attributed to the artist himself. Misattributions may be due to innocent errors in the case of the work being made with no intention to deceive but then finding its way onto the market as an original, such as those done by students trying to learn by copying from the Masters. Or a work by a minor artist may be wrongly attributed to an artist of greater repute. Artists themselves can contribute to the confusion. Certain artists, including the Greek painter Apelles and sculptor Phidias, and french painters Boucher and Corot, signed works executed by their most talented students.[4] Fragonard copied Rembrandt, and Rubens signed many duplicate paintings produced in his workshop.

## Limited Editions

The term 'limited edition' causes further confusion. Strictly speaking, the rarity of a limited edition is imposed by the nature or the process or by the artist, and determined by artistic reasons. The term 'limited edition' is much abused to convey an unjustified value or sense of value on a really worthless object in the case of 'limited edition' reproductions or replicas. To avoid misrepresentation, museums which sell reproductions do not make their replicas to scale even though this is not expressly forbidden in the code of ethics of the International Council of Museums (ICOM). Though not yet adopted, this code endorses high quality reproductions *with* marks permanently identifying them as such. Marks identifying replicas as copies could be eradicated by an unscrupulous person to mislead a potential buyer who fails to detect that the object is a copy, or who neglects to have the object scientifically checked before buying it. Many museums produce high quality museum reproductions and insist on differences to the original in technique, materials and scale, to avoid confusion.

The print market has unfortunately experienced more than its share of misrepresentations, fraudulent practices and swindles in recent years. Reproductions are misrepresented as originals. Manually drawn 'afters' — the work of copyists — are misrepresented as originals. Edition sizes are misrepresented. Signatures are forged and facsimile signatures and unauthorised restrikes exist. The print collector will need to learn about prints in order to distinguish original prints from these reproductions, as well as which prints to collect. When buying prints the same rules apply: buy from the most reputable sources, seek the advice of respected specialised print dealers, and develop your eye.[5]

You must know the difference between original prints and reproductions. It is common practice, unfortunately, for prints which are really worthless reproductions to be presented as 'limited' so-called 'artist signed' and 'numbered' prints to unsuspecting buyers. Understanding the exact terminology used in the field of prints is crucial or misrepresentation can easily occur.

Reproductions are printed by commercial printers, using commercial printing technology. Like reproductions in books and magazines, an artist's painting or drawing would have been photographed and then reproduced in thousands of copies on the printing press. The printed images are certainly prints. However, they are printed reproductions and not original prints. Because the work which was photographed was signed, the artist's signature may read clearly on the reproduction — hence the claim that the 'print' is 'artist signed'. And the 'print' may well be numbered by the printer who runs off consecutive numbers on each print up to a certain number to support the claim for the prints to be 'limited', though they may be 'limited' to thousands of identical reproductions!

Original prints are made from images the artist has created directly and originally on a printing plate which are then printed by hand to the artist's instructions, proofed by the artist, and usually limited to a relatively small number being hand-printed. Therefore, the edition or total number of the same prints is indeed limited, but also, after the edition is printed, the image on the plate is defaced to prevent more prints being made. In other words, whereas a reproduction is a copy made by a printer from a pre-existing work, an original print is a multiply-produced work made by the artist in limited number from a unique image that the artist created expressly as a print. The prints themselves are the originals. Original prints are made by artists who consider printmaking a serious art form capable of producing unique effects and imagery, and not simply a means to reproduce images.

Artists engage a variety of printmaking techniques to make their prints. Each technique features particular visual properties, familiarity with which will help the buyer when judging the quality of an impression you are thinking of buying.

All prints are made by pressing an inked matrix — a printing surface of metal, wood, stone or other material — against sheets of paper. The four basic printmaking techniques which each requires a different matrix are: lithography, silkscreen (also called serigraphy), intaglio and relief printing. Several variations of the basic techniques of intaglio (including etching, soft ground, drypoint, aquatint, engraving and mezzotint) and relief printing (like woodcutting and linocut) exist, and artists combine processes as well to produce 'mixed media' prints which can even combine photographic and commercial printing processes.

Because prints within each edition must be similar, without too much variation, the number of impressions made of a print is determined by the number which can be pulled before the matrix shows signs of wear. The size of the edition will also be influenced by the demand for the artist's work and the amount of time and money the artist or his printer can spend printing the same image over and over.

Though technological developments like steel facing allow artists to produce virtually unlimited numbers of impressions of identical quality, most original prints are produced in small limited editions ranging from as low as one to twenty impressions, though there can also be large editions of from 150 or more impressions.

From the end of the 19th century, when the practice of issuing original prints in small editions became customary, artists usually signed and numbered their prints indicating the size of the edition below the image area in the lower margin. The number reveals the size of the total edition and the individual number of each print. So '15/25' or 'XV/XXV' specifies this particular impression is number fifteen in a total edition of twenty five impressions.

Other notations on prints include 'artist's proofs' (*epreuves d'artiste*) of which there are usually about 10 per cent of the prints in an edition, usually for the artist's own use; trial or state proofs which are unique impressions revealing the stages through which the artist developed the ultimate printed image; and *'bon a tirer'* (B.A.T.) which are the trial proofs or impression the artist instructs the printer to follow as a guide for printing the entire edition.

Since the 1880s when Seymour Haden (1818–1910) and James McNeil Whistler (1834–1903) began hand-signing their prints, artists have individually hand-signed usually in pencil each impression of their printed editions. The artist's pencilled autograph is usually featured outside the image area in the lower margin. Hand-signed prints differ to those 'signed in the plate' or with signatures in the plate or stone as part of the image. To avoid confusion that can easily occur, legislation in 1975 in New York State made it an offence to describe a print as being 'signed' unless it was 'hand-signed' by the artist.

Unfortunately some artists sign posters and reproductions of their work intended to be either sold or offered at the 'affordable price' reproduction prints are only worth. These signed reproduction prints can end up selling for prices paid for signed original prints by the artist when, in fact, such signed reproductions are really worthless.

Restrikes or late impressions are additional later impressions made with or

### Fakes, Forgeries, Fraud, Replicas

without the artist's impression from the original matrix (if this has not been destroyed). Clearly not reproductions, because made directly off the surface of the artist's matrix, restrikes are usually of inferior quality to the artist's original edition. They are often unauthorised, unapproved and consequently unsigned by the artist. So long as this is reflected in the price asked when offered for sale, the sale of these restrikes is legitimate, and the price asked should also reflect the quality of each impression and the number in circulation.

Fortunately for the collector, most editions are documented. In the case of most important artists' *catalogues raisonné* document and catalogue chronologically the complete *oeuvre* (works) of an artist listing all available information on each print so thoroughly that prints can be identified by the numbers assigned to them in the *catalogue raisonné*. In the case of more contemporary, hence uncatalogued, editions all the details on each edition should be provided by the dealer selling the print, by the publisher and printer, and ultimately by the artist. Many dealers and publishers issue certificates giving full details about the edition. In the United States, Print Disclosure Statutes have been legislated in several States which require full details about the edition be given to the buyer.[6]

In the print market you seldom get more than what you pay for. Beware of bargain-priced prints which often turn out to be photo-reproductions or hand-copied translations of the artist's work in another medium, and cheap 'original' prints which are mass-manufactured in commercial factories. Avoid buying photographically made reproductions which are easy to identify by their dull flat appearance and halftone screen dot pattern resulting from photo-offset printing.

## Export Controls

There is an increasingly active international trade in illicit trafficking of artworks. Systematic looting of cultural treasures is organised by black market operators in big buying centres.

The loss of material has reached crisis level in some countries. In 1970 UNESCO drew up a convention to deal with the question of illicit international trafficking in cultural treasures.[7] Some fifty-three nations are party to the international agreement to return illegally removed important cultural objects to their countries. The Convention broadly defines cultural material to include (beyond illegal exports) archaeology, pre-history, history, literature, art and science. The Convention also proposes forms of protection beyond those concerning illegal international traffic. These include national inventories of protected cultural property, support for collecting institutions, rules for curatorial conduct, educational measures, controls on antique dealers and supervision of archeological sites, as well as conservation, security, presentation and public education. Britain, France, Switzerland and Japan have, to date, refused to sign the Convention.

## Collecting Art

From August 1988 in Australia, regulations for the protection of moveable cultural heritage came into effect to ensure that the rarest and most significant objects of Australia's movable cultural heritage are protected. The Protection of Movable Cultural Heritage Act 1986 was established to protect Australian national cultural heritage from the permanent export of irreplaceable material. Export and import controls regulate the movement of important cultural objects, and reciprocal arrangements with other countries for the return of illegally exported material are provided.

There are two classes of heritage material. Class A objects are those objects so rare and important as to be considered inalienable (such as Aboriginal objects) and these cannot be removed except with a certificate of exemption for temporary import and re-export. Class B objects are rare and irreplaceable objects which require export permits and these include Aboriginal heritage, fine art, decorative arts and graphic material. A national cultural heritage control list details these categories with the criteria by which export controls are exercised. The only objects so far restricted from export are objects of Australian Aboriginal heritage classified as Class A objects, and these include bark and log coffins, human remains, rock art and dendroglyphs. There are no fine art objects defined as Class A objects that are not to be exported. All other objects can be freely exported. However, items with current market values beyond specified amounts are listed as Class B objects and may not be exported without an export permit or certificate. Class B objects include Australian and Australian-related objects, and foreign objects of fine art which are generally not Australia-related, are made by a foreign artist, and have been in Australia for not less than 35 years.

There is no restriction on any object made by a living artist or on object less than 30 years old. The following Aboriginal and other Australian or Australia-related objects require export permits if their current Australian market values exceed the amounts given below:

| Item | Current Australian Market Value Not Less Than$ |
|---|---|

**Division A — Aboriginal & Other Australian or Australia-related objects**

| | | |
|---|---|---|
| 1 | Objects of Aboriginal fine art | 5,000 |
| 2 | Paintings | 150,000 |
| 3 | Watercolours, pastels, drawings, sketches and similar works | 30,000 |
| 4 | Prints, posters, illustrated books, photographs and other works of art with potential for multiple production (including cast metal or moulded ceramic sculptures) | 7,000 |
| 5 | Sculptures other than sculptures referred to in Item 4 | 30,000 |
| 6 | Stained glass objects | 10,000 |

| | | |
|---|---|---:|
| 7 | Tapestries | 20,000 |
| 8 | Objects of Fine Art not otherwise referred to in this Division, being objects (such as objects of folk art) made outside formal European traditions of fine art | 10,000 |

**Division B — Foreign Objects**

| | | |
|---|---|---:|
| 9 | Any painting held in Australia for not less than 35 years and still held in Australia | 500,000 |
| 10 | Watercolours, pastels, drawings and similar non-multiple works of art held in Australia for not less than 35 years and still held in Australia | 100,000 |
| 11 | Prints, posters, illustrated books, photographs and similar works of art with potential for multiple production (including cast metal or moulded ceramic sculptures) held in Australia for not less than 35 years and still held in Australia | 40,000 |
| 12 | Sculptures held in Australia for not less than 35 years and still held in Australia | 40,000 |
| 13 | Tapestries and stained glass objects held in Australia for not less than 35 years and still held in Australia | 20,000 |

To date, only one item has been refused export. This is *The Bath of Diana*, an 1837 oil painting by John Glover (1767–1849), bought in good faith at auction by an American buyer for A$1.76 million — a record for an Australian painting. The painting was barred from export in 1989 because it was considered by a panel of experts appointed to advise The National Cultural Heritage Committee to be the only painting by Glover in Australia depicting Aboriginal landscape. This is the first time that the export of a painting has been forbidden under the Movable Cultural Heritage Act of 1986.

A number of countries have laws restricting exports of cultural property regarded to be of national importance. Early attempts to protect a 'national heritage' of Western Art include Grand Duke Ferdinando de Medici's edict of 1601 forbidding export from Florence of the works of 18 listed Masters which included the High Renaissance giants whose works were regarded as a significant 'ornament' which the State should not dispense with, including among them Michelangelo, Raphael, and Correggio. Interestingly the edict blithely passed over all the names that made the glory of Florentine art, from Cimabue and Giotto to Ghirlandaio and Botticelli.[8]

Pope Sixtus IV had forbidden export from Rome of any classical work of art before this. Peter the Great forbade export from Russia of Scythian antiquities. As is to be expected, these edicts were circumvented by many clever devices. There is the legendary story of Philadelphian millionaire P.A.B. Widener who smuggled the magnificent Van Dyke portraits of the Cattaneo family, now in Washington's

National Gallery, by rolling the canvases into a cylinder attached to the chassis of his car alongside the car's long, wide exhaust pipe. Even today valuable paintings are often taken out of their frames and hidden under worthless ones. Signatures are painted over so the work will appear to be done by a lesser artist. The fact that the art world has always been shrouded in secrecy helps thefts. Dealers almost never reveal the names of their clients, their suppliers or the price paid. No systematic procedure exists for determining whether an art work has been exported illegally. The Italian government maintains a National Catalogue of Artistic and Cultural Goods which identifies objects subject to export regulations. The Metropolitan Museum of Art, in New York, sends a letter to the appropriate ministry of culture requesting any information that government has regarding the provenance of an art object. If a vendor objects to the museum sending such a letter and is himself unable to provide the necessary information, the museum will terminate negotiations over the questionable object. Sotheby Parke Bernet includes an express warranty in its consignment agreements specifying that the property is transferred free from the claims of any government.

Great Britain has seen a lengthy exodus of works of art. The British market in antiques and works of art turns over about £800–£900 million a year. Great Britain's enlightened art-export policy grants export licences to those objects more than a hundred years old which, if considered of national importance by a special reviewing committee, are temporarily embargoed from export to give a British institution the chance to raise funds to match the export-price. If no such funds are raised, export licences are granted. A sale for export is merely delayed, generally for three to six months, while British galleries are given an opportunity to match the foreign offer. If no matching offer is forthcoming the original sale goes ahead. Each year there are over 5,000 applications for export licences, about 50 of which are valued highly enough to have their applications subjected to review. About two thirds of the objects reviewed are judged sufficiently important to have their export licences suspended to give heritage groups or museums a chance to buy them instead.

There exists in the United Kingdom several organisations which may be called upon to contribute the funds necessary to buy for the nation significant works which come onto the market. The National Art Collections Fund is an independent charity established since the beginning of the century, with 18,000 contributing members. The National Heritage Memorial Fund receives £3 million a year from the government. Others include the Pilgrim Fund, and a government fund administered by the Victoria and Albert Museum.

Australia's Protection of Movable Cultural Heritage Act established a national cultural heritage fund to facilitate the acquisition of Australian protected objects prohibited from export. Important objects of the national heritage refused export permits will be acquired, wherever possible, for display in a public collection.

Inherent here is recognition of an individual's right to enjoyment of property while establishing the nation's right to restrict the movement of that property where it represents an irreplaceable part of the cultural heritage. Arrangements are administered by the National Cultural Heritage Committee appointed by the Minister of the Department of the Arts, Sport, The Environment, Tourism and Territories. The committee advises on the national cultural heritage control list, on maintaining a register of expert examiners, on the operation of the export and import controls, and on allocations from the fund. Under these arrangements it remains to be seen what becomes of Glover's *The Bath of Diana*.

With the event of a borderless European Community in 1992, there is grave concern that the removal of customs controls between the 12 Economic Community nations could lead to wholesale plundering of European storehouses of art treasures, most especially from Italy where art theft is big business. Experts fear with the free movement of goods within the European Community and no customs checks, there will be nothing to stop truck-loads of art passing out of Italy, despite Italy's tough laws on the exporting and importing of works of art. Italian government officials have begun talks with their European counterparts in a bid to get important works of art exempted from the new rules, which stipulate the free movement of goods within the EEC. The EEC Executive Commission is currently working on guidelines for the protection of national treasures when customs between the twelve member countries are abolished in 1992. The difficulty is in getting international agreement on the definition of what constitutes a national art treasure and what should therefore be protected from being sold.

# FOOTNOTES

## Chapter 1. Collecting

1. The word museum comes from the *Mouseion*, the superb library the first Ptolemy built in Alexandria and dedicated to the Muses. Ever since the word came into use in Western Europe, all sorts of private collections, from the most artless Wunderkammern to the greatest princely art collections, have been called 'museums'. The modern 'Museum Age' as we know it began following three events: the conversion of the Uffizi into a true public art museum by the will of the Medici in 1743; the further organisation of the Uffizi as a true art museum by the Grand Duke Pietro Leopoldo; and the establishment of the forerunner of Vienna's Kunsthistorisches Museum in the Belvedere Palace by the Emperor Josef II.

2. Just about every great public art museum in Europe today is basically a converted princely art collection. The last major conversion occurred in Russia in 1852, when Tsar Nicholas I opened the Hermitage. The royal collection in England and the Liechtenstein collection in the vaults of Vaduz Castle are now the last princely collections of the old type. The British Museum was established by an act of Parliament in 1753, and is the earliest Western art museum ever founded *de novo* with public revenues. Another Act of Parliament set up London's National Gallery and provided funds to buy the foundation collection made by the founder of Lloyds, Sir John Julius Angerstein.

   The many art museums of the modern Western World may be broadly divided into those founded to keep private art collections permanently intact; plus princely art collections converted into national or municipal collections, like the Uffizi, the Prado, the Hermitage, and many more in Europe; plus museums publicly founded at public expense, like the British Museum; and museums founded by private enterprise, directed by a board of rich private supporters, and municipally and state-aided, like the Metropolitan in New York, founded in 1870. Examples of public collections created by private collectors include The Netherlands Kroller-Muller Museum and Sculpture Park, Europe's largest, which attracts 450,000 visitors each year, at the Hogeveluwe National Park in Otterloo. There is also West Germany's newest and most unusual art museum, Hombroich, of 39 acres on an island in the Erft River just east of Dusseldorf, housing through six pavilions the decade old collection of German real-estate developer Karl-Heinz Muller.

3. The Mellons provide a good example of private benefaction. Andrew W. Mellon, the steel magnate, was founding benefactor of the National Gallery of Art in Washington. His son Paul Mellon served as the National Gallery's first president then chairman of the Board of Trustees, a position he held until 1985, when he was elected an Honorary Trustee for life. Over the years he has donated more than 700 important works to the National Gallery, including 17 wax figures by Degas, and made possible the construction of the East Building. He

also actively supports the Virginia Museum of Fine Arts in Richmond and has contributed substantially to the expansion projects of that museum, as well as donating to it approximately 1,500 works of art. Additionally since 1977 he has given to the Yale Center for British Art more than 1,200 paintings, 20,000 prints and drawings and a rare book library in excess of 20,000 volumes. A keen Anglophile, Mellon's 18th and early 19th century paintings by Hogarth, Stubbs, Gainsborough, Constable, Turner *et al.* come close to matching in quality, if not in quantity, the British collection at the Tate.

4.     Charles Blackman, *For a Child*, oil on canvas 127 x 102 cm, signed lower right. Alan McCulloch, *Encyclopedia of Australian Art*, Edition 1 and 2, Hutchinsons, Melbourne.

5.     Edgar Degas, 'Shop Talk', *A Documentary History of Art* Vol.III *From The Classicists to the Impressionists: Art & Architecture in the Nineteenth Century*, Elizabeth Gilmore Holt, Editor, Anchor Books, 1966.

6.     An example of how contemporary American Masters dominate the prints market is illustrated by the recent progress of Jasper John's *Flags 1* in salerooms. For example, Jasper John's *Flags 1* sold at Christie's in May 1987 for US$71,500 (est. US$35–45,000); in November 1988 it fetched US$242,000 (est. US$60–70,000) at Christie's and then US$275,000 (est. US$75–95,000) at Sotheby's, a record for the artist and for a contemporary print. In May 1989 *Flags 1* reached US$308,000 (est. US$200–250,000) at both auction houses. With great modern prints becoming scarce, new highs are easily reached for the most popular images by the most popular artists. The print market is no longer the Cinderella of the art market. Today there is a growing demand for 'a terrific image', whether in a print or a sculpture or a drawing or painting. If the work is very good, it does not matter what medium it is in.

7.     Kate Halley, *Bob Sredersas*, Wollongong City Gallery, 1989.

8.     Sotheby Parke Bernet & Co., *Mentmore*, 5 vols. (London, 1977), vol.I, Catalogue of French and Continental Furniture, Tapestries and Clocks; vol.II, Catalogue of Works of Art and Silver, vol.III, Catalogue of Vincennes and Sevres and Other Continental Porcelain and Italian Maiolica; vol.IV, Catalogue of Paintings, Prints and Drawings; vol.V, Catalogue of General Contents of the House.

9.     In 1958, Cézanne's *Boy in a Red Vest*, sold for US$616,000, the highest price then ever bid on any single painting at an auction. More or less academic and anecdotal paintings brought extremely high prices until World War I, but their vogue distinctly passed.

10.    For courses available, and a suggested reading list to begin with, see Appendix. Also check with your local museum what courses and lectures they offer.

## Chapter 2. The Art Market: Auctions

1.  Collecting art became popular with the bourgeoisie in the 17th century. Sales increased everywhere. Italy and Holland produced the most paintings and had the largest sales and lowest prices. Much higher figures were reached in London and Paris where entire Italian collections were sold en bloc. Auctions were frequent, particularly in France and England. The first auction held by the famous James Christie the Elder (1730–1803) took place on 5 December 1766, in rooms in Pall Mall. Christie's catalogues and those of the equally famous Sotheby's are an index of English and international taste during two centuries.

2.  Richard Hislop, Annual *Art Sales Index*, through the 1987–88 auction season analysed 1,700 catalogues from 20 countries to conclude the biggest auction players were the USA (45%), UK (31%) and France (12%) followed by Sweden (only 2.8%), Italy (2.2%), Germany (1.7%), Switzerland (1.2%) and Australia (1%). Estimated turnover through 1988 in Australia of Christie's, Sotheby's and Leonard Joel of Melbourne is A\$55 million.

3.  *Andy Warhol sale*, Sotheby's, New York, 23 to 30 April 1988, (Art Nouveau and Art Deco, jewellery and watches, collectibles, jewellery, furniture, paintings, American Indian art, contemporary art, Americana, paintings, drawings and prints). Andy Warhol, *Collection of Jewellery and Watches*, Part 2, 4 December, 1988, New York. Andy Warhol Contemporary Art, *22 Lots from the Collection of Andy Warhol*, 2 May, 1988, New York. Two months after these auctions curators, while moving two file cabinets at Warhol's Manhattan townhouse, discovered hidden away in the false bottom of a drawer a secret stash of jewels which brought US\$1.64 million at auction, the proceeds of which went to the Andy Warhol Foundation for the Visual Arts.

4.  Elton John sale, Sotheby's, 6 through 9 September 1988. Elton John, Volume 1, *Stage, Costume and Memorabilia*, London 6 September 1988. Elton John, Volume 2, *Jewellery*, London 6 September 1988. Elton John, Volume 3, *Art Nouveau and Art Deco*, 7 September 1988. Elton John, Volume 4, *Diverse Collection*, 8–9 September 1988.

5.  Worldwide inflation and inadequate tax incentives make a mockery of a privatised arts industry. Without grants, increased to match inflation, museums and galleries face being unable to pay their staff or maintain their buildings. They have long lost purchasing power, their acquisition funds failing to keep abreast with the escalating values of the market. Fuelled by Bicentennial fever, Australian museums and galleries have enjoyed capital grants allowing them to develop badly needed extensions and facilities which now require maintaining on funds that are inadequate and, worse, are threatened to be with-

drawn by cost-conscious governments. In Britain public subsidy in the forms of Arts Council, city and County Council grants accounts for just under 50 per cent of income, while earned income supplies about 48 per cent, with sponsorship less than three per cent. Diminishing funds are not matched by incentive funding through private sponsorship from individuals and corporations encouraged by tax deductions for charitable gifts to nonprofit organisations. Britain's National Gallery in 1987–88 had a government grant for purchases of only £2.75 million (US$4.4 million) annually.

A recent survey of American museums (surely the world's most munificently endowed) revealed that few public institutions have enough funds to meet current high price levels of important works. Outclassed by big money competition, museums are increasingly regarding collecting as a spectator sport. They are finding themselves collecting institutions unable to collect. Cleveland tops the list with US$6.5 million in its acquisitions fund for 1988. The Kimbell (Fort Worth), New York's Metropolitan Museum, and the Boston Museum of Fine Arts follow, with only three others claiming over US$1 million to spend annually. The Getty is the one exception, with close to US$140 million available annually.

In the United States (in which between 85 and 90 per cent of museum holdings are the result of gifts of works of art), the 1986 Tax Reform Act has resulted in the dollar value of gifts to American Art Museums drop from US$143 million in 1986 to US$67.1 million in 1988. French wealth tax does not take works of art into account, so recently introduced legislation (whereby such works can be bequeathed to the State without incurring inheritance tax) suits not only the rich but museum curators finding it increasingly difficult to keep up with fast-escalating art prices.

6.    Sotheby's negotiated two historic private treaty sales (which were not included in their 1988–89 sales totals) with the Soviet Union during the 1988–89 season. An important collection of 13 letters by the Russian poet Alexander Pushkin was sold to the Ministry of Culture of the USSR, who purchased them with the proceeds from Sotheby's first auction in Moscow in July 1988. As well, Lord Gowrie, Sotheby's Chairman in London, presented to Raisa Gorbachov the manuscript of Ivan Turgenev's novel *Fathers and Sons*, which had been sold to the Soviet Cultural Foundation.

7.    Figures supplied by courtesy of Richard Hislop's *Art Sales Index* for the year ended 31 July 1989. 'Christie's runs the antique cliche, "are gentlemen trying to be businessmen: Sotheby's are businessmen trying to be gentlemen."' Godfrey Barker, 'Pillars of the Art World,' *Harpers & Queen*, October 1985, p.168.

8.    Interestingly when offered by Christie's in April 1990 the painting shrank in value to fetch a more realistic A$700,000. Peter Fish, 'Why the Tax Office Loses

on Art', *Australian Business,* 16 May, 1990, pp. 26–27.

9.  See Chapter 7, page 85 through 88 for details about Export Controls.

10. John Russell, 'Clapping for Money at Auctions', *The New York Times,* Sunday 21 May 1989.

## Chapter 3. The Artmarket: Dealers

1.  Paul Jeromack, 'Old Master Paintings', *Art & Auction* September 1989, p.171

2.  *Australian Commercial Galleries Association Handbook,* listing member galleries their locations, and what they specialise in. This handbook is available from member galleries, whose premises often feature the Association logo, or whose publications often declare their membership within the Association. Otherwise the Handbook is available from The Secretary, The Australian Commercial Galleries Association c/- Bloomfield Galleries, 118 Sutherland Street, Paddington, NSW 2021.

    *Guide to Taxation Incentives for the Arts and List of Approved Valuers,* Committee on Taxation Incentives for the arts, Department of the Arts, Heritage and Environment, Australian Government Publishing Service, Canberra.

3.  For an account of this scandal and its repercussions see Lee Seldes, *The Legacy of Mark Rothko,* New York, 1978. A year after Rothko's suicide in 1970, the executors of his estate were charged with conspiring with Marlborough Gallery director Frank Lloyd to defraud the multi-million dollar estate through self-dealing. Following six years of litigation, the executors and Lloyd were found guilty and ordered to pay US$9.2 million in fines and damages.

4.  Laura De Coppet & Alan Jones, *The Art Dealers,* Clarkson N. Potter, New York, 1984. p.58.

5.  For more on Durand-Ruel, see Footnote 4 to Chapter 4.

6.  Robert Wraight, *The Art Game,* London 1965.

7.  The Kahnweiler Gallery had by 1914 amassed an incomparable stock of early Cubist paintings. As an enemy alien, Kahnweiler had no redress when his stock was sequestered in wartime by the French state. When the war was over, Kahnweiler's stock was auctioned in Paris. Prices were horribly and unforgettably low. The auction was an example of the isolated great auction offering an abundance of great art that went down in history as a catastrophic failure.

8.  Ambroise Vollard, *Recollections of a Picture Dealer,* Dover, New York, 1978.

9.  Sidney Janis, *Abstract & Surrealist Art in America,* Runal & Hitchcock, New York, 1944.

10. For more details on the relationship between artists and money see Rudolf and

Margot Wittkower, *Born Under Saturn: The Character and Conduct of Artists: A Documented History from Antiquity to the French Revolution*, W.W. Norton & Company, 1963, Chapter Xl, 'Between Famine and Fame'.

11.     Giorgio Vasari, *Lives of the Artists*, Penguin, 1981.

12.     David Throsby and Devon Mills, *When Are You Going to Get A Real Job?: An Economic Study of Australian Artists*, Australia Council, 1989.

13.     The collection of Baron Hans Heinrich Thyssen-Bornemisza, whose holdings of 14,000 Old Master, European and American paintings and works on paper are acknowledged to be the finest in private hands next to those of Queen Elizabeth II, is administered by a salaried curator (with a salaried staff of ten including a full-time conservator) charged with realising the Baron's plans for acquisitions, exchanges, exhibitions and long-term care of the collection. Other 'private' and Foundation collections managed by professional private curators include the Saatchi Collection, London, and the Eli Broad Family Foundation in Santa Monica (with its 22,600 square foot study centre with exhibition space and contemporary art library). Both these are collections of contemporary art.

## Chapter 4. The Contemporary Market

1.     Edouard Manet, 'Reasons for Holding a Private Exhibition,' *A Documentary History of Art*, Volume III, *From The Classicists to the Impressionists, Art and Architecture in the Nineteenth Century*, Elizabeth Gilmore Holt, Editor, Anchor Books, 1966.

2.     At the November 1988 auctions, records were written and rewritten for many post-war artists. At Christie's on November 9, a single-session evening sale made a total of US$37,292,200, with only four lots bought in, while at Sotheby's the following night an evening session totalled US$50,036,250, not counting an additional US$16,313,000 for six contemporary paintings from the Collection of Mr & Mrs Victor Ganz, and only six lots went unsold. At Christie's, Jasper Johns' *White Flag*, from the Tremaine Collection, reached US$7 million, a record for a contemporary work of art and for a living artist, which was overtaken the next night at Sotheby's when Johns' *False Start* fetched US$17.5 million.

3.     There are many well-known instances of artist-collector friendships that have been part of the development of extraordinary collections, like for example the 19th century American collectors Louisine and Harry Havemeyer. Through their friendship with artist Mary Cassat (1845–1926) they discovered the modern French school called Impressionism, and the Havemeyer Collection was born. They brought the first Degas and the first Monet to reach America. They

delighted in making their own choices, eagerly responding to new or unknown artists. Today the walls of New York's Metropolitan Museum and Washington's National Gallery and many other museums throughout the United States, all sparkle with works by Degas, Manet, Cézanne, Monet, Daumier, Courbet, El Greco and Goya that were first owned by the Havemeyers. Their daughter-in-law Doris Havemeyer died in 1982. The sale of paintings in her estate through Sotheby's, New York brought more than US$15 million. This sale is regarded by many as the auction that, more than any other, launched the rise in art prices that has yet to abate. For the story of their collection see Frances Weitzenhoffer *The Havemeyers: Impressionism comes to America*, Harry N. Abrams, New York, 1986.

4.   Paul Durand-Ruel (1831–1922) succeeded his father and became the dealer of such still unknown or little appreciated masters as Corot, Millet, Courbet and Boudin. After 1871, he began buying the works of the Impressionists, stoically enduring scorn and contempt from the very clients who he had led to appreciate the Barbizon school but were now unwilling to share his new enthusiasm for the Impressionists. Being the same age as Manet, and through his intimate acquaintance with the works of the preceding generation, Durand-Ruel recognised in the Impressionists the logical successors of Corot, Courbet and Boudin before most others did. Durand-Ruel was for many years practically alone in recognising the merits of the Impressionists. For accounts of this history, see John Rewald, *The History of Impressionism*, Museum of Modern Art, 1973.

5.   Ambroise Vollard, *Recollections of a Picture Dealer*, Dover Publications, 1978.

6.   Jean Campbell, *Early Sydney Moderns, John Young and the Macquarie Galleries 1916–1946*, Craftsman House, 1988.

7.   Komon greatly advanced the interests of many artists and made many valuable contributions to the development of Australian art. Alun Leach-Jones, 'Rudy Komon 1908–1982 An Appreciation', *Art & Australia*, Vol.20 No.3 Autumn 1983, p.329.

8.   Andre Emmerich; Laura de Coppet and Alan Jones, *The Art Dealers*, 1984, p.57.

9.   Such theme shows include *The Australian Sculpture Triennial*, initiated and held by The National Gallery of Victoria, offering a view of current sculpture and trends. *Fields to Figuration*, Australian Art 1960–1986, a survey of 26 years of Australian art from The Gallery's collection was also staged by the National Gallery of Victoria (from 21 February to 29 March 1987). *Australian Perspecta*, was launched in 1987 at the Art Gallery of New South Wales. The exhibition is held biennially, surveying recent Australian art.

10.  Joseph Beuys (1921–1986) is the European equivalent of Andy Warhol as a suc-

cessor to Marcel Duchamp in creating a cult of personality. Both Beuys and Warhol used the idea of art as religion, together with a clever grasp of what gives politicians and rock stars charisma. Using identifiable symbols — Beuys' hat and workers' clothes, Warhol's white wig and equally pseudo-proletarian jeans — together with specific references to religious symbols in their art, they turned themselves into legendary icons and they enjoyed a level of public fame reserved for the greatest of the Old Masters.

11.   Leo Castelli; Laura de Coppet and Alan Jones, *The Art Dealers* 1984, p.103.

12.   Knoedler's is one of the grand dealers of this century. Rival to the legendary Duveen, Knoedler's advised many clients they shared with Duveen, such as Mellon and Frick.

13.   The number of galleries in New York City alone exceeds this! Veteran collectors can identify the best galleries. It is worthwhile to seek their advice as to which galleries they best recommend the new collector to visit.

14.   David Throsby and Devon Mills, *When Are You Going to Get a Real Job?: An Economic Study of Australian artists.* Australia Council, 1989. David Throsby, 'Artists' Incomes: Then and Now', *National Association for the Visual Arts Newsletter*, June 1989.

15.   In a comparison of the policies on government subsidies of the arts, the *New York Times* recently found that the country that spends the most on the arts is the Soviet Union, which gave US$4.4 billion to the arts and media in 1988. The next biggest spender was Italy, which allocates US$2 billion a year to culture — much of it, however, to conservation and restoration of historic monuments. Next came France and Germany with annual arts budgets of US$1.6 billion. Mexico's Council for Culture has a US$200 million budget, while the United States has allocated US$323. 4 million to the two federal arts endowments for 1990. Great Britain spent US$702 million on the arts in 1989. Japan spent US$290 million in 1989 on culture, but only US$46 million went to contemporary art. *The Journal of Art*, vol.2, No: 1, September–October 1989.

16.   Shane Simpson, *The Artist and The Law*, The Law Book Company, Sydney, 2nd edition 1989.

17.   *SPADEM*, 12 Rue Henner, Paris 75009: one of several artists' collection agencies. Another is Design and Artists Copyright Society, DACS, St Mary's Clergy House, 2 Whitechapel, London E17QR.

## Chapter 5. Art As Investment

1.   It took three-and-a-half minutes for Van Gogh's *Irises* to sell for US$49 million — US$53.9 million with the buyer's premium added. That is US$14 million a

minute. Records are brief: at Christie's November 1988 sale a record for a contemporary work of art and for a living artist was paid for Jasper Johns' painting made of encaustic and newsprint on three attached panels. *White Flag* fetched US$7,040,000. The record was overturned one night later when Johns' *False Start* brought US$17,050,000.

2. Godfrey Barker, 'Turning Bond Street Upside Down', *The Daily Telegraph*, 11 September, 1989, p.16.

3. Impressionism was the derisive name given to the most significant artistic phenomenon of the l9th century and the first of the Modern Movements. The name was derived from a painting by Claude Monet, *Impressionism, Sunrise 1872*, representing the play of light on water. The occasion of the derision was the first Impressionist Exhibition held in 1874. Other independent Impressionist Exhibitions followed in 1876, 1877, 1879, 1880, 1881, 1882 and 1886.

4. *Van Gogh in Arles*, 18 October through 30 December 1984. *Van Gogh in Saint-Remy and Auvers*, 25 November 1986, through 22 March 1987. See catalogues documenting both exhibitions by Ronald Pickvance, The Metropolitan Museum of Art, Harry N. Abrams, New York.

5. After Robert Scull's death in 1986, his widow Ethel sold 130 works of which 13 established record prices for American artists. Most pictures sold over estimates and the sale totalled US$8.5 million, the highest for any single collection of contemporary art at auction at the time. Other examples of extraordinary appreciation which excited the avaricious imagination include New York collector Ben Heller's Jackson Pollock *Blue Poles* bought in 1956 for US$32,0000 and sold in 1973 for US$2 million, realising a compounded annual rate of return of 28 per cent; and Mr & Mrs Burton Tremaine's 1959 Jasper Johns' *Three Flags* bought for US$900 and sold in 1980 for US$1 million realising a compounded annual rate of return of 40 per cent.

6. *Paintings, Collection of Mr & Mrs Victor W Ganz*, Sotheby's New York, 10 November, 1988.
   *Pablo Picasso Retrospective*, The Museum of Modern Art, New York, 22 May through 16 September 1980; Picasso Museum, Hotel Salé, Le Marais, Paris. The Museum also features the remarkable last works of Diego Giacometti (1902–1987).
   Paintings by Picasso held the record as the most expensive pictures (after Van Gogh's *Irises*): *Yo Picasso* by the 19 year-old Picasso ranks second in world prices, and *Au Lapin Agile* 1905 became the third most expensive painting in the world when it sold at Sotheby's for £25.9 million, US$40.7 million to Walter H. Annenberg. *Acrobat et Jeune Arlequin* 1905 sold in November 1989 ranks fourth and the sixth most expensive Picasso auctioned is the 1901 *Maternité* sold at Christie's, New York in November 1988. Then on 20 November, 1989, a

large Blue Period painting *Les Noces De Pierrette* sold in Paris for FF 315 million (US$51.7 million) making it the second highest price paid for any work of art.

7.  Paul Jeromack, 'Old Master Paintings', *Art & Auction*, September 1989, p.170.

8.  Sotheby's, New York, Contemporary Sale, 4 November 1988. Ellsworth Kelly (b.1923), painter and sculptor, figures significantly in the history of non-gestural abstraction. His work with its array of flat, sharp-edged forms and unmodulated colour is a hybrid of the biomorphic and the geometric traditions. Unconcerned with the spontaneity of Abstract Expressionism, in the 1950s Kelly painted preconceived, hard-edged silhouettes of shapes from nature, in the manner of Henri Matisse's cutouts.

9.  A Japanese buyer, Shigeki Kameyama of the Mountain Tortoise Company, paid a world record price for a living artist in November 1989, paying A$26.45 million for Willem de Kooning's 1955 *Interchange*. Willem de Kooning (b.1904) is one of the giants of Abstract Expressionism. Ironically (in view of the painting's title) Kameyama, a Tokyo dealer found himself unable to meet the US$20.7 million he bid for the painting. When Sotheby's refused Kameyama an Alan Bond type financing deal, Kameyama consigned to Sotheby's a number of paintings to offset his debt.

    Through the 1980s the Japanese have enjoyed what is called in Japanese *a Kaneamari gensho* — an 'excess of money phenomenon', and many of these fortunes have been lured toward the international art market. Sally Richardson, 'Who Says the Japanese don't like Imports?', *The Australian*, 25 November, 1989.

    At Christie's Doheny sale of 15th century books the most expensive printed book was bought by a Japanese group, the Maruzen Publishing House of Tokyo. This was a surprise because Maruzen's name had not been heard at auction before, nor had there even been the slightest intimation that the Japanese were after European incunabula. On 27 June, when Habsburg-Feldman, S.A., the new Geneva auction house, had its first major auction devoted to Galle glass of the highest order, Japanese buyers bought 60 per cent of the pieces. From a fully trilingual catalogue printed in English, French and Japanese, the record piece, *Feuille de Rhubarbe*, was picked up by a Japanese buyer, negotiated at the end of the sale after it missed its reserve by a hair at SF1.5 million (US$1.1 million).

10. Sotheby's, *The Return of Marco Polo*. Auction in The Forbidden City, Sunday, 5 June 1988, Beijing.

11. Svetlana Alpers, *Rembrandt's Enterprise, The Studio and The Market*, Thames & Hudson, 1988.

12. Robert Hughes, *The Shock of the New*, BBC, 1980, p. 383. Also Robert Hughes,

'Sold', *Time Australia*, 27 November 1989, pp. 60–67.

13.  Robert Hughes, 'On Art & Money', *New York Review of Books*, 6 December 1984.

14.  Gerald Reitlinger, *The Economics of Taste: The Rise and Fall of Picture Prices 1760–1960*, Volumes I to III, London 1961; 'Art As Investment' *London Economist Intelligence Unit Report*, 1979.

15.  The Frick Collection, which in 1985 marked the 50th anniversary of its opening to the public, spans five centuries of Western art with only 172 paintings in the collection. With an operating budget of around US$4 million, the Frick has not bought a painting since 1968. Henry Clay Frick had an almost infallible eye for quality. Each work in the Frick collection, of masterpieces of European painting and sculpture and 18th century French furniture, is a fully executed masterpiece. They are displayed so the visitor can enjoy a quiet and personal relationship with individual rare and exquisite objects. A detailed study of Frick (1849–1919) the collector, his relations with Knoedler and with the British dealer Joseph Duveen (1869–1939) has yet to be undertaken. Miss Helen Clay Frick, who disliked New York and who severed her association with the Frick Collection in 1951, eventually suing the trustees for violations of her father's will, kept his records in a bank vault in Pittsburgh. She would answer direct queries by mail, but access to records was, and has remained, extremely restricted. The artworks are now being catalogued and should yield valuable information about the upper echelons of the art business in the early years of this century. Joseph Duveen ranks as one of the most successful dealers of all time. He was responsible for building up the collections of the American millionaire collectors — Andrew Mellon, Samuel Kress, J.P. Morgan, the Widener family — men and women with an appetite for art and long cheque books but no particular education in the arts. Duveen's career testifies to the fact that all dealers should have the twin aims of providing a service and building a profitable business. See *The Frick Collection: Handbook of Paintings*, New York, 1978; S. N. Behrman, *Duveen*, Hamish Hamilton, London, 1932, p.125; Edward Fowles, *Memories of Duveen Brothers: Seventy Years in the Art World*, Times Books,1976. Colin Simpson, *Artful Partners, Bernard Berenson and Joseph Duveen*, Macmillan, 1986.

16.  Sotheby's experts advised the Fund on its collection — essentially a Sotheby's-formed collection — and Sotheby's auctions are also the usual venue for the Fund's art dispersals. Much criticism was levelled at British Rail and Sotheby's for this. It was asked why the British Rail Pension Fund allowed itself to be advised by the auctioneer that was acting as the contractual representative of sellers and whose primary duty is to vendors.The precise arrangements of the Fund/Sotheby's deal have never been made public. Sotheby's and British Rail have a separate company, Lexbourne, which oversees all the Fund's art

transactions. Though the general assumption is that Sotheby's have exclusive rights to sell the collection, the Fund has sold a number of works privately, among them illustrated manuscripts to J. Paul Getty, Jr and 19 Old Master drawings to the Art Institute of Chicago in May, 1989.

17. *Impressionists and Modern Art*, The Property of the British Rail Pension Fund. London 4 April, 1989, Sotheby's, London.

18. Other Art Funds include that announced in 1981 by a New York-based doctors' group called the Physician Planning Service Corporation which planned to set up a US$5 million limited partnership to invest in art, with funds to be provided by participating doctors, dentists and others. Advice was to be supplied by a panel of collectors of American art. Investment groups more or less inspired by the British Rail Pension Fund are now appearing in Europe, targeting Impressionist, Modern and Contemporary art. One example is Finaco Art, an art-investment consultancy partly owned by Finacor, the largest stock and currency brokers in Continental Europe. In partnership with three French dealers (experts in Old Masters, Impressionist and Modern Masters), Finacor Art will advise on buying and selling art on a commission basis. Interestingly, the British Rail Pension Fund gained another US$4.5 million to profit handsomely on one of its most eccentric purchases: a 16th century album of 20 wash drawings by Frederico Zuccaro bought for US$600,000 in the mid-1970s was bought at Sotheby's, New York in early 1990 by Finacor Art.

19. *A guide to taxation incentives for the arts and list of Approved Valuers*, Committee on Taxation Incentives for the Arts, Department of Arts, Heritage and the Environment, Australian Government Publishing Service, Canberra.

20. In 1988 Artemis sold Nicholas Poussin's 1651 painting, *The Finding of Moses*, once owned by the Duc de Richelieu and later by Robert Clive of India, to the National Gallery, London, and the National Museum of Wales, Cardiff. This was the first time that two British institutions combined their purchasing power to acquire a painting jointly. This acquisition demonstrates the recent changing responses within museums to an increasingly expensive art market.

21. Robert Hughes, 'The Anatomy of a Deal: How Alan Bond bought a $53.9 million painting, with more than a little help', *Time Australia*, 27 November 1989, pp. 69–70.

22. Rene Gimpel, *Diary of an Art Dealer*, Universe Books, New York, 1987, p.232.

## Chapter 6. Protecting Your Treasures

1. Most modern paper is produced from mechanically ground wood pulp. This ground wood paper is strong enough to survive the printing and binding processes. However, because of the presence of wood impurities it can rapidly

become discoloured and brittle. The life of paper can be further jeopardised by the acidic sizes used in the manufacturing process, air pollution, excessive heat, light and humidity.

The Australian Libraries and Information Council estimated in 1987 that the total preservation cost for microfilming and treating Australian book and manuscript collections, in public institutions, stood at over A$230 million. The technology now exists to produce bleached chemical wood papers which are alkaline and sized with neutral synthetic sizings. If stored and handled properly, these papers should be stable and usable for several hundred years. An American National Standard for the Permanence of Paper for Printed Library Materials was published in 1984. An increasing number of American publications are being printed on archival paper. The infinity symbol set within a circle identifies paper which confirms to the 1984 standard.

2.   See Appendix for listing for conservators.

3.   The exhibition *Van Gogh in Saint-Remy and Auvers,* was held at the Metropolitan Museum of Art, New York, 25 November 1986–22 March 1987. This exhibition followed on the heels of the exhibition *Van Gogh in Arles* held at the Metropolitan Museum of Art, New York, 18 October–30 December 1984.

4.   In Australia for assets to which Capital Gains Tax applies, taxpayers are required to keep records necessary to ascertain the date the person acquired the asset; any amount that would form part of the cost base of the asset i.e. consideration for acquisition; incidental costs of acquisition and disposal; capital expenditure on improvements to the asset; capital expenditure to establish, preserve or defend title to the asset; and the date of disposal and consideration. Penalties (A$2,000 fine under Section 160ZZU), apply for not keeping adequate records for Capital Gains Tax purposes. Records must be kept for seven years after the date of sale. With listed Personal Use Assets such as Antiques and Paintings, any gains made are taxable. Losses can only be deducted against any other capital gains or income. All listed personal use assets acquired before or after 19 September 1985 should be recorded and include, where possible, proof of the date of acquisition (e.g. insurance listing). For those acquired after that date keep relevant cheque butts, bank statements, credit card slips, suppliers' invoices and insurance records.

5.   The International Foundation for Art Research, Inc (IFAR) was founded in 1968. IFAR publishes ten times a year the *Stolen Art Alert,* that lists all works reported to it as stolen, and in most cases includes with an accompanying photograph details regarding the item, and the circumstances surrounding the theft. The *Stolen Art Alert,* contains between 100 and 150 entries on stolen art objects and is updated by an annual *Index of Stolen Art*. IFAR also publishes emergency flyers to disseminate information about easily traceable stolen objects. Such

objects include those that are easily identifiable because they are unique, published and well documented, or of great interest to a highly specialised market. *The Stolen Art Alert* is distributed to approximately 500 IFAR members including art dealers, private individuals, libraries, museums, and law enforcement agencies. Statistics based on the 1980 listings in the *Stolen Art Alert* indicate that out of a total of 1,649 stolen objects reported, 207 were reported to IFAR as recovered, representing a 13 per cent recovery rate. See 1980 'Art Theft Statistics', *Stolen Art Alert*, March –April 1981.

Art-theft archives offer a simple procedure for purchasers who want to verify an art work's title. The Art Dealers' Association of America (ADAA), a non-profit organisation of select art dealers, has maintained an extensive archive of stolen art as a public service since 1971. The archive is devoted primarily to the fine arts including paintings, drawings, prints, sculptures and photographs. Its information is maintained in files organised by category of art and by the artist's name. Any individual, museum, art dealer, insurance company, or other institution can report a theft to the archive, which publishes a monthly notice containing descriptions and photographs of stolen paintings, drawings, prints, and sculptures. The notices are circulated among 1,500 art dealers, museums, major auction houses, professional art associations, law enforcement personnel, and art publications around the world. Between 1971 and 1977, the ADAA published 49 bulletins reporting 3,215 stolen works of art.

6.    Bridgid Grauman, 'A Secret Cache', *Art News*, Summer 1989, p. 59.

7.    *A guide to taxation incentives for the arts and list of Approved Valuers*, Committee on Taxation Incentives for the Arts, Department of Arts, Heritage and the Environment, Australian Government Publishing Service, Canberra.

## Chapter 7. Fakes, Forgeries, Frauds, Replicas

1.    Mark Rogerson, *The Dali Scandal*, Gollancz, London. Pierpont, 'Salvador Dali and the Printing Press,' *Australian Business*, 27 September 1989, pp.36–37.

2.    Alvin S. Lane. 'The Case of the Careless Collector', *Art in America*, October–November 1965. Albert E. Elsen. *Origins of Modern Sculpture: Pioneers and Promises*, 1974. Bonnie Rurnham, Editor, *The Protection of Cultural Property*.

3.    Panned by critics when Degas's bronze figure of a dancer was first shown at the 1881 Impressionist exhibition in Paris, the sculpture had been bought in 1971 for US$380,000. Concerned with the protection of the integrity of the original work of art, numerous authorities in the United States drafted the 1974 College Art Association's *Statement on Standards for Sculptural Reproduction and Preventive Measures to Combat Unethical Casting in Bronze*. This statement

## Footnotes

has provided a useful reference and influenced more recent United States legislation to offer consumer protection against abuses in the promotion and sale of limited edition originals. See *Art Journal*, No.1, Fall, 1974.

4.   One of the oldest riddles of 19th century art is the production of The Fountainbleu School master, Jean Baptiste Corot. Records show he painted approximately 3,000 works, yet there are over 4,000 alleged Corots presently in the United States alone. Authentication of any painting by Corot is confirmed by catalogue entry in the 1905 Robant *catalogue raisonné* and certificate from photo archivist Michel Dieterle. Other 19th century artists whose works have been definitively catalogued include Pissarro and Sisley; authentication is less clear for other artists such as Gauguin, Renoir, and Géricault.

5.   There are many excellent references on prints, reading of which will help to clarify the many commonly-held confusions over 'prints' and 'originals'. Two good guides are Bamber Gascoigne, *How to Identify Prints*, Thomas & Hudson, 1986 and Felix Brunner, *A Handbook of Graphic Reproduction*, Hastings House Publishers,1984.

6.   For each print you purchase you should obtain a bill of sale clearly stating the title of the work, name of the artist, and particulars of the work such as the image's *catalogue raisonne* number; the date or year the print was made; the printing process employed; whether the print is an original; the size of the edition, the edition's number on the print; whether the image exists in other editions; whether the print was hand signed by the artist, unsigned, or signed in the plate; whether the print is a restrike or an art reproduction; the price charged; and any exchange and refund privileges, if any.

7.   *The UNESCO Convention on the Means of Prohibiting and Preventing the Illicit Import, Export and Transfer of Cultural Property*, adopted by the UNESCO General Conference at its 16th session in Paris on 14 November, 1970.

8.   Other protected artists were: Andrea del Sarto, Domenico Beccafumi, Rosso Fiorentino, Leonardo Franciabigio, Perino del Vaga, Pontormo, Titian, Francesco Salviati, Bronzino, Daniele da Volterra, Fra Bartolomeo, Sebastiano del Piombo, Filippino Lippi, Coreggio and Parmigianino.

# APPENDIX: COLLECTORS MARKETPLACE DIRECTORY

## INTERNATIONAL SERVICES AND ASSOCIATIONS

**International Foundation for Art Research (IFAR)**
46 East 70 Street, New York, NY 10021
Telephone: (212) 879 1780
IFAR was incorporated in 1968 to provide authentications to collectors on paintings. Over the years, IFAR's function has changed, and although its staff still work on authentications a large part of their efforts go towards gathering and disseminating information on stolen art and forgeries. IFAR also publishes two periodicals, *Art Research News* and *Stolen Art Alert*.

**CINOA (Confederation Internationale Des Negociants En Oeuvres D'Art)**
27 rue Ernest Allard, Brussels, Belgium
The International Art Dealers' Association is a non-profit-making organisation founded in Amsterdam in 1936. Its purpose is to promote good feeling and goodwill between dealers in all member countries and to consult on any international matter relating to antiques and works of art. The headquarters were later transferred to Brussels and have remained there ever since. There are thirteen member states at present: Belgium, Holland, New Zealand, Eire, France, Western Germany, Austria, Italy, South Africa, Great Britain, United States of America, Sweden and Switzerland.

**Art Dealers Association of America (ADAA)**
575 Madison Avenue, New York, NY 10022
Telephone: (212) 940 8590.
The ADAA, a group of well-established dealers, was formed in 1962. The Association has roughly 120 members who sell for the most part fine arts — that is, paintings, drawings, etchings, prints, and sculpture. Membership is by invitation rather than application. The Association gives out two annual awards, one a $5,000 award for outstanding contribution to art historical study, and the other a $20,000 fellowship to a doctoral student at a United States university whose studies focus on American or European fine arts. The ADAA also sponsors a series of panel discussions on the art world each November. Their publication, the *Art Theft Archives*, is a free service that lists art recently stolen. ADAA is a member of CINOA.

## AUSTRALIAN SERVICES AND ASSOCIATIONS

**Australian Protective Service**
PO Box 1920, Canberra City, ACT 2601
Telephone: (062) 753596; Fax (062) 753823
The Australian Protective Service has been involved in the protection of cultural property for the past two years. Initially this involvement was the provision of armed protection for touring Commonwealth indemnified exhibitions. The involvement was soon expanded to include security surveying of art galleries and museums, and in April 1988, the transfer of responsibility for approving security arrangements of proposed Commonwealth indemnified exhibitions from the Australian Federal Police to the APS.

**Australian Commercial Galleries Association**
c/- Bloomfield Galleries, 118 Sutherland Street, Paddington, NSW 2021
Telephone: (02) 326 2122

**Department of Arts, Sport, the Environment, Tourism & Territories**
(Taxation Incentive Scheme for the Arts)
GPO Box 787, Canberra, ACT 2600
Telephone: (062) 74111

**Art Museums Association of Australia**
Suite 10, Level 4, 422 Collins Street, Melbourne, Victoria 3000
Telephone: (03) 600 0240; Fax: (03) 602 2008
Established in 1965, the Association develops and promotes professional standards for art museums and those who work in them. The AMAA represents all 128 Australian public art museums. Its four main programme areas include professional development, professional support and resources, publications and advocacy. The Association works to establish and promote standards of excellence with the art museum profession.

**Antique Dealers Association of NSW**
354 Dowling Street, Paddington, NSW 2021
Holds an annual antiques fair and regular education courses.

**Antique Dealers Association of Victoria**
PO Box 24, Melbourne, Victoria 3144

## CONSERVATION

**State Conservation Centre of South Australia**
Department for the Arts
70 Kintore Avenue, Adelaide, SA 5000
Telephone: (08) 223 1766, (08) 223 1456

**Australian Institute for the Conservation of Cultural Material**
GPO Box 1638, Canberra, ACT 2601
Telephone: (062) 414044

## BROKERS SPECIALISING IN FINE ARTS INSURANCE

**Gow-Gates Insurance Brokers Pty Ltd**
PO Box 680, Parramatta NSW 2150

**Frank B Hall Australia**
27th Floor, 201 Kent Street, Sydney, NSW 2000

**Indemnity Corporation Pty Ltd, Insurance Brokers**
PO Box 206, Rozelle NSW 2039

## ART PACKERS & SHIPPERS

**Pace Express Pty Ltd**
Unit 1, 476 Gardeners Road, Mascot, NSW 2020
Telephone: (02) 669 5144, Fax: (02) 669 6850 (imports); (02) 669 6034 (exports)

**Grace Art**
551 Gardeners Road, Mascot, NSW 2020
Telephone: (02) 669 2099

*Appendix: Collectors Marketplace Directory*

**Woollahra Art Removals**
PO Box 275, Woollahra, NSW 2025
(02) 669 2688, (02) 328 2186

## COURSES

**The Centre for the History of the Fine and Decorative Arts**

*London*
30 Holmbush Road, London SW15 3LE
Telephone: (01) 788 8491 Fax: (01) 788 5636

*Melbourne*
7 Parkin Street, Glen Iris, VIC 3146
Telephone: (03) 824 7424, 266 1879

*Sydney*
36 Queens Park Road, Bondi Junction, NSW 2022
Telephone: (02) 389 6653

Conducts courses covering the history of the fine and decorative arts and architecture, including a full-time one year diploma course at the Victoria and Albert Museum in Modern and Contemporary art, design and architecture. Specialists from the academic and commercial fields of the arts provide the appropriate expertise. They also conduct a residential course studying the English Country House from 18th century Combe House in Somerset.

## BOOK SUPPLIERS

Museum bookshops especially those of the Australian National Gallery, the Art Gallery of New South Wales, and the National Gallery of Victoria offer a good selection of Museum and Gallery exhibition catalogues, artist monographs, and books and journals.

**The Arts Bookshop**
1067 High Street, Armadale, VIC 3143
Telephone: (03) 822 2645; Fax: (03) 822 5157
Specialist in the visual arts ranging from Renaissance to contemporary art. Regularly publish mail order catalogue.

**Art Salon Bookshop**
15 Crossley Street, Melbourne, VIC 3000
Telephone: (03) 662 2918
Specialises in overseas catalogues from major museums and architectural books.

**Berkelouws**
'Bendooley', Hume Highway, Berrima, NSW 2577
Telephone: (008) 04 6240
Especially good for out-of-print, hard-to-get books and journals, particularly limited edition publications.

**Craftsman House**
Upper Level, 108 Pacific Highway, Roseville, NSW 2069
Telephone: (02) 416 4469; Fax: (02) 416 4190
Publishers of Australian art books.

**Gleebooks Bookshop**
191 Glebe Point Road, Glebe, NSW 2037
Telephone: (02) 660 2578, (02) 660 2333

**Hordern House**
77 Victoria Street, Potts Point, NSW 2011
Telephone: (02) 356 4411; Fax: (02) 357 3636
Excellent for the collector of antiquarian and original material.

**Lamella Art Books**
333 South Dowling Street, Darlinghurst, NSW 2011
Telephone: (02) 331 4501
Museum and gallery exhibition catalogues and books on modern art, photography, design
and architecture.

## INFORMATION GUIDE — INTERNATIONAL PUBLICATIONS

*Apollo*
22 Davies Street, London.W1

*Art & Antiques*
89 Fifth Avenue, New York NY 1003, USA
Monthly magazine of the international art markets. Urbane, wide-ranging, with particular
emphasis on sales activity in the United States.

*Art & Auction*
250 West 57th Street, New York NY 10107, USA
Published ten times a year; previews and reviews of auctions, calendar of sales, reviews of
art books and exhibitions, profiles of collectors. The magazine of the international art
markets, covers the business of buying and selling and publishes an annual International
Directory for collectors.

*Art Diary*
The World's Art Directory (Ed. G. Politi)
Via C Farini 68, 20159 Milan, Italy
391 2 688.7341
Published annually in Milan listing artists, galleries, museums. Emphasis is on
contemporary art.

*Art in America*
980 Madison Avenue, New York, NY 10021
Monthly journal of the arts in America, principally Visual Arts. The August issue of the
magazine is an annual guide to galleries, museums and artists of contemporary art.

*Art International*
77 rue des Archives, 75003 Paris, France
Quarterly journal of International Art.

*Art Investment Guide*
Richard Hislop, Editor,
Art Sales Index Ltd,
Pond House, Weybridge, Surrey, KT 13, England
Published three times a year; reports on major auctions, analysis of market trends.

**The Burlington Magazine**
6 Bloomsbury Square, London. WC1A 2LP

**The Journal of Art, International Edition**
PO Box 693, New York, NY 10013-0693, USA
Monthly; published in Turin and New York. Useful covering of the European scene.

**Modern Painters**
10 Barley Mow Passage, Chiswick, London W4 4PH

**The Print Collectors' Newsletter**
Jacqueline Brody, Editor
72 Spring Street, New York NY 10012, USA
Published six times a year; print-related news and reviews, auction price lists.

## INFORMATION GUIDE — AUSTRALIAN PUBLICATIONS

**Agenda**
PO Box 4177, Melbourne University VIC 3052
Telephone: (03) 344 4819, (03) 344 6961
Review format tabloid newspaper published bi-monthly covering visual arts, cinema and
theory with an emphasis on readable but theoretical criticism.

**Art Almanac**
5/171 Darlinghurst Road, Darlinghurst, NSW 2011
Telephone: (02) 332 3225
A useful monthly listing of all galleries in Sydney, Brisbane, Canberra, Melbourne and
Adelaide with details of new exhibition programmes for each month.

**Art & Australia**
Fine Arts Press Pty Ltd
Suite 2, 653 Pacific Highway, Killara, NSW 2071
Telephone: (02) 498 4933
Australia's national visual arts magazine, published quarterly covering important aspects of
the visual arts, particularly contemporary painting and sculpture, as well as the history of
Australian art.

**Artline**
PO Box 94, West End. QLD 4101

**Art Link**
363 Esplanade, Henley Beach, SA 5022
Telephone: (08) 356 8511; Fax: (08) 235 1280
Quarterly of Australian contemporary art activity and issues in Australia, with particular
emphasis on performance art and art using new technology. Nine years old, the longest
running journal of contemporary Australian art.

**Art Monthly**
c/- Arts Centre Australian National University, GPO Box 4, Canberra, ACT 2601
Telephone: (062) 48 0321
Australian and international art monthly, this is the Australian edition of Britain's long-
established journal of the same name. A useful source of information, news and listings of
recent activities through the visual arts. Interviews, lively reviews and regular columns on
arts education, arts law and the saleroom.

**Art Text**
PO Box 259, Paddington, NSW 2021
Telephone: (02) 339 9535, (02) 332 2997
Quarterly publication covering Australian contemporary art with particular emphasis on critical theory.

**Australian Journal of Art**
Published by the Art Association of Australia c/- Department of Visual Arts, Monash University, Clayton, Melbourne 3168

**Australian Arts Guide**
Editor Roslyn Kean, Third Edition, 1989.
One of a series of *Art Guide Publications*, covering art centres worldwide

**Australian Antique Trader**
PO Box 1171, Brookvale, NSW 2100
Newspaper published monthly. Reports on auctions and saleroom activity and previews forthcoming sales.

**Australian Collectors Quarterly**
Published by Australian Consolidated Press, 54 Park Street, Sydney 2000
Telephone: (02) 282 8731

**Craft Arts**
PO Box 363, Neutral Bay Junction, NSW 2089
Telephone: (02) 908 4797
Covers contemporary craft and related arts such as sculpture in Australia. This is Australia's largest selling visual arts magazine with sales of 15,000 per issue. Features well illustrated articles on artists and their works with gallery listings and reviews.

**Imprint**
172 Roden Street, West Melbourne, VIC 3003
Telephone: (03) 328 2140, (03) 328 3578
Quarterly journal of the Print Council of Australia. Very good cover of Australian printmakers and printmaking with informative articles, reviews and exhibition listings.

**Photofile**
Australian Centre of Photography
Dobell House, 257 Oxford Street, Paddington, NSW 2021
Telephone: (02) 331 6253
Quarterly published through the Australian Centre of Photography and devoted to critical writing on photographic art. Includes feature articles and reviews.

**Pottery in Australia**
68 Alexander Street, Crows Nest, NSW 2065
Telephone: (02) 436 1681, (02) 436 1184
Long established quarterly on ceramics — really a potter's trade journal with frequent articles on production techniques and materials as well as marketing.

**Tension**
1 Oban Street, South Yarra, VIC 3141
Telephone: (03) 240 0654
Bi-monthly, well designed colour magazine, with feature articles on contemporary visual arts.

*Appendix: Collectors Marketplace Directory*

## AUCTIONEERS AND AUCTION PRICE INDEXES

### Auctioneers

Auction catalogues are available individually or by annual subscription. Catalogue prices and information on upcoming sales may be obtained by writing to the catalogue subscription departments of each company.

### Ader Picard Tajan

12 Rue Favart, 75002 Paris
Telephone: (011.33.1) 42618007

### Compaigne Des Commissaires-Priseurs De Paris

Auctions are held at the Hotel Drouot, 9 Rue Drouot, 75009 Paris, Telephone; (01) 42461711 and at 15 Avenue Montaigne, Paris 75008, Telephone: 48002020.

The world's largest auction salesroom where two thousand sales are held of more than 400,000 items annually. A collective enterprise of 70 separate auction offices, sales occurring in either buildings. Called a chaotic bazaar as many as 16 sales can occur simultaneously in the afternoons. Drouot Richelieu is the principal and most active location with an average of six to ten thousand visitors daily to non-specialised 'jumble-sale' auctions, 50 per cent of which are uncatalogued, offering an insane mix of merchandise.

For more information contact the *Gazette de l'Hotel Drouot*, a weekly tabloid available on French newstands. Catalogues are available from the auctioneers.

### Christie's

*Christie, Manson & Wood Ltd*
8 King Street, St James, London SW1Y 6QT, England

*Christie's, New York*
502 Park Avenue, New York, NY 10022, USA

*Christie's (Australia) Limited*
298 New South Head Road, Double Bay NSW 2028
Telephone: (02) 326 1422; Fax: (02) 327 8439
Christie's in Australia hold three painting auctions annually, usually in March, July and September. Two are held in Melbourne and one in Sydney.

### Geoff K. Gray

34 Morley Avenue, Rosebery NSW 2019
Telephone: (02) 669 2622; Fax: (02) 667 4839
Less specialised auctioneer with four painting sales each year usually in March, June, September and November.

### Guernsey's

136 East 73rd Street, New York, NY 10021 USA
Telephone: 212.7942280
An 'alternative' auction house with sales mainly of objects like a sale in 1984 of 125,000 Cuban cigars stored in Spain since the 1950s.

### Habsburg, Feldman

S.A. Box 125
202 Route de Grand-Lancy 1213, Onex, Geneva, Switzerland.
Telephone: (022) 7572530

**James R. Lawson**
212 Cumberland Street, Sydney NSW 2000
Telephone: (02) 241 3411; Fax: (02) 251 5869
Holds five painting sales each year usually in March, May, July, September and November. Also holds regular weekly sales every Friday morning, monthly decorative arts sales and regular specialised sales. In 1988 instituted successful sales of modern works. Also known for interesting turn-up of Australian prints in their sales.

**Kornfeld & Company**
Laupenstrasse 41, 3008 Bern, Switzerland

**Leonard Joel**
1195 High Street, Armadale, VIC 3143
Telephone: (03) 202 654 (03) 201 040 Fax: (03) 822 8573
Holds three painting sales each year.

**Phillips**
101 New Bond Street, London, WlY OAS
118 Queen Street, Woollahra NSW 2025
Telephone: (02) 328 1343; Fax: (02) 326 1305
Australian representative of London auctioneer. Will arrange buying and selling in London particularly of Australian material and bring to Australian attention any material surfacing in Britain from their London department or one of their twenty provincial offices. Also to find English and European works in Australia for despatch to London and disposal in their various sales.

**Rushton Fine Arts**
Rushton House, 184 Day Street, Darling Harbour, NSW 2000
Telephone: (02) 261 5533; Fax: (02) 267 5096
Holds two painting sales annually, usually in April and November.

**Sotheby's**
*Sotheby Parke Bernet & Co*
34–35 New Bond Street, London WlA 2AA, England

*Sotheby Parke Bernet Inc*
980 Madison Avenue, New York, NY10021, USA

*Sotheby's*
13 Gurner Street, Paddington, NSW 2021
Telephone: (02) 332 3500
Sotheby's in Australia hold three painting auctions annually, usually in March, August and November. Two are held in Melbourne and one in Sydney.

**Spinks**
53 Martin Place, Sydney, NSW 2000
Telephone: (02) 27 4729; Fax: (02) 233 6009
Deals in stamps, coins, war medals, some antiques. Does not deal with paintings.

*Appendix: Collectors Marketplace Directory*

## AUCTION PRICE INDEXES

Several annual directories of auction prices are available to collectors in most reference libraries or by subscription from the publishers. These directories enable collectors to keep up to date on current prices and check price trends over several years by comparing back issues.

Richard Hislop, Editor, *Annual Art Sales Index*
Art Sales Index Ltd, Pond House, Webridge, Surrey KT13, England. A comprehensive annual guide to international auction prices. Hislop's computer holds details of 34,000 auctions.

*Art Expo* Annual, Phaidon Publishers
The International Review of the major exhibitions and events of the past year.

*Christie's Review of the Season*, Annual, Phaidon-Christie's

*Gordon's Print Price Catalogue*, Martin Gordon Inc.,
25 East 83rd Street, New York, NY, 10028
Reference for international prints.

*Sotheby's International Price Guide*, Annual, The Vendome Press

Ted Craig, *Australian Art Auction Records*, Vol.6 1987–1989,
Australian Art Sales, Sydney, 1989
Currently into its sixth volume, lists Australian Art Auction Records.

Selma Smith, Editor, *The Printworld Directory*, Contemporary Prints & Prices, Fourth Edition, 1988–1989.
International Print/Price reference.

*International Art and Antiques Yearbook*, a worldwide dealers' and collectors' guide to the antiques trade published by Art and Antiques Yearbook Publishers, London. Lists dealers, dealers' associations, art and antique periodicals, antique fairs.

## BIBLIOGRAPHY

The list that follows includes all books and articles mentioned in the text, in addition to many others considered useful to collectors.

### Maintaining a Collection

Dolloff, Francis W., and Perkinson, Roy, L., *How to Care for Works of Art on Paper*, Museum of Fine Arts, Boston, 1979.

### Market Trends

*Art as Investment*, London Economist Intelligence Unit, London, 1979.

Mahon, Gigi, 'Unveiling Sotheby's Art Index', *Barron's*, 9 November, 1981.

Reitlinger, Gerald, *The Economics of Taste: The Art Market in the 1960s*, Barrie and Jenkins, London, 1970.

Reitlinger, Gerald, *The Economics of Taste: The Rise and Fall of the Objets d'Art Market Since 1750*, Holt, Rinehart and Winston, New York, 1965.

Reitlinger, Gerald, *The Economics of Taste: The Rise and Fall of the Picture Market, 1760–1960*, Holt, Rinehart and Winston, New York, 1964.

**Miscellaneous**

Hughes, Robert, *The Shock of the New*, Knopf, New York, 1980.

Behrman, S. N., *Duveen*, Hamish Hamilton, 1951.

Burnham, Bonnie, *The Protection of Cultural Property: Handbook of National Legislations*, International Council of Museums, Paris, 1974.

de Coppet, Laura, and Jones, Alan, *The Art Dealers*, Potter, 1984.

Fowles, Edward, *Memories of Duveen Brothers, Seventy years in The Art World*, Times Books, 1976.

Gimpel, Rene, *Diary of an Art Dealer*, translated by John Rosenberg, Hodder & Stoughton, 1966

Lynes, Russell, *The Tastemakers — the shaping of American popular tastes*, Constable/Dover, 1980

Myers, John Bernard, *Tracking the Marvellous*, Random House, 1983.

Hughes, Robert, 'On Art and Money', *The New York Review of Books*, 6 December, 1984.

Seldes, Lee, *The Legacy of Mark Rothko*, New York 1978.

Vasari, Giorgio, *Lives of the Artists*, Penguin 1981.

Wittkower, Rudolf and Margaret, *Born Under Saturn: The Character and Conduct of Artists: A Documented History from Antiquity to the French Revolution*, W.W. Norton & Company, 1963.

Wraight, Robert, *The Art Game*, 1965.

**European Paintings**

Alpers, Svetlana, *Rembrandt's Enterprise: The Studio and the Market*, Thames & Hudson, 1988.

Fritz, Novotny, *Painting & Sculpture in Europe 1780–1880*, 1960 Pelican History of Art, Penguin, New York.

Holt, Elizabeth Gilmore, Editor, *A Documentary History of Art*, Anchor 1966.

Rewald, John, *The History of Impressionism*, Museum of Modern Art, 1973.

Pevsner, Nikolaus, general ed., *Pelican History of Art* series, Penguin, New York (formerly Baltimore).

**Medieval Art**

Pope-Hennessy, John, *An Introduction to Italian Sculpture*, Phaidon, New York, 1972.

**Photographs**

Newhall, Beaumont, *The History of Photography from 1839 to the Present Day*, Museum of Modern Art, New York. 1964.

**Primitive Art**

Newton, Douglas, *Masterpieces of Primitive Art*, Knopf, New York, 1978.

**Prints**

*Directory 1988*, Australian Artists Producing Prints, Print Council of Australia Inc., 1989.

## Appendix: Collectors Marketplace Directory

Gilmour, Pat, *Understanding Prints: a contemporary guide*, Waddington Galleries, 1979.

Russell, John, 'A Connoisseur's Guide to the Fine Art of Print Collecting', *New York Times*, 22 June, 1979.

Zigrosser, Carl, *Prints and Their Creators*, A World History, New York 1937, Revised 1974.

### Twentieth-Century Art

Arnason, H.H., *History of Modern Art: Painting, Sculpture, Architecture*, Abrams, New York, 1968.

Barr, Alfred H., Jr., *What is Modern Painting?*, Museum of Modern Art, New York, 1943.

Elsen, Albert E. *Origins of Modern Sculpture: Pioneers and Promises*, 1974.

Haftmann, Werner, *Painting in the 20th Century*, Praeger, New York, 1966.

Rose, Barbara, *American Art Since 1900: A Critical History*, Praeger, New York, 1967.

### Australian Art

Haese, Richard, *Rebels and Precursors, The Revolutionary Years of Australian Art*, Allen Lane, 1981.

Hughes, Robert, *The Art of Australia*, Penguin, 1966.

McCulloch, Alan, *Encyclopedia of Australian Art*, Hutchinson, 1984.

Smith, Bernard, *European Vision and The South Pacific, 1768–1850*, Oxford University Press, 1960.

Smith, Bernard, *Australian Painting 1788–1970*, Oxford University Press, 1971.

# INDEX

Académie Royale de la Peinture 52
Ader Picard Tajan 40, 94, 151
Apelles 120
Arensberg, Walter 29
Art Consultants 55, 56
Art Dealers' Association of America 50,
    57, 142, 145
ARTEMIS 85, 140
Art Fairs 56–8
Art Gallery of New South Wales 63, 135
Art Investment Funds 82-86, 140
Artmarket 8
Artist's Proofs 122
Art Subsidies 136
Art Theft Archive 105
Art Thefts 103–108
Attalus I of Pergamum 1
Auction
    bidding 23–24
    catalogues 31
    celebrity sale 27–28
    costs 32, 35
    history 21
    market size 38, 71
    'Ring' 26
    sale categories 30
Australia Council 66, 136
Australian Commercial Galleries
    Association 49–50, 58, 133
Australian Institute for the Conservation
    of Cultural Material 98
Authentication 17

Barnes Collection 3
Barnes, Dr Albert C 7
Bastianni, Giovanni 116
Beatty, Helen Chester 75
Beit, Sir Alfred 104

Benivieni Bust 116
Berenson, Bernard 13
Beuys, Joseph 64, 135–6
Bierce, Ambrose 89
Blackman, Charles 5, 130
Blaue Reiter 4
Bloom 90
Bon a Tirer 122
Bond, Alan 36
Bonham's, London 94
Booth, Peter 10
Boucher, François 120
Boudin, Eugene 52, 135
Bouguereau, Adolphe-William 16–17
Boyd, Arthur 9, 42
Brack, John 62
Braque, Georges 53, 64
British Antique Dealers Association 57
British Museum 129
British Rail Pension Fund 82, 139–40
Broad, Eli Foundation 134
Brown, Joseph 42, 107
Bruskin, Grisha 10
Buffet, Bernard 41
Bunny, Rupert 22, 42–43

Caravaggio, Michelangelo Nerisi da 12
Carmichael, Rodick 10
Carnavalet, Musée 104
Cassat, Mary 134
Castelli, Leo 53, 64, 136
Catalogues 63, 131
Catalogues raisonné 123
Cataloguing 102–3
Cézanne, Paul 16–17, 41, 130, 135
Charles I 2, 7
Chase Art Fund 83–4
Cherry, Wendall 75

Chicago International Art Exposition   57
Cognac-Jay Museum   3
Conder, Charles   10
Connoisseurship   11, 15
Conservation   95–98
  and insurance   112
Consultants   55–6
Contemporary Art Market   59
Copy   118–9
Copyright   69
Corot, Jean Baptiste   52, 120, 135, 143
Correggio, Antonio   125
Costakis, George   12
Courbet, Gustave   52, 135
Courtauld Institute   2
Courtauld, Samuel   2
Crackle   90
Crating   101
Crooke, Ray   10

'Dali Scandal'   118, 142
Della Palla, Giovani Battista   52
Damasippus   52
Daumier, Honoré   135
Da Vinci, Leonardo   99
Daws, Lawrence   9
Dealer Galleries   48
Dealers   28–30, 32, 45
Degas, Edgar   6, 14, 37, 54, 104, 129, 130,
  134, 142
  *Lithe Dancer, 14 Years Old*   41, 119
De Kooning, Willem   37
  *Interchange*   71, 138
  *Woman*, 1953   76
Del Sarto, Andrea   54, 115
De Maistre, Roy   9
De Menil, Francois   29, 74

Derain, Paul   53
Dobell, William   107
Dorrance, John   37
Dossena, Alceo   116
Drawing   6, 13
  old master   47
  storage   95
  framing   92–95
Droit de Suite   70
Droit Moral   70
Drouot, Hotel   39–40, 151
Drysdale, Russell   9
Duchamp, Marcel   4, 136
Dufy, Raoul   41
Durand-Ruel, Paul   52–53, 62, 135
Durer, Albrecht   52
Duveen, Lord   52, 54, 82, 136, 139

El Greco   3, 135
Emmerich, Andre   52, 54, 62, 135
Environmental Hazards   89
*Epreuves d'artiste*   122
Everton House Sale   21
Export Controls   123–127

Facsimile   119
Fairweather, Ian   9
Faking   3, 115–119
Fauves   3
Forgery   119
Fox   90–1
Fragonard, Jean Honoré   15, 120
Framing   92–5
Fransella, Graham   10
Frick Museum   42, 82, 139
Fry, Roger   82

Gardner, Mrs Jack (Isabella)   13,
Gardner, Isabella Museum   13
   theft   104
Gersaint   52
Getty Museum   36, 42, 83, 132
   *Aphrodite*   106
Getty, Paul   12
Gimpel, Rene   54, 86, 140
Glover, John   43
   *Bath of Diana*, 1837   125
Goodman, Marian   45
Grosvenor House Antiques Fair   57–58
Guimet, Musée   2, 104

Haden, Seymour   122
Haring, Keith   53
Havemeyer Collection   134
Heritage Act   43
Hinton Collection   3
Hodgkins, Frances   9
Hughes, Robert   81, 138–9, 140
Humidity   90–91
Huntington Library   3

Impressionism   13, 137
Insurance   108–112
International Art and Antique Loss
   Register Ltd (IAALR)   106
International Council of Museums (ICOM)
   120
International Foundation for Art Research
   (IFAR)   103, 141, 145
*International Imaginary Museum*   117
Interpol, Art Program   106

Janis, Sidney   53, 133
Japanese Collectors   76–7, 138
John, Augustus   10

John, Elton   27, 131
Johns, Jasper   8, 130
   *False Start*   71, 74, 134, 137
Johnson, Stowers   12

Kahnweiler, Daniel-Henry   53, 61, 64, 133
Kelly, Ellsworth   76, 138
Kimbell Museum   76, 132
Knoedlers   64, 82, 136
Koestler, Arthur   115
Komon, Rudy   62, 135
Kress, Samuel   2, 139
Kroller-Muller Museum   107, 129

LaserNet   106
Laurencin, Marie   41
Lees, Derwent   10
Léger, Fernand   53
Leroi-Gourhan, Andre   1
'Limited Edition'   120–123
Lloyd, Frank   45
Loan Acknowledgement   101
Loan Agreements   100–101
Loans   98–102
Lodoli, Fra Carlo   12
Long, Sydney   12
Louvre   104
   *Benivieni Bust*   116
'Luminists'   7

Maastricht, European Fine Art Fair   58
Maillol, Aristide   54
Majorelle, Louis   8
Makin, Jeffrey   10
Manet, Edouard   37, 59, 104, 134, 135
Mantegna, Andrea   42
Marlborough Gallery   50, 133
Marmottan Museum   104

Matisse, Henri   54
Matting   93-4
Medici, Cosimo De   2
Meissner, Bruno   76
Meissner, Kurt   47
Mellon, Andrew W   7, 129, 139
Mellon, Joseph   2
Mentmore Sale   15, 130
Metropolitan Museum, New York   73,
   101, 126, 129, 132, 137, 141
Michelangelo, Buonarroti   54–5, 125
Miller, Godfrey   9
Millet, Jean François   52, 135
Miro, Joan   53
Monet, Claude   37, 73, 135, 137
   thefts   104
Morgan, J Pierpont   86, 139
Morgan Library   3
Museum Exhibitions and Values   101–2
Museum of Modern Art, New York   4

National Art Collections Fund   126
National Centre for Cultural Heritage
   Science Studies   98
National Gallery, London   16, 42, 129,
   132, 140
   *The Leonardo Cartoon*   99
National Gallery of Scotland   83
National Gallery of Victoria, Melbourne
   63, 107
National Gallery, Washington   125–6, 129
National Heritage Memorial Fund   126
Nolan, Sidney   9, 42

Paper   90
Pastiche   119
Petit Palais   104
Phidias   120

Picasso, Pablo   14, 41, 54, 63, 64, 115
   *Acrobat et Jeune Arlequin*   71, 75, 137
   *Weeping Woman* 107
   *La Cage d'Oiseaux*   75
Pontormo, (Jacopo Da Carruci)   41
Price Indexes   80, 153
Prices
   Australian   42–3
   Old Master   41–2
   Records   30, 37, 71, 46, 76, 83, 134,
   136–7
Prints   14, 16, 120–123
Private Treaty Sales   33, 132
Prouté, Paul   47
Provenance   5, 119–120
Pugh, Clifton   10

Raphael   12, 54, 115, 125
Rembrandt, van Rijn   81, 104, 120, 138
Renoir, Pierre Auguste   5, 14, 54, 62, 73
   *La Promenade*, 1870   83
   Theft   104
Replicas   120
Reproduction   119
Restoration   18–19
   insurance   112
Restrikes   122–3
Reitlinger, Gerard   81, 86, 139
Revision, Revaluation   3, 7
Reynolds, Joshua   12
Romano, Giulio   115
Rosa, Salvatore   81
Rosenquist, James   28
Rothko, Mark   50, 133
Rubens, Peter Paul   42, 55, 120
Ruskin, John   1
Russell, John   43
Russell, John Peter   22

*Index*

Saatchi Collection   134
Sackler, Arthur   29
Scull, Robert and Ethel   28, 74
Shafrazi, Tony   53
Simon, Norton   13
Sodoma, Giovanni Antonia Bazzi   55
Solander Boxes   95
Soviet art   10–11
SPADEM   70, 136
Spoerri, Daniel   71
Sredersas, Bob   12, 130
State Conservation Centre, South
    Australia   98
Stein, Gertrude   63
Stella, Frank   8
Stolen Art Alert   103
Storage   95
Storrier, Tim   10
Strada, Jacopo   52
Streeton, Arthur   42
Surmoulages   119

Tanguy, Pere   53, 62
Tate Gallery   9
Taxation Incentives   84–5, 132, 133, 140
Thaw, Eugene   47
Thermal Shock   90
Thyssen-Bornemisza Collection   134
Titian   12, 13, 55
Tiunick, David   47
Toulouse-Lautrec, Henri Marie
    Raymond de   14
Traill, Jessie   30
Turner, James Alfred   9
Turner, J.M.W.   21
Tzara, Tristan   40

Uffizi Museum   115, 129
UNESCO Convention   123, 143

Valuations   112–114
Van Gogh, Theo   54
Van Gogh, Vincent   41, 54, 62, 137
    *Irises*   29, 36, 37, 71, 136
    *Portrait of Dr Gachet*   5, 74
    *Sunflowers*   40, 71, 73, 74–75, 101
    Theft   107
Van Meegeren, Hans   116–117
Vasari, Giorgio   55, 134
Velasquez, Diego Rodriguez de Silva   82
Vermeer, Jan   104
Veronese, Paolo   12
Victoria and Albert Museum   126
Visual Artists and Galleries Association
    69
Vlaminck, Maurice   53
Vogel (Dorothy and Herbert) Collection
    51
Vollard, Ambroise   53–54, 62, 133, 135

Wallace Collection   2
Warhol, Andy   5, 45, 136
    Sotheby's Andy Warhol Sale   27, 131
Watteau, Antoine   52
Wertheim, Maurice   29
Whistler, James McNeil   122
Whiteley, Brett   9
Widener, Joseph E   2
Widener, P.A.B.   125
Wilde, Oscar   1
Williams, Fred   62
Wollongong City Gallery   12

*Index*

Yale Centre for British Art  130
Yasuda Fire and Insurance Company,
    Tokyo  75
Young, John  62, 135

Zola, Emile  53